401(k) Day Trading

401(k) Day Trading

Trading

The Art of Cashing in on a Shaky
Market in Minutes a Day

RICHARD SCHMITT

WILEY

John Wiley & Sons, Inc.

Published by John Wiley & Sons, Inc., Hoboken, New Jersey.
Published simultaneously in Canada.

For general information on our other products and services or for technical support, please contact our Customer Care Department within the United States at (800) 762-2974, outside the United States at (317) 572-3993 or fax (317) 572-4002.

Wiley also publishes its books in a variety of electronic formats. Some content that appears in print may not be available in electronic books. For more information about Wiley products, visit our web site at www.wiley.com.

Library of Congress Cataloging-in-Publication Data:

Schmitt, Richard, 1956–
  401(k) day trading : the art of cashing in on a shaky market in minutes
a day / Richard Schmitt.
      p.   cm.—(Wiley trading series)
  Includes index.
  ISBN 978-1-118-08541-7 (cloth); ISBN 978-1-118-12821-3 (ebk);
  ISBN 978-1-118-12822-0 (ebk); ISBN 978-1-118-12823-7 (ebk)
  1. 401(k) plans—Management.   2. Retirement income—United States—Planning.
3. Day trading (Securities)—United States.   4. Portfolio management—United
States.   I. Title.   II. Title: 401(k) day trading.
  HD7105.45.U6S359 2011
  332.024'0145—dc22   2011015867

Printed in the United States of America

10   9   8   7   6   5   4   3   2   1

To Mom, who told me that I could.
To Dad, whose fantastic spirit is my compass.
To Wendy, who made it so that I did.

Contents

Preface

Have you ever felt like an outsider hoping to get a glimpse of what actually is going on behind the scenes in your 401(k) plan? Wading through all of the financial and legal jargon involved in participating in a 401(k) plan can be an overwhelming and not all that exciting task. Who knows—maybe it could be like a sausage factory, and you would not want to know what goes into it. This is not really the case. Instead, you should appreciate that government policy makers, plan sponsors and their staff, and other experts put much thought, time, and energy into developing, implementing, and administering savings vehicles to help you save for a secure future. This book is your backstage tour through retirement savings vehicles, such as 401(k) plans, showing you how to profit in these current uncertain times through day trading your retirement savings portfolio.

Like sausage, these plans are made up of a myriad of ingredients, such as layers of savings and investment options, interwoven with structure, like tax law and other rules. It is all in how the ingredients are used that makes the difference between producing a mediocre or an exceptional result. Over time, sausage makers have modernized their operations to make more sausage with the same amount of ingredients. That is good news for its primary ingredient—the pigs—whose numbers are not being depleted as rapidly.

Likewise, financial institutions have adopted technology to efficiently administer more 401(k) accounts. Yet, for all the technology devoted to administering 401(k) plans, it is the individual 401(k) account holders who are still leaving money on the table—they are not making the most of their investments in their 401(k) accounts. To take a lesson from the sausage makers, it is time for 401(k) account holders to adopt a new approach in using the same old ingredients to yield more product.

The goal of most investors is to accumulate wealth through the investment of savings. To do this requires some planning and strategy. First and foremost, 401(k) investors need to save; for without savings, there are no investment opportunities. Then they need to invest their savings so as to get the best return on investment. Ideally they accomplish this through careful selection of securities and impeccable timing of their purchases and sales. This is easier said than done. In reality, the investment selection and timing processes can be pretty subjective and challenging even to investment professionals.

Yet there are certain elements of the investment process within your control, and every 401(k) investor's control, that can better your chances of generating higher returns on your hard-earned savings. It is always wise to follow conventional investment theory emphasizing portfolio diversification and a long-term perspective toward investing. At the same time, you need to take care to lessen your exposure to risk as you age and your investment time horizon shortens. Security becomes paramount as you get older and have less time to turn around any poor investments that do not pan out.

The 401(k) plan offers you a special environment with additional opportunities to build retirement wealth. Not only can you enjoy the convenience of automatic savings through payroll withholding, but you also consequently enjoy the benefits of dollar-cost averaging for stock purchases made on a regular periodic basis from payroll savings. Then you generally get to invest in professionally managed investment options carefully selected by your employer. In addition, 401(k) plans as well as other retirement savings plans offer you special tax treatment and cost savings not available through regular savings and brokerage accounts.

Another area of opportunity within the investment process garnering more attention, as well it should, is the control of investment expenses. Year after year, expenses reduce investment performance and eat away at account balances on which investors may eventually rely for support in their retirement. Given the right information in a transparent way, you and every other investor can improve your investment returns by managing your investment expenses. This means you need to select investment options that charge expense levels worthy of the returns they generate—not necessarily the lowest-cost funds, but funds whose performance justifies the expense charged.

Enter the concept of day trading your retirement accounts. Day trading offers you yet another way to get more out of your retirement savings portfolio in these uncertain times. This is not the type of day trading a full-time trader does to turn a quick profit from intraday price movements on sometimes exotic securities bought and sold on a rapid-fire basis. Instead, with day trading retirement savings accounts, you take only minutes a day to make a single daily fund exchange.

The day trading strategy is a really old concept wrapped in a new package built for the cost- and tax-friendly environment offered by 401(k) and other retirement savings plans. Its underlying premise relies simply on the old adage of buying low and selling high. The new package is the part relating to the proper timing, amount, and direction of each trade that produces gains in these current uncertain times.

The day trading strategy addresses the questions necessary to execute a trade within a retirement savings plan: what fund options to exchange, which direction the fund exchange is to take, how much to exchange, and when to submit the exchange instructions. Its ability to build retirement wealth in an uncertain market is fueled by the day-to-day changes in the stock market. As will be demonstrated, it is the elegance of simple arithmetic that enables day trading to generate gains in the type of unsettled, sideways market that this author predicts for the near term through at least 2020.

Most investment strategies depend on stock picking. The day trading strategy focuses on the bottom line. Day trading is more of a quantitative strategy that bases trading decisions on daily stock market fluctuations rather than on technical or fundamental analyses of individual securities or market sectors. In a way, it could be considered a form of swing trading on market trends that sets up or captures gains with only one daily fund exchange. The whys and the wherefores of the market twists and turns are not nearly as important as the disciplined execution of the process over time.

As with any profession, the investment community has developed its own jargon that could take years to learn. Fortunately, day trading deals primarily with basic trading concepts, like exchanging funds between stock and cash. Each day you either buy stock with cash or sell stock for cash. In short, you need to buy and sell stock at the right time (which will be defined herein). Beyond the basics, investing, like driving a car, can become more about the experience.

Nonetheless, this book explores the rationale behind day trading and the retirement savings vehicles that make it all possible. In the course of its discussion, some financial terms and 401(k) and other retirement savings plan terms will be introduced along the way and be displayed *in italics*, as well as defined in the Glossary at the back of the book.

A global positioning system (GPS) can be useful in driving a car (or golf ball) from where you are to where you want to be. The GPS continually monitors your location and adjusts its instructions to tell you which direction to go and how far. You can think of the day trading strategy as your own personal GPS for directing your retirement portfolio trades. You already know your destination is wealth accumulation. Under the day trading strategy, your reading of the daily change in the stock market will guide you in the direction (i.e., buy or sell) and amount of each daily trade.

Market volatility will cause your trades to go back and forth in incremental amounts based on your readings of the daily market changes.

Until now, day trading 401(k) accounts has been sort of a dirty little secret that plan administrators would rather you not know about. For many years, some 401(k) investors have engaged in a type of frequent trading that plan administrators see as putting other account holders and themselves at a disadvantage. Trading costs passed along to all shareholders may increase if a particular fund's inflows do not equal its outflows. In turn, fund prospectuses note that uneven cash flows into and out of funds brought about by frequent trading make it harder for fund managers to invest fund assets.

Most important, though, is that frequent fund exchanges by participants in retirement savings plans necessitate more record-keeping and systems capacity on the part of fund companies. Although your 401(k) plan may offer daily fund exchanges, the plan administrator surely does not expect everyone to do just that. Establishing enough systems capacity sufficient to handle all potential trades would be like building roads to smoothly accommodate all rush hour traffic—a novelty in most major cities.

Just as a bank does not keep all of its depositors' savings in the vault reserves ready for withdrawal on a moment's notice, plan administrators do not maintain enough systems capacity to handle all of its account holders making fund exchanges every day. Consequently, 401(k) plan administrators have already stepped in to establish some pretty effective policies and rules designed to thwart day trading in the name of facilitating orderly investment management. If you sit passively by, these rules could keep you from realizing your retirement dreams.

You understand that rules generally act to discourage you from hurting yourself or others. Mom always said not to hit your brother. The posted speed limit is 65 miles per hour. However, independent-minded Americans do not always follow rules very well, especially when a worthwhile cause like wealth accumulation is at stake. The bold ones have always said that rules are made to be broken. Perhaps to the disappointment of the rebel in you, no rules will be broken here. By following the day trading strategy described in this book, you will be strictly abiding by the rules as they stand. You will not even be attempting to bend the rules, although you may dance around them on a fairly regular basis. So, really, stop hitting your brother, and slow down!

To work, day trading must accommodate the structure of the rules established by plan sponsors, plan administrators, fund companies, and the government. In most retirement savings plans, you can effectively trade only once per day, because all fund exchange orders, regardless of when they are submitted before the close of the market, are executed each business day at the market close. As a result, the retirement savings day trading strategy calls for only one trade just before the end of each day.

Of course, there are some plans that facilitate more frequent trading with real-time trades of individual securities like stocks, bonds, and exchange-traded funds (ETFs) through self-directed brokerage accounts. However, unlike the mutual fund options offered in a 401(k) plan, you would generally pay any trading costs you incur, and your resulting investment returns would be reduced accordingly. Then it becomes up to you as to whether undertaking a more frequent trading strategy is worth the risk, time, and trouble.

The essence of day trading retirement savings accounts lies in the methodical execution of daily fund exchanges to remove the emotion from each trading decision (and frankly save you a bunch of time). 401(k) and other retirement savings plans offer the type of favorable conditions that make it possible to derive value from each daily trade over the long term. The reward of higher investment returns in these uncertain times goes to those patient investors who stick with day trading.

Day trading retirement savings in an uncertain market is just one way to get the most out of your participation in 401(k) and other retirement savings plans. It is intended only to serve as a supplement to a sound underlying investment strategy encompassing prudent asset selection, risk management, and expense control applied to all household assets.

This book presents the environment, rationale, and process on which day trading relies to juice retirement portfolio returns. It offers practical information everyone can use in building a retirement portfolio. In addition to introducing some basic tenets of investment management that also apply to day trading, it covers topics ranging from saving for retirement to expense management before describing the process and nuances of day trading retirement savings.

It starts with a discussion of the unique features of retirement savings plans that make day trading possible. From there, it turns to why these plans have taken such a prominent role in retirement planning. Some background on 401(k) plans and investment options found in such plans is next, followed by a discussion of investment strategies. Then the case for the value of day trading in uncertain times is presented. With this as a backdrop, the basic premise for day trading and its execution strategy are laid out. Finally, it concludes with some crystal-ball gazing as to what could become of all this.

Along the way, the book will lay out clues **(in bold type)** as in the genre of a murder mystery. Only these clues will not lead you to a conclusion of who-done-it. You already know that you will be doing it. Rather, the clues will lead you to how day trading is actually done.

Any views and opinions expressed in this book are those of the author. This book is not intended to provide any tax or financial advice. As such, any reliance on the views and opinions presented herein is at your own risk. Any financial plan should consider your own personal circumstances. Before undertaking any action, you should consult with your tax and financial advisers to determine whether that action would be suitable for managing your retirement portfolio.

Acknowledgments

Any work requires the perseverance and understanding of those around you. Luckily, I have been blessed on a daily basis with the most awesome support of family and friends in the completion of this project. I cannot thank enough my wonderful wife and four brilliant children for their thoughtfulness and contributions to this project and the rest of my life.

Many thanks also go to Bill Falloon and his most capable team at John Wiley & Sons, notably Jennifer MacDonald, Vincent Nordhaus, and Tiffany Charbonier, for recognizing and nurturing the expression of a new way to approach the investment of retirement savings.

Last, thank you for providing an audience for an idea whose time has come.

401 (k) Day Trading

PART I

Introduction

CHAPTER 1

Game On

Making Something Out of Nothing

Remember, you don't have to buy at the very bottom or sell at the very top to be a successful investor [but it sure helps].

—Charles Osgood, KCBS commentary,
April 13, 2009

The boy plays video games. When Dad first hooked up the video game console, the little shaver experimented to learn how to play his games. With experience, the boy picked up some strategies and techniques on his own. He was not about to read any instruction manuals beforehand. After playing over a period of time, he eventually developed some proficiency. However, he wanted to do better. He wanted to become the next professional gamer, like his "manny" (a male nanny). So, like most people these days, he consulted the Internet. There he found the latest "cheats" on many of the games he plays. It seems that gamers are a somewhat friendly bunch who like to share cheat codes to help others in the community do better in their games.

Video games are basically a bunch of rules embedded in computer code acted out on a video screen. Each gamer's action (toggle turn, button push, etc.) has a consequence that may be good or bad. A cheat code represents a series of special commands that can enhance the skill level or appearance of characters within the game to gain an advantage. For example, a gamer playing a certain basketball video game could use a cheat to outfit his entire team with new shoes. As we like to believe in real life, it is the shoes that make the video basketball star the best he can be.

Now Dad became concerned when he first heard of his son's use of so-called cheats. After all, the boy was not brought up to gain an unfair advantage through nefarious measures. Rules are rules and must be followed by both sides in a fair contest. They dictate the way the game must be played. So the boy sat Dad down to explain (in his own way) that cheat codes were used to take advantage of not-so-apparent rules already built into the game. They were meant to be used to increase the skill level of the players. He compared their use to coaching, saying they were more like a coaching strategy than a ploy to gain an unfair advantage.

So Dad accepted the coaching argument. Everyone acknowledges that good coaching is a key component to achieving success. Even John Wooden, the Wizard of Westwood, used to coach his legendary UCLA basketball teams on every last detail, down to the proper way of putting socks (not shoes) on. To my knowledge, nobody ever called that cheating. It was more like getting the best out of what you had within the rules of the game.

There is also a way to gain an edge in managing retirement savings. It involves *day trading* tax-deferred retirement savings accounts, such as *401(k) plan* accounts. It is just that the term "cheat" usually does not lend itself to a positive connotation in most environments, perhaps other than gaming. It may sound exciting to school kids playing video games, but conjures up visions of Internal Revenue Service (IRS) audits to the rest of the population. So hereafter, "cheats" will not be the preferred term used to describe a way of taking full advantage of existing rules in managing assets in tax-deferred retirement savings accounts. Rather, the clever use of a way to maximize the tax and cost benefits afforded retirement savings accounts to enhance a retirement portfolio's investment returns is deserving of a more favorable term.

How then would you describe a way to get better returns under retirement savings plans that allow employees to avoid taxation on savings and investment earnings until distribution? "Scheme" (as in Ponzi) is really too strong a term in the United States, even though it is used to refer to jolly old retirement plans in Great Britain. A tax attorney might prefer the term "loophole," because of its connotation as a clever way to legally avoid taxes. You could also refer to it as a "method," "technique," "system," "approach," or "strategy." Even better yet, you could call this new way of managing retirement savings an "art" for its simple elegance in enhancing return on investment in uncertain times.

The process of managing assets in a retirement portfolio is a little like becoming proficient in video games. Because the way you manage the investment of your retirement savings accounts now may affect how you live in the future, it really is more than just a game. However, like a game, managing your retirement savings account investments has its own set of rules and terminology established by employers, plan administrators, and the government. You need to follow these rules, or you will be kicked out of the game (i.e., suspended from investing in a fund option, which is a much nicer way to put it). It is up to you to take every advantage available within the rules of the game to get the most out of your retirement portfolio. If you take exception to comparing wealth accumulation to a game, please consider any further game references herein as purely coincidental (and lighten up).

So you join a 401(k) plan offered by your employer, whether ready or not. You may be hesitant to join the plan, because you are uncertain about either how much to save or how to allocate your contributions among the available plan fund options. Some plans make it easy for you by automatically enrolling you in the plan when you first become eligible and depositing your contributions into a designated fund. Other plans wait for you to enroll, at which point you will need to direct the allocation of your contributions to your preferred fund options.

Once you have decided how much to put into your 401(k) plan, you will probably notice that your paycheck reflects a withholding of your own contributions that are directly deposited into an individual account in your name. For plans allowing participants to direct the investment of their individual account funds, there are two decisions to make. First, you will need to allocate your contributions among the plan's available fund options (especially if you enrolled yourself or if you were automatically enrolled by your employer but wish to have your contributions invested other than in the default fund selected by your employer).

Second, as you build an account balance from contributions and any accumulated earnings, you may redirect the investment of your accumulated balance among the plan's available fund options. These two investment decisions, relating to the allocation of your (1) new contributions and (2) already existing account balance among the plan's alternative fund options, have a profound impact on the future growth of your account.

Managing your retirement savings encompasses both of these investment allocation decisions. Day trading comes into play with respect to the ongoing allocation of only your already accumulated retirement savings accounts.

Since you may not be sure at first about the right allocation of your 401(k) contributions or account balance, you may experiment a little, or maybe you will just follow what you are told to do. If you feel a little overwhelmed by the investment management responsibility, you are not alone. In a 2008 survey, employers cited where to invest 401(k) plan assets as most confusing to their employees.[1]

Finding the right investment at the right time can be ever so tricky. Studies show that employees procrastinate when faced with choices relating to their retirement savings plan participation.[2]

At first, asset allocation is a little like errant skeet shooting: ready, fire, aim (whereas a more prudent course might involve aiming before firing). You are not quite ready to pull the trigger on fund selections, but nonetheless you need to designate how your contributions and account balance are to be spread among the available fund options once you are in the plan. So you might select your investment options anyway, leaving the work of studying the investment options to later.

It is important to use saving and investment strategies that will help you get the most out of your participation in 401(k) and other retirement savings plans, since your decisions in these areas have serious and lasting consequences that affect your account buildup. You can also use a day trading strategy within the current framework of these retirement savings plans to help you reach your retirement goals.

Day trading deals with securities. When not used to refer to something keeping you warm and safe at night, a *security* is a general term used to refer to an investment vehicle under which an investor pays money in exchange for a right to future payments from the issuer of the security. Securities come in three basic varieties, depending on the level of their processing. Just like potatoes, they can be bought raw, cooked, or twice-baked. A security can be issued raw by a company or a government to evidence a debt (as in a bond) or ownership interest (as in stock). Another type of security is cooked up by *pooling* or aggregating raw securities into a collective fund, such as a *mutual fund*. The third type of security resembles a twice-baked potato where cooked mashed potatoes are wrapped in an already-baked potato skin, in that this security is formed by wrapping or pooling already-pooled collective funds to form a fund of funds, such as a target-date fund.

The day trading strategy works effectively in most 401(k) plans, as well as other tax-deferred retirement savings vehicles covering individuals and employees of governmental, educational, nonprofit, partnership, sole proprietorship, and other entities. All of these retirement savings plans, otherwise known as *defined contribution retirement plans*, look a lot like savings accounts, but with tax advantages. These account-based plans offer participants the opportunity to defer taxation of plan balances, composed of contributions and investment earnings, until distribution.

Day trading derives its value from the execution of daily *fund exchanges* within the favorable tax and cost environment of a typical retirement savings plan in an uncertain market. The features commonly found in these plans facilitate taking advantage of daily swings in the market. More important, the fragile condition of a mending world economy brings about the type of conditions that feed the stock market volatility that fuels day trading.

Day trading is simple. Anyone with basic arithmetic skills can do it. In fact, it is the elegance of simple arithmetic that accounts for its success. Although you do not need a financial background to day trade, you may be curious as to why it works.

The balance of this chapter presents a preliminary discussion of the concepts underlying this day trading strategy. It starts by looking at the distinction between trading and investing. It summarizes different types of investment funds. Only then does it follow up with a discussion of the environment that makes day trading hum. This discussion touches on ways to minimize investment expenses, tax advantages of retirement savings plans, stock market volatility, and other conditions conducive to day trading. Much more is presented in the following chapters.

TRADING AND INVESTING

Among other things, this book is about trading. Thus the distinction between *trading* and *investing* becomes important at this point. A *trade* generally refers to the purchase or sale of a security, such as stock of a publicly held company. Trading is generally referred to as a series of trades over a short time period. An investment in a company begins with a trade to purchase its stock and ends with a trade to sell the stock. Whereas trading involves many trades over a short time period, investing has a more long-term perspective.

Under a 401(k) plan, personal trades and investments both occur through exchanges among the plan's fund options. Day trading retirement savings involves daily fund exchanges between different fund options with the intention of setting up or capturing short-term stock gains based on market swings.

On the surface, trading is a bit like dating, and investing is more like getting married, albeit in an open marriage. People may date quite frequently with different prospects before settling down for the long haul with the right partner once it comes time for marriage. Similarly, a security held by a trader has a shorter shelf life than one held by an investor.

As dating can be viewed as trading one partner for another on a fairly regular basis, trading in the securities markets involves buying and selling securities on a frequent basis. After a while of serial dating, you may get a feel for the type of mate you are looking for. You may even narrow down your prospects to certain distinct types, such as drinking buddies or teetotalers. Although both may make very delightful companions, you may consider there to be situations where one may be more suitable than another. At the risk of carrying this analogy just a little too far, day trading retirement savings accounts also involves narrowing your plan choices to just two types of alternative fund options and switching between them on a regular basis depending on the situation.

Marriage, in contrast, can be thought of as similar to a long-term investment. You generally go into both marriage and an investment with the intent of staying put for a long time. However, this is where the analogy begins to break down. Unlike marriage, you are not bound to have and to hold an investment until death. Also, an investment portfolio should not be as exclusive as a marriage, as many investments are necessary in a properly diversified investment portfolio. So an investment typically represents the best of intentions with respect to holding for the long term but may be dumped if conditions warrant.

This analogy breaks down further when you consider that marriage usually spells an end to dating, whereas the day trading strategy can be carried out simultaneously alongside a sound investment strategy. In this case, day trading for short-term gains can be considered a supplement, rather than a prelude or alternative, to investing for long-term wealth accumulation. Along the lines of this open-marriage-with-dating context, day trading in a disciplined manner should be considered an integral part of managing retirement savings in these uncertain times.

In summary, trading generally deals with buying and selling securities over a short period of time. By contrast, a long-term investment is made with the intent of holding a position or fund to increase the value of the account over time. It is the intent of the holding period (rather than the actual holding period) that distinguishes a (short-term) trade within the realm of (long-term) investments.

Both investment and trading strategies can be used to accumulate wealth over the long term. An investment strategy establishes the foundation of asset holdings for the long term, while the day trading strategy capitalizes over time on short-term market swings through daily fund exchanges between two different asset classes.

ENVIRONMENT

Day trading takes place in the special financial environment offered by 401(k) and other retirement savings plans where trades do not trigger immediate taxes or direct expenses.

Fund Composition

Each trade involves transferring existing retirement savings account assets from one fund option to another. The day trading strategy generates gains from daily fund transfers between investment options composed of securities in different asset classes with different risk and liquidity characteristics.

Asset Classes Nothing in life lasts forever, unless you own. Duration makes the difference. Take the case of an owner and a renter. An owner enjoys the ride and gets to keep whatever is left over, whereas a renter gets to take a ride and returns it when it is done. The distinction derives from the difference between perpetual and temporary rights.

Stock confers perpetual (but transferable) ownership in a company to a stockholder, whereas a *fixed income security* evidences a temporary obligation to repay a debt holder for a loan to the debtor. Stockholders have perpetual rights to a company's future earnings (in the form of any *dividends*, *capital appreciation*, and return of capital upon sale). Debt holders get the rights to repayment of a debt in the form of a temporary fixed income stream (comprising any dividends and a return of principal) over a specified *term*. In a sense, stockholders own a piece of a company, and debt holders (or holders of fixed income securities) rent a piece of a company (although, in a more conventional sense, it could be considered that the company is renting money from the debt holder).

Using this distinction between perpetual and temporary rights, assets available for investment can be categorized into two broad types: stock and fixed income. The fixed income type can be further broken down into *bonds* (including *notes*) with longer repayment terms or more liquid *cash* with a short or nonexistent term. Although bonds and cash are still just different forms of debt, they are often segregated into separate asset classes for classification purposes. So you will generally see assets classified into one of three classes: stocks, bonds, or cash.

Risk Each of these three broad asset classes has its own risk characteristics that affect its potential returns. *Risk* represents the volatility of a particular investment's return in relation to that of the market.[3] A higher-risk investment offers a wider variation in returns from day to day than a lower-risk investment. Less risky investments generally offer lower returns in exchange for stability of returns and liquidity over the long run.

Over time, stocks have experienced the most volatility in returns and thus are generally considered the riskiest of the three classes. Bond returns have been less volatile than stocks and consequently carry lower risk. **Cash has been the least volatile and therefore is considered to have the lowest investment risk of the three asset classes.** In short, the three asset classes can generally be ranked from highest to lowest in risk level as follows: (1) stocks, (2) bonds, and then (3) cash.

Liquidity   *Liquidity* refers to the ability to sell an investment at a moment's notice with little or no loss of principal. However, easy access to cash in on an investment comes at the price of offering a lower return. Cash best fits the bill as the most liquid of asset classes, followed by stocks and bonds.

Most investment advisers wisely suggest that you invest your retirement savings for the long term in a diversified portfolio of stocks, bonds, and cash. This time-tested investment strategy tends to produce the most consistent year-to-year returns by balancing the underlying risk and liquidity characteristics of the asset classes when properly allocated.

Fund Options

Almost all 401(k) and other retirement savings plans enable portfolio diversification by offering fund options that pool securities from one, two, or all three asset classes. Each alternative fund option comes straight up or blended, depending on whether its composition within its market basket of securities is dedicated to only one of the stock, bond, or cash asset classes, or is composed of a combination thereof. Most large plans include a separate fund option dedicated to each asset class and additional balanced fund options blending one or more asset classes.

Plan fund options typically come in the form of mutual funds, *institutional funds*, and separate accounts managed by registered investment companies, banks, and insurance companies. These collective funds pool the investments of one or more investors, offering the advantage of professional management at a reasonable cost. Each fund's objective will determine whether it is either *passively managed* to track a *market index* or *actively managed* to seek the best returns through investment selection and market timing.

Many plans offer employer stock as an investment option, especially for employer contributions. Some plans also offer *target-date funds*, which use investors' time horizons until retirement as the basis for the allocation of asset classes within the fund. For investors looking to put the management of their accounts on autopilot, these funds, also known as *life cycle funds*, have an asset class mix (and associated risk) that shifts over time from a stock-heavy balance with higher risk at younger ages to a more conservative blend with more fixed income securities as retirement nears. These target-date funds operate as a fund of funds, serving as a wrapper around other mutual funds or institutional funds offered by the investment manager for the plan. This additional layer of management, of course, results in additional expenses of the wrapper fund, as well as those of the underlying funds, being passed along to shareholders.

All of these fund options commonly found in 401(k) plans are valued only once at the end of each day. Less prevalent are plans incorporating fund options, such as self-directed brokerage accounts or exchange-traded funds (ETFs), that allow more frequent trading. Unlike most plans offering only mutual fund type options valued only once each day at the close of the market, a plan with self-directed brokerage accounts or ETFs offers participants the ability to trade their accounts throughout the day on a real-time basis.

Most 401(k) and other retirement savings plans do not offer the kind of exotic investment alternatives found elsewhere in the market (for good reasons to be discussed later). So you generally will not find stock options, derivatives, or commodities funds offered under your plan. In fact, very few retirement savings plans stray outside of offering professionally managed mutual funds, institutional funds, or separate accounts as fund options.

The management of your retirement portfolio requires your attention on how to allocate your retirement savings accounts among various fund options. Fortunately, part of the fund selection process has already been done for you by your plan sponsor or, more likely, its investment committee. Without even considering institutional funds and separate accounts, as of the end of 2010, there were about 7,600 mutual funds in the United States from which to choose.[4] From the fund universe, your plan sponsor has carefully selected a menu of funds to offer as investment options under your retirement savings plan, taking into account each fund's risk, potential returns, and other factors. Even under the most limited of investment options offered under your plan, you usually can still use day trading to take advantage of swings in the market.

Fund Expenses

The two types of explicit expenses charged for investing in a fund are sales loads and ongoing expenses. Although uncommon in 401(k) plans, a sales load is a one-time charge paid to a financial adviser at the time of the purchase (in the form of a front-end load) or sale (in the form of a back-end load) of the fund. Ongoing expenses include the operational and trading costs incurred in running the fund. Operational costs cover investment management, administration, accounting, marketing, and other costs involved in the ongoing operation of a fund. Trading costs result from the fund manager's purchase and sale of securities in carrying out the fund's objectives. Ongoing operational and trading expenses are passed along to shareholders as a reduction in gross returns.

Each fund within your account is charged with its applicable share of operational and trading expenses for the fund. Operational expenses are computed as the fund's *expense ratio*, a percentage, applied to assets under management within the fund. The amount of trading costs that are also passed along to all shareholders depends on the fund's *portfolio turnover*, or amount of buying and selling of securities by the fund manager. You bear your share of these expenses regardless of whether you make money by investing in the fund.

Fund companies pass along these ongoing fund expenses covering operational and trading costs to shareholders as a reduction from the fund's gross investment returns. These fund expenses are typically charged as a percentage of assets under management. Depending on the type of expense, they can vary by the plan size, management style, or portfolio turnover.

Plan Size   Plan funds come in different sizes. Like your local fast-food operation that used to offer what it called a super size with more fries per dollar, the shareholders in larger plan funds are usually charged lower expenses as a percentage of assets invested. Operational expenses passed along to shareholders in the form of an expense ratio usually vary by fund class inversely to the size of the plan's investment in that particular fund. Thus institutional fund shares offered as investment options under larger plans will have a lower expense ratio than retail shares of the same fund. An institutional class fund option with $10 million invested in it by a plan is likely to have a lower expense ratio than a retail fund of the same variety within another plan but with only $10,000 in assets invested.

Regardless of your individual account size, you share in the expense savings afforded institutional funds when its lower expense ratio (percentage of your account assets) is deducted from the returns credited your account. You get the advantage of being part of something bigger when the expenses charged to your modest (or emerging, as you may like to call it) account for its management and administration are less than they would have been if it were not combined with your fellow participants' accounts invested in the same fund.

Management Style   As noted previously, *passively managed funds* track a market index, and *actively managed funds* seek the best returns through investment selection and market timing. Both types of funds charge investment management and administrative expenses as well as trading costs that are passed through to shareholders as a deduction from gross returns.

A passively managed fund holds a market basket of securities that is simply intended to track a market index, such as the Standard & Poor's 500 (S&P 500) index. The reduced scope of a passive fund's investment management and trading activities can translate into minimal management fees and trading costs passed along to shareholders, resulting in only slightly lower investment returns than the market index itself that it is intended to track.

In comparison to passively managed funds, actively managed funds generally incur the additional cost of paying high-priced investment managers as well as higher trading costs, which are passed along as fees that reduce the fund's return. Perhaps because of the higher cost of investing in actively managed funds, studies show that most actively managed funds do not outperform the broad market on a consistent basis.[5] It turns out that the higher costs taken out of actively managed funds' investment returns place them at a disadvantage to passively managed *market index funds* from the outset that most can never quite seem to overcome. If an active manager does not indeed add value to a fund, you end up paying more and getting less in an actively managed fund.

Portfolio Turnover   Investment funds incur trading costs, such as brokerage commissions, for the purchase and sale of securities within the fund portfolio. The trading costs incurred by a fund are affected by shareholders' net fund exchanges (i.e., purchases and redemptions) and dividend reinvestments.

Passively managed funds incur trading costs to keep fund investments aligned with the underlying market index after adjusting for fund purchases and redemptions and any changes in the index's lineup. Actively managed funds incur additional trading costs related to the fund's portfolio turnover resulting from the purchase and sale of securities necessary to carry out its investment manager's security selection and market timing calls. Depending on a fund's portfolio turnover, this added layer of trading costs to carry out its fund manager's strategy can significantly increase an actively managed fund's trading costs. Without this added layer of an actively managed fund's trading costs, a passively managed fund will generally incur fewer trading costs than an actively managed fund in tracking a market index.

These expenses resulting from a fund's aggregate trading activity are passed along to all shareholders as a deduction from the fund's gross returns. Each shareholder incurs a proportionate share of the fund's aggregate trading costs based on his or her account size, without respect to the individual's own transactional activity. **Individual fund investors generally do not directly bear the trading costs associated with their own fund exchanges, with some exceptions (as described later).**

If you buy shares in a mutual fund with a sales load from a broker, you may very well pay a sales commission. As a retail customer, you may not be in a position to buy directly from the fund company in order to avoid paying the broker to serve as an intermediary in the transaction. If you have ever heard the radio advertisement of your direct diamond importer, you know that buying direct from its wholesale warehouse eliminates the middleman, allowing the importer to pass the savings along to you. As a 401(k) participant, you too can avoid the middleman, in this case, the broker—and the broker's sales commissions and redemption charges—when you make a fund exchange through the plan.

Comparing expense ratios and trading costs of funds is important in that each dollar paid as an expense to a fund company is a dollar never again to be seen by you as a shareholder. Over time, these expenses paid year after year to fund companies rather than credited to your retirement portfolio may have a profound effect on how well you will live in retirement. **So it really is important that you consider investing in the lowest-cost funds within your 401(k) portfolio that meet your objectives.**

Taxes

Taxes are a good thing when you consider their use to build roads, educate children, defend freedom, and send people to the moon. However, most people will agree that they pay more than their share of taxes. Consistent with this philosophy, tax advisers promote strategies to help people avoid or reduce taxes and pay them later (not forward) as much as legally possible. A 401(k) or other retirement savings plan is just the ticket to help you achieve the goal of paying less current tax and deferring payment of taxes.

Taxes can get quite sticky and are always subject to change. Although there is an ever-expanding body of law dealing with the operation of 401(k) and other retirement savings plans, the taxation of these plan accounts is relatively straightforward in comparison to the taxation of holdings in brokerage accounts. More important, the preferential tax treatment afforded retirement savings plans presents a compelling case for their use in saving for retirement.

The principal tax advantage available under these plans relates to the timing of the tax due on contributions and investment earnings within individual accounts. When you deposit part of your wages into a normal brokerage account, the amount of your deposit is what is left over after paying taxes. Then you get taxed on your investment earnings each year. However, a 401(k) plan allows you to deposit that entire amount into your individual account before taxes are withheld. Any employer contributions also go into the account untaxed. This power of pretax contributions is then compounded over time with nontaxable earnings until distribution.

Investment earnings can generally be broken down into capital gains, dividends, and interest. A realized *capital gain* is the gain from the sale of a security at a price higher than its original purchase price. A *capital loss* occurs when the sale price is less than the purchase price and may be used to offset other capital gains or other income to an extent. A *dividend* is typically a quarterly distribution of earnings (on stock) or a promised semiannual interest payment (on a bond). Interest income (as from a bank account) is also distributed periodically.

In a taxable account, the different forms of investment earnings may be nontaxable, partially taxable, or fully taxable as income, depending on the issuer (as in municipal or corporate bonds), holding period (as in short- or long-term capital gains), and tax preference (as in qualified vs. nonqualified dividends). Interest and short-term capital gains on the sale of securities held less than a year are generally taxed as ordinary income. Dividends may be taxed at a preferential rate or not at all. The sale of an appreciated security held at least one year generates a long-term capital gain that is generally taxed at a preferential tax rate. Any income tax on dividends and interest is due in the year of receipt, and any capital gains tax due is due upon sale of the security generating the capital gain. In short, the amount and timing of taxation varies by the source of the investment income.

Unlike the different tax treatments afforded different forms of invest-ment earnings in a taxable account, a 401(k) or other retirement savings account's investment earnings (as well as employee pretax contributions and employer contributions) generally escape current taxation. Instead, taxes are deferred until receipt of a plan distribution. Regardless of the timing or source of the investment earnings within the retirement savings account, the taxable portion of the account is subject to tax as ordinary in-come upon distribution in cash to a participant. It does not matter whether the investment earnings are from dividends, interest, or capital gains.

Realized capital gains from an individual's redemption of fund shares caused by a participant-directed exchange from one fund to another within a retirement savings plan escape current taxation. Likewise, realized capital gains on the sale of securities traded by a fund's investment manager over the course of a year (that typically get assigned to fund shareholders) are not currently taxable to individuals holding that fund in their retirement savings accounts. Both are generally taxed as ordi-nary income upon eventual distribution to the individual.

However, taxes on such gains may be further deferred by rolling over the account distribution into an *individual retirement account* (IRA) or other retirement plan. Participants receiving a distribution of employer stock from a 401(k) plan may also be able to further defer taxation of any unrealized gains on the stock.

Just as important as tax and trading cost avoidance is to the effective-ness of day trading a retirement savings portfolio is the day-to-day volatility of the stock market.

Stock Market Volatility

How easy would it be to manage your investment portfolio if the stock market headed straight up? All you would have to do is put all of your money into stocks and watch your portfolio grow in value. It seems that some people actually believed this to be the case until a dramatic market decline or two reminded them of the risk involved in investing in stocks.

Instead, the stock market is unpredictable. Its volatility should come as no surprise, as stocks represent the asset class with the most risk. The market goes up some days and down others. Yet, even though there have been declines, the stock market has shown a resiliency over time to bounce back from declines. Its general trend has been to go up over the long term, although it tends to fluctuate quite a bit along the way.

Various indexes measure the aggregate value of segments of the stock market. The index widely regarded as the best measure of the U.S. stock market is the *Standard & Poor's 500 (S&P 500) index*. Covering about 75 percent of the U.S. stock market, the S&P 500 index is a composite average of the market value of 500 of the largest U.S. companies doing business in a cross section of industries. It is updated continuously throughout each day the stock exchanges are open.

One way to represent the volatility of the U.S. stock market would be to depict the changes in the level of the S&P 500 index over time in a graph. Figure 1.1 presents a history of the level of the S&P 500 index over the past 50 years (through 2010). The vertical height of each point on the squiggly line in Figure 1.1 represents the level of the daily closing value of the S&P 500 index, as you go horizontally forward in time. The volatility of the stock market is depicted by all of the up-and-down spikes shown in this 50-year history of the index.

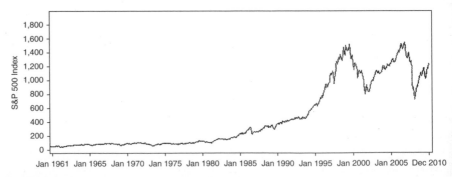

FIGURE 1.1 Standard & Poor's 500 Index History
Source: Standard & Poor's 500 Index Historical Chart, http://moneycentral.msn.com.

The S&P 500 index has increased at an annual average rate of about 6.3 percent per year, excluding dividends, over this 50-year period ended December 31, 2010. Along the way, its investment returns, whether measured on an annual basis or otherwise, have fluctuated quite a bit. Its largest annual calendar year advance of 34.1 percent was in 1995. Its largest annual calendar year decline of 38.5 percent occurred in 2008. The S&P 500 index also experienced some dramatic daily changes. Over this same period, its largest daily gain on a percentage basis was 11.6 percent on October 13, 2008. Of course, one cannot easily forget its largest daily percentage loss of 20.5 percent on October 19, 1987.[6] The market can be quite volatile on a daily basis and seems to get moreso in uncertain times.

The increased volatility of the stock market has come in the form of bigger swings in the market, combined with an increased number of changes in the direction of the market. This volatility may further be characterized as a string of extended periods of wobbly movement ending up with little or no net change, broken up by some brief periods of sizable changes. For the most part, though, the direction of the market measured over long periods has been relatively neutral, or *sideways*. Yet the sharp advances, interspersed among the longer periods of volatile but sideways movement, have historically driven the market to higher levels.

You have only to look back to 2010 to observe an extended period of sideways volatility in the stock market over the preceding decade. By comparison with the bull market of the 1990s, turbulence rocked the stock market during the first decade of the 2000s, with ascents to new highs followed by declines to lows last experienced a decade or more earlier. There also was an era of more than 18 years up to mid-1982 when the market stumbled along before settling back into the price range where it all started in 1964. In the past 50 years, these and other extended periods of volatile but sideways movement have predominated in the stock market about three-fourths of the time.[7] Unsettling as it may have been on a day-to-day basis, these volatile markets presented trading opportunities to take advantage of short-term movements in stock prices in an otherwise sideways market.

Among other factors, the impact of demographic patterns on consumer spending suggests that the U.S. economy, and consequently the stock market, will idle through 2020. Accounting for about 70 percent of the U.S. *gross domestic product*, consumer spending drives the U.S. economy. As the free spending of the retiring baby boomers (born between 1946 and 1964) wanes, the world waits for the next generation of spenders, the millennials generation (born between 1977 and 1997), to hit their stride while grappling with paying down unprecedented national and personal debt. These and other challenges present significant obstacles to achieving much in the way of economic growth or associated stock market advances in the near term.

To participate in the market advances that may eventually come, you need to be continuously invested in stocks. In addition, you will now have a way to cash in on more prevalent sideways markets by harnessing daily stock market fluctuations through day trading.

RATIONALE

Day trading draws on fundamental principles of investment management to exploit daily market volatility.

Retirement Savings Account Management

Having gotten this far into the book, you must be either a saving voyeur observing others defer current pleasure in favor of a better future or the real thing socking money away on a regular basis. Assuming the latter, congratulations on having the foresight to save for retirement in a 401(k) or other retirement savings account. There will be no chastising here about what you already have or have not put aside as savings in your 401(k) plan account. It is not anyone's business but your own to assess or address the proficiency of your retirement saving skills, or lack thereof. Whatever your perspective, chances are you would not mind making the most out of what you already have in your 401(k) account(s).

Yes, you should save for retirement, and more is better. However, saving is only part of the formula for successfully meeting your retirement goals. You also need to manage the accumulation of your savings in your retirement portfolio. Success in managing your retirement savings accounts comes from following a sound investment strategy supplemented by day trading. Not to be overlooked, managing risk and minimizing investment expenses are also key elements in getting the best returns in your retirement portfolio.

Managing investments would be a whole lot easier and more profitable if you could remove all emotion from the process and follow a simple, methodical process. The investment and day trading strategies described later will establish such a methodical process for managing your retirement portfolio. This approach works in layers. You start first with an investment strategy to generate long-term wealth, and then you overlay a day trading strategy to enhance your returns.

Investment Strategy   The underlying investment strategy is based on time-tested investment principles that have served investors for years. These principles include portfolio diversification, dollar-cost averaging, portfolio rebalancing, and reduction of risk as you age. These basic principles espoused by most investment professionals serve as the underlying foundation of sound retirement savings account management.

Portfolio *diversification* comes from not holding all your eggs in one basket. When done right, asset class diversification reduces a portfolio's risk. By holding different securities that do not move in concert, diversification buffers the impact of market shifts on your overall portfolio.

Dollar-cost averaging refers to buying securities at regular intervals. Regular 401(k) contributions withheld from pay each pay period facilitate these periodic purchases at then current prices, thus eliminating market timing guesses as to the best time to buy. The resulting cumulative purchases under dollar-cost averaging result in more shares being bought when prices are low and fewer shares bought when prices are high.

Along these lines of dampening the effect of market volatility, you may choose to periodically *rebalance* your accumulated account assets so as to keep a consistent allocation of your account assets proportionately distributed among plan funds if earnings in one or more funds have outpaced those in other fund(s). In effect, you transfer money from a higher-performing fund to another lesser-performing fund to get back to your initial target asset allocation. Relying on the underlying concept of buying low and selling high, rebalancing ensures that you preserve gains from a market run-up by selling stock after the market has risen and you set up future gains by buying stock after the market has declined.

Any investment strategy for your retirement savings should involve a gradual reduction of risk as you get closer to retirement. Unlike retirees depending on their retirement savings for current income, young investors have a longer investment horizon before they will need to draw on their retirement savings. This longer investment horizon allows young investors to take on more risk in their quest for higher returns. So when you are younger, your investment portfolio should be heavily weighted toward stocks, the riskiest of the three asset classes. Your youth gives you a long time frame to reap the potential long-term appreciation of stocks and the ability to wait out any short-term hiccups in the market. As you age and get closer to retirement when you will need to start drawing on your retirement savings, you should be investing more in secure investments by gradually reducing your exposure to stocks in favor of less risky assets such as bonds and cash.

Day Trading Strategy   The day trading strategy draws additional returns out of a portfolio's underlying investments. It does this through a formulaic approach that dictates what and when to buy and sell. After all, that is all you really need when it comes to managing investments. It is the day trading part of the account management strategy that has not gotten the attention from 401(k) account holders that it so justly deserves. By most appearances, trading for the short term to enhance returns in retirement savings accounts seems to be at odds with the long-term perspective espoused by most investment professionals for managing retirement savings.

Yet carried out over the long term, day trading provides a great way to take advantage of market volatility within the unique environment offered by 401(k) and other retirement savings accounts. Under this day trading strategy, you make daily fund exchanges within retirement savings accounts that will capture the positive returns in a fluctuating market, while avoiding all direct trading costs and immediate income taxes.

Like an insatiable gold-digger looking for the next victim, day trading is easy, cheap, and opportunistic. In the parlance of the financial world, it also fits the bill of a successful investment or trading strategy, because it is simple, cost-effective, and profitable.

Simple   The simplicity of a strategy determines its effectiveness. The transparency of the strategy's underlying logic and its ease of use facilitate its translation into a routine that can be carried out quickly without much thought. In turn, such an efficient and methodical routine promotes the regular usage of the strategy that leads to a successful result.

Day trading involves systematic fund transfers between stocks and cash. Its simplicity comes from dealing with only these two fund options. Forsaking all other options in the strategy, day traders use a simple formula that dictates the amount, direction, and timing of daily exchanges between stocks and cash. The strategy does not mess with esoteric investments, sector weightings, or style selection. Its success comes from the ease with which it can be used on a regular basis over time.

Cost-Effective   The most cost-effective way to day trade involves the use of a stock market index fund and a cash-type fund. These funds may not offer the potential pop promised by more expensive actively managed funds, but then neither do the vast majority of actively managed funds live up to their hype. In view of the questionable value of actively managed funds that typically do not beat or even match the returns of index funds, the day trading strategy sticks to the use of market-tracking stock index funds and stable cash-type funds with their lower investment management and trading expenses.

Trading costs are another consideration. Frequent trading within a taxable brokerage account can get quite expensive due to brokerage commissions and fees as well as taxes associated with trades. (After all, your broker has to eat, and the government needs to keep those roads in good repair.) In fact, such trading expenses and taxes can greatly reduce or even eliminate any potential profits generated through frequent trading within a brokerage account.

However, day trading within retirement savings accounts makes use of cost and tax advantages not otherwise available in taxable brokerage accounts. Retirement savings accounts offer a unique environment free of direct trading costs and immediate taxation of gains. More specifically, the advantages to you as an individual trading in a retirement savings accounts are:

- You do not incur any direct trading costs for making fund exchanges done the right way (to avoid frequent trading restrictions, as explained later in Chapter 8) within a retirement savings account. Instead, each fund's trading costs associated with rejiggering the fund to accommodate the net sum of all shareholders' fund exchanges are shared among all fund shareholders.
- You do not bear any immediate tax consequence resulting from trading activity within a retirement savings account. Any realized capital gain triggered by a fund exchange is not taxed until distribution.

This retirement savings account day trading strategy is unique in the way it uses low-cost funds, avoids direct trading expenses, and defers taxes.

Profitable   Most sound retirement investment advice centers around a *buy-and-hold investment strategy* with little or no active trading. By contrast, day trading your retirement portfolio involves daily fund exchanges to take advantage of market uncertainty. The premise underlying day trading's ability to generate gains in a fluctuating market relies solely on how arithmetic creates something from nothing. The timing of your trades allows you to capture temporary gains, only to convert them to more lasting gains, over a period when the market is otherwise neutral.

When it comes to the stock market, this much is known: it will go up, go down, or remain the same each day. Day trading sets up and preserves gains resulting from stock market volatility. The gains garnered under the day trading strategy come from executing fund exchanges based on the day-to-day swings in the stock market. It uses the market's fluctuations to set up profit opportunities when the stock market declines and to preserve profits made when the stock market advances. It is as simple as buying low and selling high to generate gains within retirement savings accounts. The more volatile the market is, the more opportunity there is to profit under this strategy. Using stock market index and cash funds, the day trading strategy uses the volatility of stocks and the stability of cash to enhance returns over time in a sideways market.

PROCESS

Day trading avoids restrictions intended to thwart its very existence through the methodical application of a simple process that can be carried out in minutes a day.

Day Trading Prerequisites

There are certain plan ingredients conducive to the success of day trading. These prerequisite features relate to the availability of 401(k) and other retirement savings accounts, fund options, daily valuation of accounts, and daily exchange privileges. Fortunately, most 401(k) and other retirement savings plans incorporate the features you need to day trade.

Plan Type   Most tax-deferred retirement savings plans are ripe for day trading. Although references throughout this book may refer to 401(k) plans that are primarily sponsored by corporations, other types of tax-deferred account-based plans sponsored by different entities will work just as well. The types of defined contribution plans in which you may day trade include:

- 401(k) plans, tax-deferred profit sharing plans, money purchase plans, and target benefit plans, sponsored by corporations and other entities.
- *403(b) plans*, sponsored by public school systems and other nonprofit organizations.
- *457 plans*, sponsored by state and local government employers and certain tax-exempt organizations.
- Solo 401(k) plans and Keogh (HR-10) defined contribution plans sponsored by sole proprietorships and partnerships.
- Simplified employee pension (SEP) plans, savings incentive match plans for employees (SIMPLE plans), and old salary reduction simplified employee pension (SARSEP) plans, sponsored by other small employers.
- Individual retirement accounts (IRAs), established and maintained by individuals.

Once you determine that you are covered under one of these types of retirement savings plans, you need to make sure it is the type of plan that allows you personally to direct the investment of your account assets. You can day trade only in plans that allow you to make fund exchanges within your individual accounts. Therefore, plans under which the assets are managed by the plan sponsor, instead of you, cannot accommodate day trading.

Consequently, day trading is not possible with *defined benefit pension plans* promising an *annuity* or lump sum benefit at retirement from plan assets managed by a plan sponsor. Absent your ability to make fund exchanges or otherwise take any role in managing plan assets, you are not in a position to day trade under a *pension* plan. The types of pension plans under which day trading is not possible include traditional pension plans, cash balance plans, pension equity plans, life cycle pension plans, retirement bonus plans, or mobility plans. Do not be fooled by the appearance of some defined benefit pension plans under which individual accounts are maintained. Since their underlying assets are still managed by the plan sponsor, you cannot day trade with these pension plans.

You may want to check with your plan administrator or check your plan documentation as to the type of plan under which you are covered so that you may determine whether it can accommodate day trading.

Number of Accounts   In order to day trade, you need to have saved and accumulated balances in at least two different retirement savings accounts. More accounts are even better. Your accounts from your current and former employers, as well as IRAs, must be maintained in the types of retirement savings plans that allow free daily fund exchanges.

If you have not succumbed to the barrage of solicitations to consolidate the accounts from your former employers' plans, you are in a position to use these accounts for day trading.

Available Fund Options   Day trading requires that each retirement savings account must offer at least two alternative investment fund options into which you may direct the investment of your account. Although most plans offer a variety of fund options, daily fund exchanges will be made exclusively between only two options: a stock fund and a cash-type fund. Again you are in luck, as virtually all plans offer stock and cash-type funds as alternative investment options.

Daily Account Valuation   Mutual funds and other investment funds offered in retirement savings plans are typically valued once per day at the market close. Yet some plans are valued less frequently, such as quarterly, or more frequently, such as on a real-time basis, as with self-directed brokerage accounts and exchange-traded funds (ETFs). Day trading relies on each retirement savings plan offering a daily valuation of accounts. That is, each of the alternative investment funds held in your accounts will be updated at the end of each and every business day with the day's contributions, disbursements, fund exchanges, and, most important, investment gains or losses. Day trading uses these daily updated account valuations to work its magic through daily fund exchanges.

Daily Exchange Privileges For day trading to work, any fund exchange you submit needs to be executed on the basis of each fund's closing price for the day on which your direction is made prior to the close of the market. This daily fund exchange privilege is critical, as daily exchanges into or out of stock funds will set up or preserve gains when the stock market drops or rises.

Most retirement savings plans offer daily exchange privileges between stock and cash-type fund options that are valued daily. If your retirement savings plan does not have these attributes, you may want to suggest some changes to your employer or plan sponsor. Otherwise, you may have to rely on other strategies to manage your retirement savings portfolio.

JUICING RETURNS

Managing a retirement savings portfolio is no easy task. Aside from saving, you should have an overall investment strategy to assist you in managing risk and minimizing expenses through an appropriate allocation of your retirement account assets among available investment options. Any investment strategy must also consider your investment time horizon until retirement. The way you deal with your savings levels, expense management, risk management, and investment time horizon significantly influences whether your retirement savings goals will be met.

As a practical and inexpensive way to supplement a sound investment strategy, the day trading strategy draws upon the nature of uncertain markets and people's reaction to them. Done the right way, day trading in response to market volatility over an extended period enhances a retirement portfolio's investment returns. Its daily rebalancing of a retirement savings portfolio's asset allocation between stocks and cash through fund exchanges sets up and captures stock market gains by buying low and selling high.

The day trading of a balanced retirement savings portfolio will outperform any static portfolio in a sideways market, which may very well be the case for the second decade of the twenty-first century (i.e., 2011–2020). Otherwise, in a rising market, it also can align with an investment strategy goal of reducing portfolio risk as you age (and your investment horizon shortens as you approach retirement) through an increased allocation to lower-risk funds.

It is important that the day trading strategy support and supplement a sound investment strategy. Having only touched on the basic concepts underlying how day trading can supplement a sound investment strategy, there is more to be discussed on the mechanics of how those concepts can be used in harmony. Only then will you be able to decide if day trading will work for you.

Ready or not, you are responsible for making sure your retirement savings will last a lifetime (or two, if you consider your spouse or partner). As a result, investing and trading within the context of retirement savings accounts will be more important than ever. In the process, you will need to address how you will formulate an approach for managing your retirement savings accounts. How did you ever wind up with this investment responsibility?

PART II

Environment

CHAPTER 2

The Shift

Pensions to 401(k) Plans

*The art of progress is to preserve order amid change
and to preserve change amid order.*
                                        —Alfred North Whitehead

S ure there would be the reunions, but it was his last day with his colleagues at the company that had employed him for 35 years. He had just accepted an early retirement package and was about to venture forward into an unknown phase of life. They shared the customary cake, the presents, and then some heartfelt words. What was left unsaid at the party was the most important of details: he would receive a pension guaranteeing him income for life. For that he was grateful.

There used to be a day when a hardworking employee was rewarded with a gold watch and a pension upon retirement after a long career with an employer. My, how times have changed! People change jobs so often these days that loyalty awards are becoming a thing of the past. The traditional pension is also on its way out of favor, as defined contribution plans, such as 401(k) plans, have supplanted them as the primary type of retirement plan. So the gold watch and pension have been replaced with a handshake and a 401(k) account. By the way, you will need that handshake for good luck in making sure your 401(k) account lasts a lifetime.

Retirement is not what it used to be. Retirement used to be that time of your life when you stopped working for pay and instead relied on Social Security, employer-sponsored retirement plans, and accumulated savings to sustain your lifestyle. Reaching age 65 was considered a turning point in making the transition from work into retirement. Now even Social Security is at risk. If you had a pension, your career could comfortably end with a full pension starting at the normal retirement at age 65. Now, if you cannot count on Social Security and pensions, you will be left with relying on your 401(k) accounts and savings, which may not be enough to support you in retirement.

In addition, Americans are living longer and healthier lives, turning this notion of retirement on its head. Due to medical advances and lifestyle choices, many seniors are remaining active well beyond age 65 and cannot quite settle into retirement at any set age. In a study conducted by Age Wave for Charles Schwab & Company, 71 percent of survey respondents of different ages said they plan to work in retirement.[1]

Meanwhile, employers are establishing programs to encourage these healthy and active seniors to continue working full-time or part-time while transitioning into retirement. A July 2008 study of 140 midsize and large companies found that 61 percent of the companies already offer, or plan to offer, phased retirement programs enabling employees to ease into retirement in stages. These programs generally allow employees to start collecting retirement benefits as they reduce their work hours.[2]

Some seniors still work to supplement their income, while others do it to keep a sense of purpose in their lives. You may decide to work for other reasons, such as the need to stay independent. As much as you love your children and they love you, they probably are not too interested in being a source of your support (or housing) in retirement.

With pensions in decline and the future of Social Security in question, you are the one who needs to make sure you can support yourself for the rest of your life once you actually do retire. Since you will no longer be earning wages from the sweat of your brow—that's why it's called retirement—you will instead have to rely for support primarily on your own retirement savings, although other income sources may also be available.

HOW MUCH RETIREMENT INCOME IS ENOUGH?

Making sure you have enough money once you have really retired is a scary proposition. First you have to know how much to save, then how to invest it, and finally how to draw it down. If you are like most people, you will want to sock away enough money over time so that you can support a lifestyle similar to what you have enjoyed prior to retirement.

Once you stop working, your expenses for commuting, work clothes, and income taxes will decrease. If your house is paid off and the kids are grown, your monthly housing costs and support obligations are less. Yet after retirement, some expenses, like travel, health care, and long-term care, may increase. In view of these factors, there is a theory that on average you will generally want to make sure that you will have an income stream in retirement of at least 70 percent of what you earned just before retirement. Of course, the desired level of this *replacement rate*, at which your retirement income replaces your preretirement pay, varies for each individual depending on income, lifestyle, and other factors.

SOURCES OF RETIREMENT INCOME

The traditional sources of an individual's retirement income are derived from:

- Social Security.
- Employer-sponsored retirement plans.
- Personal savings.

You and your employer make mandatory and voluntary contributions throughout your career to fund these federal, employer, and individual programs that support you in retirement. When you stop working, you may receive a combination of income and savings from these three sources and perhaps others to support you in retirement. An agency of the federal government pays Social Security benefits; an employee benefit trust or other custodial account sponsored by your employer pays retirement benefits; and your personal savings accounts provide the rest of your retirement income.

In theory, this shared responsibility of providing your retirement income from three different sources lightens the load for any one particular payer. However, changes in demographics and a shift in government policy toward more individual empowerment have dramatically altered the retirement income landscape. As a result, more and more people are finding, and will find, that how they live in retirement primarily depends on how much they personally saved and how they invested it.

The three traditional sources of retirement income—Social Security, retirement plans, and personal savings—have all been undergoing some significant changes that will transform their relative importance in securing your future in retirement.

Social Security

The Old-Age, Survivors, and Disability Insurance (OASDI) program, otherwise known as the U.S. Social Security system, currently covers more than 90 percent of the American workforce.[3] The Social Security system provides retirement, survivor, and disability benefits, primarily in the form of a monthly annuity, to qualifying workers and their beneficiaries.

Social Security was established in 1935 primarily to pay lifetime benefits to retired workers after having attained age 65. Social Security retirement pensions are calculated under a complicated formula that generally takes into account a worker's highest 35 years of indexed covered wages. The formula is applied to the average of each of the worker's highest 35 years of wages up to the applicable Social Security taxable wage base, as adjusted for wage inflation. The weighting of the formula results in higher Social Security pensions as a percentage of preretirement pay for workers retiring from low-paid jobs than for workers retiring from more highly paid jobs.

Social Security retirement benefits are payable as a monthly pension beginning at the Social Security retirement age, which was originally established as age 65 but is in the process of being raised to age 67 by 2027. Reduced retirement benefits can start as early as age 62. Supplementary benefits are also paid to retired workers with spouses, eligible children, and other dependents, as well. Once annuity benefits commence, they are adjusted for increases in the cost of living. You can find out more about your Social Security benefits by referring to the Social Security Administration's web site at www.ssa.gov.

For these benefits, workers and their employers pay contributions into the Social Security system. Worker contributions are made through payroll withholding of a Federal Insurance Contributions Act (FICA) tax. Covered workers and their employers each contribute a 6.2 percent (of the 7.65 percent) FICA payroll tax on wages up to the current year's Social Security taxable wage base ($106,800 for 2011) toward the pension, disability, and death benefits portion of the Social Security benefits, except for 2011, when the worker's FICA payroll tax rate is cut to 4.2 percent of covered wages, while the employer's rate of 6.2 percent remains unchanged. The remaining FICA tax of 1.45 percent of all wages (with no cap) payable by an employer and its employees goes toward Medicare benefits. Self-employed persons pay the combined worker and employer rate on net income after an offset of one-half of the combined tax.[4]

The Social Security system is generally funded on a pay-as-you-go basis, where taxes paid by workers and their employers cover the pension payments due to recipients, with relatively little left over in reserve. As such, this pay-as-you-go funding method represents more of a wealth transfer system from young workers to older retirees and other recipients. Social Security's funding drastically differs from that required of private pension plans, which build a reserve during employees' working careers in advance of their retirement that is sufficient to pay their retirement benefits.

When Social Security first started in 1935, the FICA payroll tax paid by workers was originally set at 1 percent of wages up to $3,000. In the beginning, there were 40 workers paying into the system for every retiree collecting payments. Since the average life expectancy of American males and females born in 1900 was 46 and 48 years, respectively,[5] it was expected that any retiree making it to age 65 would not be collecting Social Security benefits for very long. As this FICA tax paid by workers was quite sufficient to meet the benefits due to retirees, Social Security's pay-as-you-go funding method worked out quite nicely in the early years.

Ongoing FICA taxes easily covered Social Security retirement payments, even in the case of the great deal enjoyed by Social Security's first retiree, Ida May Fuller, a legal secretary from Ludlow, Vermont. She paid into the Social Security system at a rate of 1 percent of her pay for a little more than two years until her retirement at age 65. After paying Social Security taxes totaling the princely sum of $24.75, she retired to become the recipient of a monthly Social Security check in the amount of $22.54 in January 1940. She continued to receive her monthly $22.54 Social Security checks for the next 35 years until her death at age 100. She ended up collecting almost $23,000 in Social Security benefit payments, almost 1,000 times what she had paid into the system in the short time it was in effect before she retired.[6] Quite a good deal indeed!

That was only the auspicious beginning for Social Security. Since that time, Social Security has been expanded to provide disability and death benefits as well. Fast-forward to the not-so-new millennium. With improvements in longevity, the life expectancy at birth in 2006 is 75 years for males and 80 years for females.[7] With Americans living longer and having fewer babies, the ratio of workers contributing into the system to beneficiaries receiving payments is around three to one as of 2009. FICA taxes have been raised, but not enough to cover the additional benefits and growing number of recipients. These expanded benefits along with a continuation of the trend of the decreasing ratio of workers paying taxes into the system to retirees collecting benefits under the system portend troubles ahead for the Social Security system.

Over the years, much attention has been directed toward the solvency of the Social Security system by your legislators and the press, and for good reason. Various fixes, including the 1983 Social Security Amendments, have been implemented to address the system's funding problems. Changes, such as including additional groups of contributing members, raising taxes through tax rate and wage base increases, and delaying normal retirement from age 65 to 67, serve to provide only a temporary funding solution.

Social Security has been a wonderful program for those who have already received benefits. Now demographics present a situation where a declining number of workers causes the tax base to decrease while an increasing retiree population causes the benefit rolls to increase. As a result, the current FICA taxes paid by workers cannot sustain the benefit payments promised to retirees, spouses, disabled retirees, and beneficiaries. The Social Security program cannot continue in its present form without some pretty major changes in taxes and benefit levels.

No matter how you slice it, Social Security will not be there as much for you and your children as it was for your parents. In fact, 2010 marked the first year where Social Security tax payments made by workers did not cover benefit payments. Projections show that tapping the interest on the minimal Social Security trust fund reserves and the trust fund itself is expected to provide full benefits until 2037. After that, workers' taxes will be enough to cover only 75 percent of benefit payments.[8] Other hard decisions on Social Security program changes will have to be made soon.

In short, the Social Security system relies on young workers' taxes to support retirees' and beneficiaries' Social Security pensions. As the number of workers declines relative to the increasing number of retirees and beneficiaries, this wealth transfer system will become untenable. Again taxes will need to be raised, and/or benefits will need to be cut. Therefore, you should not count on Social Security being around in its current form for much longer, as solvency will continue to be an issue as the ratio of workers to retirees decreases. If a deal is too good to be true, it usually is (in the long run).

Ready or not, change is going to happen to the Social Security system, and benefits are likely to be reduced in some form. You may want to take this into account in planning for your retirement.

Employer-Sponsored Retirement Plans

You may also be covered under retirement plans sponsored by your employer. Such retirement plans offer tax breaks to both you and your employer. Depending on the type of plan, the money you and/or your employer put into the plan may not be taxed currently. All such contributions are deposited into a trust, custodial account, or insurance company separate account established for the exclusive purpose of providing benefits under the plan. Any investment earnings on that money within the trust are not taxed currently. Income tax on your plan contributions and any investment earnings that were not already taxed will generally be deferred until your eventual receipt of a plan distribution unless you roll it over to another similar plan or individual retirement account.

Employers offer retirement plans to their employees as an important component of their benefits package. In addition to the goodwill generated with their employees, companies generally receive a corporate tax deduction for their contributions and expenses incurred for the plan when they file their corporate tax returns.

Retirement plans generally come in two varieties: defined benefit (pension) plans and defined contribution plans. First came defined benefit pension plans. In its simplest form, a defined benefit pension plan provides retirees an *annuity*, or income stream, in an amount determined by plan formula. Then came defined contribution plans. A defined contribution plan provides set (or discretionary) contributions deposited into a funding vehicle under which individual participant accounts are maintained.

Defined Benefit (Pension) Plan   As a defined benefit plan, the traditional pension plan provides lifetime pensions to retiring workers. A pension payable in the form of a life annuity begins upon a participant's retirement and continues for the rest of his or her lifetime. Other optional benefit forms, which also guarantee annuity payments for a surviving beneficiary's lifetime or for a certain duration, may also be available.

Traditional pension plans promise each participant an annuity benefit at retirement determined under a formula defined by the terms of the plan. The amount of the ("definitely determinable") annuity income is typically based on the participant's service, pay (in many cases), and retirement age. For example, the monthly retirement income under a pension plan that provides an annuity beginning at age 65 in the amount of 1 percent of pay per year of service to a participant who earned $60,000 per year during a 10-year career would be $500 (= 0.01 × 10 years × $60,000 annual pay/ 12 months per year) beginning at age 65.

Most corporate and union-sponsored pension plans are funded entirely by the employer without requiring any contributions from employees. Federal law prescribes funding standards and contribution deadlines that these companies must satisfy to fund their pension plan obligations. State and local government pension plans typically require employees to contribute toward their pensions as a condition of plan participation, with the balance of the funding covered by tax revenues.

Plan contributions made over the course of each participant's career are accumulated with investment earnings for the purpose of building up an asset reserve sufficient to prefund the value of each participant's pension by the time it starts. These contributions by the employer (and the employee, if applicable) are deposited into a trust or other funding vehicle, the assets of which are managed by the plan sponsor to produce investment income that will reduce its funding obligation.

Taking into account the plan assets already accumulated, plan population demographics, the pensions promised to existing participants, and various assumptions, an actuary determines the annual employer contributions necessary to fund the full value of participants' pensions by the time of their retirement. This annual employer contribution calculation takes into account assumptions regarding expected plan investment returns, future plan benefit levels, and how long benefits will be paid to plan participants (if they are paid at all). This employer contribution calculation also takes into account how the actual plan experience, including investment results, matches up against the assumptions going into prior contribution calculations. Any gains resulting from favorable plan experience (as compared to what was assumed) offset future employer contributions. On the flip side, worse-than-expected plan experience increases future employer contributions.

In effect, the employer plan sponsor guarantees the promised pension payments regardless of actual plan experience by making up the difference through additional future plan contributions. This means that a shortfall in plan investment experience or the unanticipated continuation of annuity payments to long-lived retirees is all made good by the employer. The employer is ultimately responsible for ensuring that enough assets are accumulated to meet the pension benefits promised under the plan. Furthermore, a quasi-governmental insurance program run by the Pension Benefit Guaranty Corporation (PBGC) backs the promised benefits, within limits, made by companies sponsoring pension plans.

Both active and retired participants can take some comfort in these employer and governmental guarantees of pensions already accrued. By law, plan sponsors cannot cut back these accrued pensions. To the extent their pensions are funded and within the limits guaranteed by the PBGC, retirees can sit back and relax while collecting on the pension plan's promise of monthly benefits without worrying about whether the underlying plan assets are sufficient to maintain the promised monthly stipend for life. It is the employer that is concerned about managing the underlying plan investments so that there will be enough assets to keep paying pensions due under the plan. In other words, the employer is assuming the investment risk as well as the longevity risk associated with how long retirees will be around to collect those monthly pension payments.

Traditional defined benefit pension plans favor older employees in the way their costs are allocated. They can also be expensive to maintain due to funding requirements imposed by law as well as the general aging of the workforce for the companies that still offer such plans.

Due to the expense of maintaining traditional pension plans, other pension plans such as cash balance plans, pension equity plans, and life cycle plans—not to be confused with life cycle funds in 401(k) plans—have sprung up in their place. These modern plans offering lump sum distributions of individual account balances (as well as annuities) to participants are typically designed to cost less than their predecessor traditional pension plan and provide a more equitable distribution of costs for employees regardless of age.

These account-based plans may resemble defined contribution plans in the way individual accounts are maintained, but are still considered defined benefit plans. Their promise of a fixed-percentage contribution or pay credit and/or interest credit each year retains the character of a defined benefit plan due to the provision of definitely determinable benefits. It is the employer that still bears the investment and longevity risks under these plans. This distinction becomes important as the discussion now turns to defined contribution plans.

Defined Contribution Plan   A defined contribution plan, such as a 401(k) plan, maintains an individual account for each participant into which employee and/or employer contributions are made. The assets underlying these individual accounts are held in a plan trust or other funding vehicle that is invested in securities and thus are subject to any gains and losses of the plan's underlying investments. Some defined contribution plans offer only one investment option selected by the plan sponsor. However, the more typical defined contribution plan—like a 401(k) plan—offers employees individual control over the investment of their accounts among various fund alternatives. Whatever vested balance results from the accumulation of employee and employer contributions and investment gains or losses within the individual account by the end of a participant's employment is the ultimate benefit under the plan.

A defined contribution plan generally offers benefits in the form of a lump sum. Although 401(k) plans may provide for distribution only in the form of a lump sum benefit, they may also offer other optional benefit forms, such as annuities. The amount of any annuity would be based on a conversion of the available lump sum benefit to an equivalent annuity income stream.

From an employer's perspective, a defined contribution plan offers the advantage of limiting its commitment to providing just the plan contributions defined under the plan. Depending on the type of plan, the contributions could be fixed or even discretionary in nature.

Under a basic type of defined contribution plan known as a money purchase plan, the employer makes a fixed contribution commitment defined by the terms of the plan. This type of plan might commit the employer to make an aggregate plan contribution each and every year of a fixed percentage of participants' pay for the year. For example, a plan providing for an annual employer contribution of 10 percent of pay (allocated on the basis of participants' pay) would require an employer contribution to the account of a participant who had annual pay of $50,000 to be in the amount of $5,000 ($= 0.10 \times \$50,000$ annual pay).

Defined contribution plans, such as deferred profit sharing plans, may call for formula-based employer contributions related to profits. A 401(k) plan that offers employees the opportunity to save for retirement on a pretax basis (through employee pretax contributions) is a form of either a profit sharing or stock bonus plan (or a very old money purchase plan). An employer may commit to match—with cash under a 401(k) profit sharing plan or with stock under a 401(k) stock bonus plan—a certain percentage of each employee's contributions to the plan. A typical employer matching formula would provide an employer contribution of 50 percent of the employee's contributions up to 6 percent of pay.

Other profit sharing plans define employer contributions to be discretionary based on profits and thus offer plan sponsors the ultimate flexibility in a plan funding commitment. In lean years, the employer may decide not to contribute at all, and in more flush years, the employer may decide to contribute or not. Take heart, though, as an employer must eventually contribute to a profit sharing plan in order to maintain its tax advantages.

All defined contribution plans have one thing in common: the plan sponsor does not guarantee plan benefits will last a lifetime. The employer plan sponsor commits only to making the ongoing contributions that are defined under the plan. In essence, plan participants are left holding the bag on the market risk for investing their accounts, and they bear their longevity risk of outliving the assets accumulated in their accounts. The ability of a defined contribution plan sponsor to avoid exposure to market and longevity risks that are passed on to participants makes this type of plan attractive to employers. This risk avoidance attribute and relative funding flexibility of a defined contribution plan explain why many employers have switched from defined benefit pension plans to defined contribution plans over time.

In tough economic times, employers have resorted to cutting or eliminating matching contributions to their 401(k) plans. When the employer match is eliminated, the 401(k) plan becomes another form of personal savings funded only by employee contributions, but on a tax-preferred basis. After Social Security, it becomes the amount that you accumulate in personal savings, including your 401(k) accounts, that will determine the timing and quality of your retirement from the workforce. Your ability to save and manage your savings is more important than ever for ensuring a secure retirement.

Personal Savings

Saving has not historically been an area in which Americans have excelled. In fact, studies perennially show Americans to have a very low penchant for saving when compared with other developed countries in the world. It turns out that the opposite of savings—credit—has gradually become an accepted way of life, as savings gave way to spending on credit.

Various reasons have been cited for Americans' tendency to forgo savings in favor of spending on credit. Advertising has created a culture of consumption. Increasingly available credit seems to have rendered savings unnecessary, as the next essential or frivolous purchase was just another credit transaction away. Furthermore, the boom in the real estate and stock markets during the 1980s and 1990s created a feeling of wealth and confidence, resulting in an increase in consumption instead of savings.

Young people are generally the worst savers—not necessarily because they figure they will be forever young and working, but because of a number of other factors. As they enter the workforce, young workers generally have less earnings from which to save. There just is not that much left over to save from the lower wages earned early in a career, after paying off debt from school, setting up a home, and starting a family. Add to that the uncertainty about how much savings is enough to face the distant prospect of retirement, and some younger workers just say no to saving.

As workers age, their wages increase, and retirement comes into better focus, they tend to have more disposable income from which to save. Their home mortgages get paid off and their children go off to live on their own. These older workers, with their larger incomes and lower housing and food costs, finally may find themselves in a position to save more.

Personal Savings Rate A measure used to gauge savings (on an individual or aggregate basis) is the *personal savings rate*, defined as personal savings divided by disposable personal income:

$$\text{Personal Savings Rate} = \frac{\text{Personal Savings}}{\text{Disposable Personal Income}}$$

Personal savings comes from whatever is left over after paying for taxes, housing, food, clothing, transportation, utilities, entertainment, health care, and interest payments. It is a residual amount after all of those expenditures are made from personal income. Looking at it from the other side, personal savings is that amount personally set aside in taxable and tax-deferred accounts. As noted previously, personal savings also includes employee contributions under retirement plans, such as 401(k) plans.

The denominator of *disposable personal income* is earnings and investment income after payment of income taxes.

Your individual personal savings rate compares your personal savings with your disposable personal income. It follows that a nation's personal savings rate is an aggregate measure of its national saving habits.

American Savers Savings rates tend to ebb and flow with the state of the economy. People spend more in prosperous times like there is no

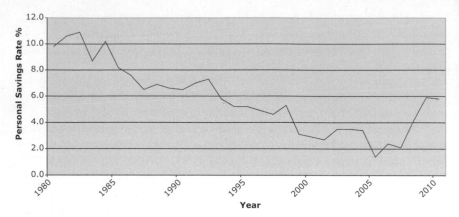

FIGURE 2.1 U.S. Personal Savings Rate History, 1980–2010
Data source: Bureau of Economic Analysis, National Income and Product Accounts
Table, Comparison of Personal Saving in the National Income and Product Accounts
with Personal Saving in the Flow of Fund Accounts, Last revised on March 25, 2011.

tomorrow, or even if there is a tomorrow, it is one surely endowed by a
steady and increasing income with no end in sight. On the flip side, people
with jobs during challenging economic times tend to save more of their pay
for a rainy day just in case it might be needed later if their income stream is
interrupted. The variation in historical U.S. aggregate savings rates is displayed in Figure 2.1, which charts the U.S. personal savings rates from 1980
through 2010.

Since 1982, personal savings rates have generally trended lower from
a high of 10.9 percent in 1982 to a low of 1.4 percent in 2005. Only recently
did workers increase their personal savings rates from that low of 1.4 percent in 2005 to almost 6 percent in 2010 as the economy remained uncertain. Even with the recent pickup in personal savings rates, though, savings
rates remain low, which does not bode well for future retirement security.
These savings rates continue to fall way short of financial planners' generic
recommendation of a 15 percent annual savings rate.[9]

As you will see in Chapter 5, your actual savings rate that is needed
to fund a comfortable retirement varies by your desired retirement income
goal, other sources of retirement income, investment returns, age at which
savings commence, expected retirement age, and actual drawdown of savings. Your risk tolerance and investment time horizon will determine your
propensity for risk in managing your savings and will affect the investment
returns you ultimately earn on your savings.

As doubts continue to loom about other sources of retirement income
(Social Security and employer-sponsored retirement plans), the need for
personal savings has become of utmost importance in retirement planning.

Saving needs to be a priority to the extent it becomes a personal cause on your part. No matter how well you manage your retirement savings, if you do not save enough, you may find yourself working longer than you had planned instead of enjoying your retirement.

TRANSITION FROM PENSIONS TO 401(k) PLANS

Now enter the era of the 401(k) plan. As a type of defined contribution plan, a 401(k) plan is basically a collection of tax-preferred savings accounts set up and maintained by an employer for its eligible employees. While working, an individual's 401(k) account gets credited with employee and any employer contributions and adjusted for net investment earnings or losses. Individuals must manage their own accounts in a way to get the most return in preparation for the day when their accounts will become a source for their support. Then after retirement, when they may start drawing upon their 401(k) accounts, they must still manage their accounts and hope they do not outlive their savings.

The past three decades have witnessed quite a dramatic shift from defined benefit pension plans to defined contribution plans such as 401(k) plans. Whereas previous generations of workers were covered more under pension plans than under defined contribution plans, now more workers are covered under defined contribution plans than under pension plans.

In 1979, about 38 percent of workers in private industry participated in defined benefit pension plans, and 17 percent participated in defined contribution plans. After three decades of a relentless decline of pension plans coupled with an explosive growth of defined contribution plans, pension and defined contribution plan coverage has pretty much flip-flopped. In 2008, 15 percent of workers in private industry were covered in pension plans, and 43 percent were covered under defined contribution plans.[10]

Many are the reasons for this shift from pension plans to 401(k) plans. Since the 1970s, frequent federal law changes and an evolving business environment have prompted retirement plan sponsors to dump pensions in favor of 401(k) plans. While some legislation reduced pension funding flexibility and increased pension administrative costs, other legislation clarified the tax benefits of 401(k) plans. Meanwhile, the transition toward 401(k) plans and away from pension plans seemed to better satisfy businesses' renewed desire to control costs, avoid risk, pay equitably, gain more appreciation for costly employee benefits, and reap previously accumulated pension gains.

From the employee perspective, 401(k) plans offered employees individual empowerment, benefit portability, and a better appreciation (aided initially by a prolonged ride in a favorable investment climate).

Legislation

In order to understand the dramatic growth of 401(k) plans, you need to consider a little legislative history. In 1974, the Employee Retirement Income Security Act (ERISA) was passed as a comprehensive reform of the retirement system in the United States. It was just the first of many laws that made it more difficult and expensive to sponsor defined benefit pension plans.

Among other things, ERISA brought some discipline to pension plan funding and established a mandatory pension insurance system that applies only to pension plans.

Reduced Pension Funding Flexibility Instead of the flexibility allowed under prior law to fund pension plans pretty much as conditions or profits warranted, pension sponsors now had to annually meet minimum funding standards in satisfaction of their pension obligations. Federal rules established funding schedules and deadlines, with penalties for noncompliance. Subsequent law changes narrowed a pension sponsor's options with respect to funding requirements. In tough times or not, such inflexibility in funding pension contributions is not at all appealing to current and prospective pension plan sponsors.

Increased Pension Administrative Costs To ensure compliance with these pension funding requirements, plan sponsors now had to hire enrolled actuaries to certify the funding of their pension plans. Furthermore, employers were required to pay annual insurance premiums to the Pension Benefit Guaranty Corporation (PBGC) to insure payment of promised pension benefits. Both measures made pensions more expensive to administer. A 1998 study concluded that administering a medium-size pension plan cost an employer about two and one-half times what it cost to administer a defined contribution plan.[11]

Introduction of 401(k) Plans Meanwhile, 401(k) plans got a boost (and their name) from the addition of Section 401(k) to the Internal Revenue Code that officially sanctioned them in 1978, although a few savings plans with similar attributes had already been established. Federal 401(k) regulations issued in 1981 clarified previously obscure rulings relating to so-called *cash or deferred arrangements*—that is, 401(k) plans—that enable employers to establish plans to allow eligible employees to prospectively elect to either:

- Receive their current wages as currently taxable pay (take the "cash").
- Or defer receipt of those wages (opt for the "deferred" portion of the "arrangement") and shelter it from current taxation until its eventual receipt.

Furthermore, these deferred wages are placed into an investment account with a trustee or insurance company. Any investment earnings on this account are not subject to income taxation until receipt of those funds by the participant in a distribution, typically upon termination of employment.

These 401(k) savings accounts essentially allowed employees to save on their own terms and manage those savings within a tax-preferred setting. The voluntary nature of these tax-advantaged 401(k) savings accounts only furthered the trend away from pension plans.

Employer Cost Control

A 401(k) plan presents an employer with more stable and controllable costs than a pension plan.

Risk Management   A pension plan commits a sponsor to make annual contributions to a trust or account that, when accumulated with investment earnings, is sufficient to pay promised pensions. Assumptions regarding assumed investment returns; surviving benefit recipients (after the effects of turnover, death, and disability); projected benefit levels (reflecting applicable future pay increases); and expected duration of lifetime benefit payments are used to develop an employer's annual pension contributions.

Any variation in the actual experience from that assumed under a pension plan is borne by the employer as a future increase or reduction in employer plan contributions. Losses from worse-than-expected experience increase an employer's future pension costs, and gains resulting from better-than-expected experience decrease its future pension costs. Any shortfall in investment earnings within the trust or account supporting the pension promises is covered by the employer, and any excess gain inures to the employer. Similarly, the risks associated with how many participants qualify for benefits, the benefit levels to which they are entitled, and how long their benefits will be paid are all assumed by the employer. In effect, the employer is assuming all of the investment and longevity risks under pension plans so that its employees can sit back and enjoy their lifetime pension guarantees.

As a type of defined contribution plan, a 401(k) plan's funding commitment on the part of the plan sponsor and its employees is defined and thus known. It is left up to the plan sponsor as to how much, if anything, it contributes to the plan, in addition to employees' contributions.

Individual 401(k) participants are on their own to manage the investment of their 401(k) accounts. Consequently, their plan sponsors are pretty much let off the hook for managing 401(k) plan assets. By leaving 401(k) account management responsibility to employees, plan sponsors consciously give up any potential investment gains in order to avoid the risk of having to make up any investment losses.

Since the employer's only commitment may (or may not) be to make a predefined contribution, it is not responsible for ensuring the adequacy of each employee's accumulated account balance to last a lifetime. The 401(k) sponsor does not assume the investment or longevity risks that a pension sponsor assumes. Under 401(k) plans, it is the employee who assumes both the investment and longevity risks.

People prefer a degree of certainty and predictability in life, some moreso than others. The type of people who work in corporate finance departments especially prefer predictable retirement plan costs. Whereas an employer with a 401(k) plan will generally experience fairly stable annual plan costs, an employer assuming the investment risk of a pension plan in a volatile market may find its plan costs varying dramatically from year to year. Consequently, employers have noticed that a properly designed 401(k) plan produces more predictable and controllable plan costs than a pension plan.

Furthermore, a pension plan sponsor's assumption of the investment management responsibility and lifetime-income guarantee may be attractive to its employees but may be considered too costly and inflexible from a business perspective. These and other factors have caused employers to cut, freeze, and eliminate their pension plans and add new 401(k) plans in their place.

Funding Flexibility   Within the context of funding a 401(k) plan, a plan sponsor may still have flexibility in the amount it contributes each year. Depending on the plan design, an employer may, or may not, commit to making a 401(k) plan contribution and may prospectively modify any such commitment. The contributions can even be discretionary from year to year, if a plan so provides. To an employer, this increased contribution flexibility under 401(k) plans represents a big advantage over pension plans, whose funding commitment is fixed (within a range) by law.

Equity   Employers are learning the hard way these days about treating employees fairly. More and more you hear about another lawsuit alleging discrimination on the basis of age, sex, race, religion, and so on—you pick your flavor of the month. It all comes down to following a policy by which employees get equal pay for equal work. Besides, equity in the workplace demands that two similarly situated employees receive the same compensation package.

This is not about socialism. The concept of equity is about providing equivalent benefits to employees with the same pay, regardless of other factors. Yet an employer may still by law provide larger retirement plan contributions to employees with higher pay or more service. A 401(k) plan meets this definition of equity, in that employer contributions are typically defined as a match of a percentage of employee contributions (which in turn may be set as a percentage of pay). Although variations may exist based on service or other factors, similarly paid employees of different ages (who contribute at the same rate) generally will receive the same employer (matching) contribution under a 401(k) plan.

Under an ongoing pension plan, a participant's pension is typically funded over the expected length of his or her career. Therefore, an older employee's pension (and each additional accrual) will be amortized over a shorter period than a younger employee's, resulting in a higher annual cost for the older employee. Then, all other things being equal, older employees receive a larger share of pension contributions than their younger counterparts. Just as Table 6.1 in Chapter 6 will show that it takes more savings on the part of an individual starting a savings program at an advanced age to prospectively fund a desired retirement income, it costs a pension sponsor more to fund a pension for an older worker.

Figure 2.2 compares employer costs as a percentage of pay for participants at various ages under generic pension and 401(k) plans that have the same aggregate cost. For this illustration, the generic pension plan is

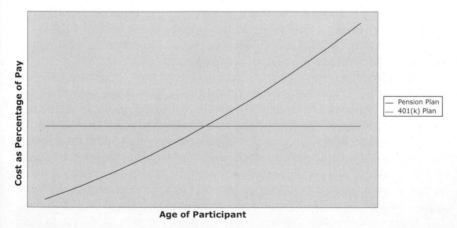

FIGURE 2.2 Comparison of Pension and 401(k) Plan Costs

assumed to provide a traditional pension of a flat percentage of earnings per year of service. The generic 401(k) plan is assumed to provide a matching contribution that turns out to be a flat percentage of pay. The specific percentages are not as relevant as the underlying cost trends for the plans.

Figure 2.2 shows that, regardless of age, all 401(k) participants receive the same employer contribution as a percentage of pay. Yet traditional pension plan participants receive a contribution as a percentage of pay that rises with age. Therefore, an older participant's pension costs more to fund than a similarly paid younger participant. On this cost-comparison basis, similarly situated employees receive more equitable treatment under a 401(k) plan than under a pension plan. Employers—and especially younger employees—embrace this concept of equity provided under a 401(k) plan, where employer contributions are spread in proportion to pay.

Effect of Aging Population on Retirement Plan Costs The U.S. population is aging. Baby boomers (born between 1946 and 1964), representing a huge cohort in the history of the U.S. population, are coming of (retirement) age. At the same time, the two demographic forces, immigration and birth rates, that could reverse this aging trend are slowing. Fewer people are coming to or being born into an America that seems to be facing more economic challenges than before. Consequently, the combination of more old people and fewer new people is raising the average age of the American working population.

If older workers' pensions cost more than younger workers' (as previously noted), an employer's pension cost increases as its workforce ages. Add to that proposition the fact that retirees receiving lifetime pensions are living longer due to advances in health care, causing the cost of paying their longer lifetime annuity streams to increase. What you find is that pension costs increase over time as an employer's workforce and retiree population both age. Unfortunately, these pension (not to mention health care) legacy costs are part of the plight that continues to force the reshaping of corporate and union-sponsored retirement plans and that now threatens the continuation of government pension plans.

By contrast, an employer's 401(k) plan cost is more manageable by design. The defined contribution nature of a 401(k) plan keeps plan costs as a percentage of pay relatively stable over time. An employer's 401(k) match set as a percentage of employee contributions may increase some for an aging population that saves more as it approaches retirement, but not nearly as much as the corresponding pension cost for an aging workforce would.

The increasing cost of pensions for the type of aging workforce and retiree population that exists today have caused pensions to lose their luster in comparison to 401(k) and other retirement savings plans. Faced with the policy decisions as to which type(s) of plan(s) to offer, employers have clearly expressed a preference for the more stable and controllable costs of 401(k) plans over those of pension plans.

Employee Appreciation

Employers like to feel the love from their employees for sponsoring retirement plans. After all, what good is money spent by an employer on a plan that its employees do not understand or appreciate?

Understanding   Most people just do not spend much time thinking about deferred annuities, which form the basis of pension plans. This lack of experience with annuities may make it difficult for the average employee to appreciate the accrual of an incremental piece of a deferred annuity for each year of work under a pension benefit formula. Then there is the matter of determining what the value of a pension payable at age 65 is really worth today, which even actuaries may not agree upon. These issues present challenges for an employer attempting to communicate the value of its pension plan to employees of diverse backgrounds. As a result, employers may well find that they do not get the goodwill or appreciation due them for devoting significant resources to sponsor a pension plan. In short, the pension plan structure is just not that user-friendly.

By contrast, the concept of a 401(k) account is something employees can wrap their arms around (and hug, especially when it goes up). After all, a 401(k) account looks a lot like a bank account, with which most working adults are intimately familiar. There really is no magic to the math of tracking an account balance's changes due to contributions, disbursements, and investment gains and losses. Account balances increase when the amounts coming in (contributions and investment gains) exceed the amounts going out (benefits, expenses, and investment losses). However, account balances can decrease as well when inflows cannot keep pace with outflows, such as when a tumbling stock market causing account losses serves as a rude reminder of the risks of investing. Nonetheless, the simplicity and transparency of a 401(k) account foster a sense of appreciation among covered employees. In turn, 401(k) plan sponsors get due credit for providing a valuable employee benefit.

People like it when you speak their language. Just ask the French, who prefer you speak their native tongue when visiting. Whereas employees can see for themselves the changes in their quarterly 401(k) account statements, they may have trouble appreciating the growth of their deferred pensions. Therefore, employers tend to get more bang for their benefit dollars spent sponsoring a straightforward 401(k) plan than a mysterious pension plan.

Power to the People   Just as an employer enjoys control over its retirement plan expenditures, employees also appreciate control of their savings
and investments within the tax-preferred setting of a 401(k) or other retirement savings plan. Their control comes in the form of deciding when, what,
and where to save for retirement.

401(k) plans are sold to employees under the label of individual
empowerment. Although pension plans offer participants a guaranteed
income for life, 401(k) plans generally offer individual empowerment
through control over the savings in their own individual accounts. The
401(k) participants get an opportunity to manage their own account assets
to beat the retirement income guarantee offered by a pension.

Along with this opportunity comes responsibility—a huge one of managing your account assets in a way that ensures there will be enough
around to last a lifetime or two (if you count you and your bunkmate).
A 401(k) plan puts you (rather than your employer) squarely at risk for
managing the assets within your individual account and for assuming the
(longevity) risk of living too long.

Your first responsibility is to save enough. Then you assume investment risk, where you benefit from any investment gains and suffer the consequences of any investment losses resulting from your management of
the investments within your plan account. Finally, when you are entitled
to receive a plan distribution, you bear the responsibility for managing and
drawing down your account for the rest of your lifetime. Unlike in a pension, your employer is not watching your back to provide you a sufficient
lifetime income after retirement. It is up to you alone.

Portability   Ladies, stand up and take a bow. Congratulations on your
part in initiating the whole concept of taking leave from work to accommodate childbearing and raising a family. You are the ones who had to in-
terrupt your careers to take time off (even if it is ever so brief) to have
children. Then you may have enlisted your beloved husband and other
members of your support network to step in and help care for the kids
while you resumed your career. These career interruptions necessitated
by working mothers and fathers leaving the workforce to care for their
families brought to the forefront the importance of retirement benefit
portability—the ability to take retirement benefits with you when you
leave an employer.

In the past, retirement benefits were just not that portable. When you
left your job, your retirement benefits were not as ready to be paid out as
you were to receive them. Rather than paying benefits upon termination
in the form of an immediate lump sum available under most 401(k) plans,
most traditional pension plans would pay benefits in the form of a deferred
annuity starting at retirement. Whereas you cannot roll over a pension

annuity to another retirement plan or individual retirement account, you can roll over a 401(k) lump sum. Therefore, the lump sum benefits typically paid under 401(k) plans are more portable than the pension annuities provided under traditional pension plans.

People leave jobs for other reasons, too. An interruption in your employment for any reason need not disrupt your ability to take your retirement benefits with you when you change jobs. The portable nature of 401(k) lump sum benefits allowing you to take them with you upon any termination of employment gives 401(k) plans another edge over traditional pension plans that pay annuities.

Favorable Investment Climate　　The introduction of 401(k) plans could not have come at a better time. Coincident with, or maybe because of, the advent of 401(k) plans in the early 1980s, the U.S. stock market began a long upward climb. This unprecedented rally continued, with only some brief interruptions, for nearly 20 years. From a low of 98 on March 27, 1980, the Standard & Poor's 500 index climbed at a whopping average annual rate of 14.7 percent to 1,527 on March 24, 2000.[12]

Whereas investment returns under a pension plan are not shared with participants but kept by a pension plan sponsor to reduce its plan contributions, a 401(k) plan's returns add directly to each individual's account. The extended favorable market conditions made most 401(k) participants look like geniuses for holding stocks in their accounts. Never mind that these fat 401(k) accounts resulted more from luck (of investing during good times) than from investment acumen. As these heady investment returns continued to build within their 401(k) accounts, it is no wonder that employees wholeheartedly embraced the concept of a 401(k) plan. No longer was a pension's lifetime income guarantee considered to be that important, compared to a 401(k)'s potential promise of outsized returns.

The support of their employees, combined with the official IRS blessing granted 401(k) plans, made it an easier decision for employers to establish 401(k) plans, and that they did. It seemed that employers, 401(k) account holders, and regulators were all mesmerized by the market's favorable investment returns generated during the formative years of 401(k) plans.

Although 401(k) participants holding stocks got clobbered by sharp market declines in 1989 and 2000, these reminders of the risks of investing in stocks soon faded in the public's consciousness, as the broad market returned shortly thereafter to new heights. The 401(k) plan's popularity took off again as market resilience overcame the public's selective short-term memory of market risks. When 401(k) investors got hit by another (more severe) market decline beginning in 2007, it was too late to overturn the public's acceptance of 401(k) plans as a way of life.

Pension Plan Termination Bonanza

This favorable investment climate of the 1980s and 1990s also had an impact on the destiny of pension plans. Working under the presumption that "this time it really is different," 401(k) investors just knew the soaring market would enable them to routinely build 401(k) accounts that would generate a larger retirement income than under a pension plan. As a result, employees and their employers turned their attention to 401(k) plans instead of pension plans.

Sensing an opportunity to shed ever-growing pension obligations, employers froze or discontinued their pension plans. In many cases, they replaced their costly pension plans with sleek, new 401(k) plans offering more controllable costs.

The outlandish market gains in the 1980s and 1990s also brought about many overfunded pension plans, where plan assets exceeded liabilities. Such pension overfunding represented an opportunity for plan sponsors to reap immediate gains. A business eyeing its excess pension plan assets as a source of business capital had a choice of either terminating its pension plan to recover all excess assets at once or take a contribution holiday to draw down the excess pension funding over time. The temptation to tap into excess assets of an overfunded pension plan through plan termination proved to be too much for many employers to resist. Consequently, many plan sponsors chose to tap their excess pension plan assets through the former route of terminating their pension plans until legislation discouraging such practice was enacted.

Nonetheless, the damage has been done, as the number of people covered by a pension plan has diminished while the popularity and growth in coverage of 401(k) and other retirement savings plans lives on.

WHAT THIS TRANSITION TO 401(k)s MEANS TO YOU

There was a day when retirement benefits were provided primarily under defined benefit pension plans. That day has passed. The transition from pension plans to 401(k) and other retirement savings plans is real. Pension plans began their decline as the federal laws changed; plan sponsors wanted more affordable, stable, and equitable retirement plan costs; and employees sought empowerment, equity, simplicity, and portability in their retirement plans. The outsized gains credited to 401(k) accounts during the favorable investment climate of the 1980s and 1990s provided newly established 401(k) plans with a honeymoon not soon forgotten by their participants.

Since the passage of ERISA in 1974, pension plans have fallen into decline, while 401(k) plans and other defined contribution plans have hit their stride. In the 1980s, employers started adding 401(k) plans to provide employees with an opportunity to supplement their pension income with tax-deferred retirement savings. Although initially intended as a supplement to pension plans, the 401(k) plan has come to replace the pension plan and instead serves as an employer's primary retirement plan in many cases. This leaves many employees with no pension and only a 401(k) account as the primary employer-provided retirement benefit. For your sake, you had better hope that Social Security and personal savings will also be there to supplement your retirement income.

Now It's Up to You ...

This shift from pensions to 401(k) and other defined contribution plans represents a distinct change in the focus of retirement plans. Whereas pensions emphasize income replacement to employees, defined contribution plans, like 401(k) plans, fix the contribution commitment of sponsoring employers. For a retiring employee, a pension's definitely determinable benefit provided at whatever cost (to the employer) is necessary certainly seems more assuring than whatever accumulates in an individual's 401(k) account at a known employer cost. Yet employers now favor the known costs of 401(k) and other retirement savings plans over the variable costs of pension plans.

The decline of pension plans, combined with the rapid growth of 401(k) plans, has led to a transfer in the asset management responsibility from professional investment managers hired by pension sponsors to invest assets underlying pension plans to individuals managing their own retirement accounts. The destiny (or adequacy) of your retirement income now rests more in your hands. It all comes down to how capably you alone, whether ready or not, manage your retirement savings and draw it down in a way so as to produce retirement income that lasts a lifetime.

But You May Need Help

Whereas the assets underlying pension plans typically receive the attention of trained investment professionals hired by the plan sponsor, the management of 401(k) assets is mostly left to individual account holders. Investment managers use their specialized training, timely access to financial information, and policy-driven strategies to manage assets on a full-time basis. Because regular folks often do not have the time, inclination, or training to manage their own retirement savings, they are not always as attentive as they should be to managing their retirement accounts.

Most people like to use the set-it-and-forget-it strategy when it comes to investing their retirement savings. Once they make their fund elections, they do not even bother to adjust them through fund transfers or redirection of ongoing contributions. Regular folks who bother to manage their accounts tend to be lunch-pail investors. Like weekend warriors confined by work to plying their athletic skills on weekends, hardworking lunch-pail investors trade their investment accounts during their available workweek hours when the financial markets are open—namely lunchtime and breaks.

In view of the differences in their approaches, it should come as no surprise that the investment returns generated by professional investment managers routinely beat those of average individual investors over time. Yet most fund managers have trouble beating the market on a consistent basis. Go figure.

In one study of companies with both pension and 401(k) plans, the assets underlying pension plans outperformed those of 401(k) plans by an average margin of a little over 1 percent per year between 1995 and 2006. On a cumulative basis, the investment returns on pension assets exceeded those of individually managed 401(k) accounts by about 14 percent over this 12-year period.[13]

Investment managers get paid well to invest pension assets in accordance with an investment policy. In many cases, staying true to the course defined by the investment policy facilitates the better investment performance of professional investment managers over individuals.

By contrast, individual investors typically lack consistency in their investment strategy, if they even have one. Instead they tend to trade on market momentum, getting subpar performance from buying a stock into a rally and selling it into a decline. Individual investors' irrational behavior manifested by inaction, lagging reactions, and knee-jerk responses to the market's movements hurts their investment performance.

Ongoing studies by Dalbar, Inc. support the notion that average mutual fund investors hurt their own investment performance by shifting into and out of stock funds at the wrong times. Dalbar has found that buy-and-hold investors in an S&P 500 index mutual fund outperformed the average mutual fund investor by just over 5 percent per year over the 20-year period ended December 31, 2009.[14] Any way you look at it, the average individual investor's irrational investment behavior and restricted access to professional investment advice cost him or her money.

Take Action

Never mind that a pension plan offers the advantage of a guaranteed lifetime income, with the plan sponsor assuming investment and longevity risks. Put aside the notion that individual investors have not shown as much competence in managing their 401(k) accounts as professional investment managers in managing pension assets. This grand 401(k) plan experiment that started years ago lives on. Now that 401(k) plans dominate the retirement savings landscape, it is ever so important to have a strategy to squeeze the most out of your 401(k) plan accounts.

If you have not already done so, you need to develop a personal investment strategy. Then you will be in a better position to either manage your retirement savings yourself or seek outside advice in managing your retirement savings. Your outside advice may come from an independent investment adviser or an online computer model. Either way, you or your personal or online adviser needs to stick to your investment strategy.

For those of you who want to take charge or get more involved in the management of your 401(k) accounts, read on. There is no magic answer here, but there are simple savings, investment, and trading strategies to help you reach your retirement goals.

A closer look at the background and features of 401(k) plans in the next chapter will give you more insight into how to maximize your benefits.

CHAPTER 3

Rules of the Game

401(k) under the Hood

I'm proud to be paying taxes in the United States. The only thing is—I could be just as proud for half the money.

—Arthur Godfrey

Think back to the day when you were six years old and woke up one sunny morning to find a bright, shiny quarter under your pillow. Try to block out the pain and suffering of losing a tooth the day before that morning of pure joy. The good Tooth Fairy had left you some cold, hard cash in exchange for an extracted body part.

Perhaps you did not realize it at the time, but getting that quarter as a gift is probably the best way you can get money. Technically, if you got the cash through other means, such as hard labor, the courts (sometimes), good luck in gambling, or nefarious measures, you would still have to pay income tax on it. It seems taxes are everywhere. Do not forget that the notorious Al Capone was jailed for income tax evasion rather than any other crimes he may have committed against society.

First, you did not have to work for the cash gift (although you may have felt some pain). Because you received it as a gift, you did not have to pay it back. Also, you paid no taxes on it, although the Tooth Fairy might have had to pay some gift taxes if she had been a lot more generous (from the IRS's perspective, not yours) in her gift. Not even a 401(k) plan can do that for you, although it comes close.

401(k) PLAN BASICS

Employer-sponsored retirement savings plans come in a variety of forms, the most popular of which is a 401(k) plan. Although different rules govern the various plan types—401(k), 403(b), 457, and Keogh—the legal framework for providing tax advantages for these employer-sponsored plans seems to be converging over time toward one platform. Smaller plans involving individual retirement accounts (IRAs) also provide similar tax advantages, but with different limits and conditions. For brevity, the discussion here focuses on the current laws affecting 401(k) plans.

If you are in a 401(k) plan, you already know it is a disco-era phenomenon that enables you to avoid current income taxes on what you save for retirement. These plans allow you to conveniently save a portion of your pay for retirement on a tax-deferred basis.

The U.S. government established the framework for these plans to encourage retirement savings through tax incentives provided to employees and their employers. Participating employees get a current tax break on their pretax contributions and on investment earnings within their plan accounts. Employers get a tax deduction for their contributions and expenses associated with sponsoring the plan.

In order to make the most of your participation in a 401(k) plan, it pays to know the rules of the game. As with any game, an understanding of the rules can help you implement specific strategies to be successful. This chapter discusses some general 401(k) plan rules and ways to take full advantage of them. It also discusses aspects of 401(k) plans critical to employing the day trading strategy that you can use to juice your returns in an uncertain market.

In its simplest form, a 401(k) plan looks like a collection of individual savings accounts subject to a bunch of rules. Each participant's individual account is credited with employee and any employer contributions and adjusted for investment earnings and losses. Any benefits and expenses paid are deducted from the account. (See Figure 3.1.)

Your savings are typically collected through payroll withholding and deposited along with any employer contributions into a trust or other funding vehicle set up to hold all plan assets in individual participant accounts. Most 401(k) plans allow their participants to control the management of their assets held within their individual accounts. Each individual 401(k) plan account is then tracked separately and subject to any gains and losses on the investments within the account.

The part of your pay that you prospectively elect to save under the plan on a pretax basis is not taxed currently. Not only does a 401(k) plan let you save a portion of your pay before it is taxed (through "pretax

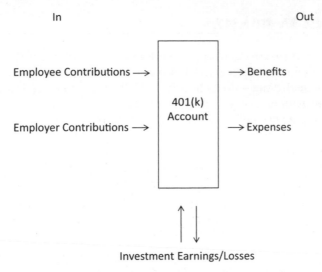

FIGURE 3.1 Cash Flow of 401(k) Account

contributions"), but some plans also allow you to save a part of your pay after it has been taxed (through "after-tax contributions" or "Roth contributions"). Many plans also provide a matching employer contribution based on your contributions into the plan.

Any employer contributions and any investment earnings credited to your account are also not taxed currently. It is only upon the eventual distribution of your account that accumulated contributions and investment earnings not already taxed get taxed as ordinary income.

A 401(k) plan is basically a tax-deferred retirement savings plan where you can save money now while you are working in order to have extra income at a time later on—at retirement—when you need income because you are not working. Also, making pretax contributions to a 401(k) plan may enable you to legally pay less tax overall as well as pay the taxes later.

Under the current marginal income tax structure applicable in the United States, you gradually pay more in income tax on every extra dollar of current income within set tiers. That means your marginal tax rate is generally higher while you are working (for pay) than when you are retired. You avoid paying tax on 401(k) savings at the higher marginal rates applicable while you are earning wages, only to be taxed later at lower marginal rates when you draw on your 401(k) savings as a retiree. This all makes sense if tax rates are not increased too much in the future when you are ready to start drawing from your 401(k) account.

401(k) PLAN DETAILS

The tax advantages afforded savers under a 401(k) plan come at a price. As with anything having to do with the tax code, 401(k) plans are subject to a variety of rules dealing with eligibility, contributions, vesting, investments, and distributions.

Eligibility

A 2009 study found that over half (51 percent) of 401(k) plans allowed their employees to immediately participate in, or contribute to, the plan upon hire. Other plans required employees to wait a short while to see if they are up to snuff on the job before allowing them to participate, especially when it comes time to dole out employer contributions. Less than one-third (28 percent) of plans required employees to be on the job for one year before becoming eligible for employer contributions.[1]

The most restrictive eligibility requirement would require regular employees to reach age 21 and complete one year of service (or more technically, the plan entry date within six months thereof) before entering the plan. Once you have reached both of these milestones of attaining age 21 and working one year with the employer plan sponsor, you would generally be eligible to start contributing into the plan.

Some 401(k) plan sponsors have carried the immediate eligibility concept further by automatically enrolling new employees in the plan (through a *default election* or *negative election*) upon hire unless they opt out. The same 2009 study reported that about one in five (21 percent) of the plans allowing employee pretax contributions automatically brought them into the plan upon hire.[2] Once in the plan, the automatically enrolled new employees contribute at a set rate into a designated fund, unless they choose otherwise.

For example, a plan may require all its new employees to contribute 3 percent of pay on a pretax basis into a target-date fund within that employee's account, unless the employee elects otherwise. Any employee subject to a default election like this may withdraw or change the terms of his or her participation at any time. Any change in an election needs to be done *in advance of* the time it is to be effective and done in accordance with plan rules.

Absent your automatic enrollment, once you are eligible to participate in a 401(k) plan, you need to follow the plan enrollment procedures to start making contributions. These procedures will require you to enroll either online or by submission of an enrollment form in advance of the commencement of your participation. During enrollment, you will essentially need to elect how much to contribute and where to invest it. You may also need to make some other elections, such as the mix of pretax, after-tax, and Roth contributions, and beneficiary designations, depending on the plan. Note that you may only prospectively designate pay that has not yet been earned to be contributed to a 401(k) plan. The plan terms dictate whether a deferral election is applicable to salary, bonuses, or other income, as well as your other available options. Check your *Summary Plan Description* (SPD) that describes the plan terms in enough detail so as to be understood by the average participant.

Employers sponsoring 401(k) plans calling for the automatic enrollment of new employees recognize the importance of getting their employees to save for retirement as soon as possible. If you are eligible to enroll in the type of plan where the enrollment decision is left up to you, start saving as soon as you are eligible. You do not want to miss out on making any possible contributions, which, when combined with employer contributions and compounded with investment earnings until retirement, can be huge. Even a delay of one year in commencing plan participation can make a significant difference in an employee's accumulated savings at retirement. For example, just missing one opportunity to contribute $5,000 to a 401(k) plan at age 25 would result in your account balance at age 65 being $35,200 short of where it would have been, assuming your account earned a 5 percent annual return.

Contributions

By definition, a 401(k) plan allows each eligible employee to save a portion of pay before it has been taxed. If a 401(k) plan so provides, an eligible employee may also elect to contribute a portion of pay after it has been taxed, either as an after-tax contribution or as a Roth contribution. Many 401(k) plans also allow employees to make additional catch-up pretax contributions (if age 50 or over) and to roll over contributions from other tax-deferred plans. Most 401(k) plans also provide some sort of employer contribution to employees' accounts, through a match or otherwise. The tax treatment upon eventual distribution of these different types of 401(k) plan contributions varies depending on the tax treatment afforded earlier upon deposit, whereas the associated investment earnings on contributions other than those of the Roth variety are taxed at distribution.

Employee Contributions Recurring employee contributions to a 401(k) plan are typically withheld from pay, whereas a *rollover* contribution may be directly or indirectly transferred from a prior plan or IRA if the recipient plan so provides. Once an employer collects the ongoing employee contributions through payroll withholding, it must deposit all employee contributions into the 401(k) plan within 15 days of the end of the month in which the contributions were withheld from pay. A rollover from a prior plan or IRA may be transferred electronically or by check. The automated payroll and fund transfer systems in effect today greatly facilitate this process.

Pretax Contributions   Employee pretax contributions are deducted from current taxable pay, and they along with any investment earnings thereon are eventually taxed at distribution. This provides a current tax break for employees making pretax contributions to 401(k) plans. For example, an employee saving $5,000 as pretax contributions out of gross wages of $50,000 would be taxed on only $45,000 in wages for that year.

Saving on a pretax basis under a 401(k) plan gives you more bang for your buck than saving on an after-tax basis. Say you are in the 28 percent federal income tax bracket and, as noted, save $5,000 out of your annual pay of $50,000. You have a choice of saving under a 401(k) plan or a taxable savings account. If you save the $5,000 as pretax contributions into a 401(k) plan and have no other withholdings, you end up with net take-home pay of $32,400 {= $50,000 gross pay – $5,000 pretax contribution – [0.28 tax rate × ($50,000 – $5,000)] income taxes} instead of $31,000 [= $50,000 gross pay – $5,000 posttax savings deposit – (0.28 tax rate × $50,000) income taxes] in take-home pay you would have if you saved in a taxable savings account. So in this example, you end up with an extra $1,400 (= $32,400 – $31,000) of take-home pay each year by investing in a 401(k) account rather than a taxable savings account. You can look at this as the U.S. government currently funding $1,400 (that you did not have to pay to Uncle Sam) of the $5,000 in payroll contributions you make each year to your 401(k) account. Thank you very much.

An employee eventually pays income tax at the time of distribution on the accumulated value of the pretax contributions and any associated investment earnings. One of the main advantages of 401(k) plans allows people to pay less tax on their retirement savings due to a presumed difference in tax rates between the time when contributions were made while working and the time when a distribution is received after retirement. An employee's last dollar of income may be subject to the 28 percent marginal tax rate while working but be in the 15 percent tax bracket when retired. Significant tax savings could result from the difference in tax rates before and after retirement.

As in the previous example, if you save $5,000 out of your annual pay of $50,000 in a 401(k) plan, you are currently paying $1,400 (= 28% federal marginal income tax rate × $5,000 401(k) contribution) less in federal income taxes that year. If you receive that $5,000 back as a 401(k) distribution later (such as at retirement) in a year when your total income is $15,000, you would pay only $750 (= 15% federal marginal income tax rate × $5,000 distribution) in federal income taxes on that $5,000 distribution. Without considering any savings in state income taxes (in states that follow federal law), you have saved $650 (= original $1,400 savings − current $750 payment) alone in federal income taxes that you will never have to pay Uncle Sam. Furthermore, any investment earnings on the distribution are subject to tax at the presumably lower marginal tax rate applicable at distribution upon retirement rather than taxed each year at applicable higher rates while working.

After-Tax Contributions Employee after-tax contributions are made from net pay after taxes have been deducted. Since they are treated as taxable before they are contributed to the plan, they are not taxed again when distributed. Any investment earnings associated with those after-tax contributions are not taxed currently but instead are taxed upon distribution.

Roth 401(k) Contributions Roth 401(k) contributions are also made from net pay after taxes (like after-tax contributions). So there is no reduction in current taxable income as a result of making either after-tax or Roth 401(k) contributions. However, the difference lies in the taxation of any investment earnings on the Roth contributions at distribution. Any investment earnings, as well as the Roth contributions themselves, are not taxed upon a qualified distribution satisfying certain conditions. The entire amount of the Roth 401(k) contributions, accumulated with any investment earnings, will generally be tax-free upon a qualified distribution at the participant's retirement, termination, death, or disability.[3]

Since the Roth contributions are taxed going in, they will not be taxed coming out of the plan. The accumulated investment earnings on the Roth contributions are also not taxed upon a qualified distribution. In a way, you can look at Roth contributions as working in reverse compared to the tax treatment afforded pretax contributions. Roth contributions are taxed first before being deposited into a 401(k) plan and later escape taxation along with any investment earnings upon a qualified distribution. However, pretax contributions escape immediate taxation before going into a 401(k) plan, only to be taxed later along with any investment earnings upon distribution.

The sum of employee pretax and Roth contributions to a 401(k) plan is limited to an annual amount set by law. For 2011, the aggregate limit on regular pretax and Roth contributions is $16,500. This limit is subject to annual increases in $500 increments for changes in the cost of living.

Because of the aggregate limits applicable to pretax and Roth contributions, you will need to decide which form(s) of contributions are the most tax-effective in your personal situation. An ability to predict future tax rates and market conditions would be really helpful in deciding which type of 401(k) contributions would work best for you. Potential reasons for favoring pretax contributions over Roth contributions include the ability to defer tax payment on contributions (and investment earnings) and maximization of the amount available for immediate investment to take advantage of the time value of money.

Roth contributions would make sense in an environment where you expect good investment earnings and increased tax rates. In this case, the tax-free nature of a Roth distribution becomes more valuable than the tax-deferral advantage afforded a distribution of pretax contributions and any investment earnings. You would end up paying less tax up front on your Roth contributions than you would upon the distribution of pretax contributions and investment earnings.

However, employee pretax contributions may be preferred in an environment where you expect to be in a lower marginal tax bracket at retirement than you are when you originally make the contributions. The case for each type of contribution becomes a little trickier when you consider the impact of investment earnings along with different tax rate change scenarios.

When an account decreases in value in a constant or declining marginal tax rate environment, Roth contributions do not get a chance to enjoy their built-in advantage of altogether avoiding taxes on investment earnings. Whereas an entire Roth contribution would be taxed up front before deposit into a 401(k) account, only the remaining value of pretax contributions after account losses would be taxed upon distribution—the portion of a pretax contribution that is wiped out by losses would never have been taxed. Therefore, pretax contributions would be the favored form of contributions in a constant or declining marginal tax rate environment when accounts decline in value from the amount originally contributed. A more extensive analysis taking into account the extent of the account loss and potential marginal tax rates would be necessary to determine the preferred contribution type in an increasing marginal tax rate environment.

After considering the possible combinations of future market conditions and expected tax rates, you may want to review your personal circumstances with your investment adviser to determine which type(s) of contributions to put into your 401(k) account.

Catch-Up Contributions   Employees age 50 or over may make additional *catch-up contributions* up to a certain limit. For 2011, the catch-up pretax contribution limit is $5,500. Therefore, an employee attaining age 50 or more in 2011 may make pretax contributions of up to $22,000 (= $16,500 regular pretax contribution limit + $5,500 catch-up contribution limit) in

2011. The catch-up contribution limit is scheduled to increase annually in $500 increments when warranted by an increase in the cost of living.

For those of you age 50 or older, if you can afford to save more with catch-up contributions, do it.

Rollover Contributions   Some plans may allow you to roll over into your current plan lump sum distributions resulting from your participation in other employers' plans and IRAs. These plans make it possible for you to consolidate your retirement portfolio by allowing rollovers of your individual retirement accounts (IRAs), 403(b) plans (generally for teachers and certain nonprofit organization employees), 457 plans (for governmental employees), or other qualified plan distributions, such as 401(k) plans and defined benefit plans that pay a lump sum. Although personally convenient from a consolidated record-keeping standpoint, there are some advantages of keeping these accounts separate.

As noted later in Chapter 8, you may want to retain your larger IRA accounts and accounts held in former employers' defined contribution plans so that you can take advantage of a day trading strategy. Accounts held in large plans typically enjoy lower fees charged for the maintenance and investment management of accounts due to economies of scale.

You may also want to avoid the temptation of consolidating accounts from prior employers' plans into an IRA. The retail fees charged individual investors in an IRA are typically higher than the institutional fees charged accounts as part of a large 401(k) plan (where the assets held are more than just those held in your account). Furthermore, the plan sponsor may pick up the administrative fees associated with operating a 401(k) plan for all participants, regardless of whether currently employed. If you are satisfied with the fund options, expenses, and other features under your former employers' plans, it may be best to retain those old plan accounts for use in day trading.

Employer Contributions   The 401(k) story only gets better when you consider employer contributions. In a 2009 study, 91 percent of 401(k) plans provided for fixed, variable, or matching employer contributions to employees' 401(k) accounts.[4]

Matching Contributions   Some employers entice their employees to save for retirement through their 401(k) plans by matching some, all, or more of what their employees save under the plan. These employer matching contributions are typically set up to provide that for every dollar the employee puts into the 401(k) plan up to a specified percentage of pay, the employer will match a percentage of that employee's contribution. The 2009 study reported that 83 percent of employers matched employee contributions to some extent in 2009.[5]

As noted in Chapter 2, a common 401(k) matching formula provides that the employer will make a contribution to an employee's individual account in the amount of 50 percent of each dollar an employee contributes up to 6 percent of pay. Under such a matching formula, an employee contributing 6 percent or more of annual pay of $50,000 would receive an employer matching contribution to his or her 401(k) account in the amount of $1,500 (= 0.50 match percentage × 0.06 employee contribution rate × $50,000 annual pay) over the course of the year.

Even if you have to beg, borrow, or steal, whatever you do, make sure you contribute at least the amount that gets the full employer match or you will be passing up free money. In a plan with a 50 percent match, this free money can add as much as a 50 percent return to your contributions, which no investment or trading strategy can do.

Other Employer Contributions   Some employers make contributions to the 401(k) accounts of all eligible employees, irrespective of whether the employees are contributing to the plan. Such employer contribution may take the form of a flat amount or flat percentage of pay allocated to each individual participant account. Although this type of employer contribution formula rewards all eligible participants, matching contribution formulas that reward savers are much more prevalent.

The aggregate amount of the employer contribution may be defined on the basis of a formula that takes into account the sponsoring company's profits or some other performance measures. Some plans even leave the amount of employer contributions to the discretion of the sponsoring company's board of directors.

Nondiscrimination standards exist to make sure a 401(k) plan's tax benefits are shared among eligible employees—both highly paid and non-highly paid. To the extent some employees do not participate enough, additional employer contributions may be made to the extent necessary to satisfy these nondiscrimination testing standards. The use of additional employer contributions represents an acceptable way to retroactively address a nondiscrimination testing problem discovered at the end of a year.

Why does an employer make contributions to a 401(k) plan? Although there are many reasons, some employers do it to remain competitive with their peers in the industry or in the local area in which they do business. Others contribute to 401(k) plans out of an obligation to ease the transition of employees into retirement. Employers also may contribute to help their 401(k) plan pass nondiscrimination tests that may otherwise prevent highly paid employees from taking full advantage of the pretax savings opportunity offered under the plan, as compared to other (nonhighly paid) employees who cannot afford to save as much.

Contribution Limits   The tax advantages of 401(k) plan contributions come with some strings attached. Not only are employees limited in the amount of regular pretax and Roth contributions ($16,500 in 2011) and catch-up contributions ($5,500 in 2011) they can make into all of their individual 401(k) accounts in any one calendar year, but employee and employer contributions to their individual accounts are subject to an aggregate contribution ("annual additions") limit, pay cap, and discrimination testing.

When a participant leaves an employer before working the requisite service period necessary to become vested under the plan, he or she leaves behind a nonvested account balance, which is distributed among remaining participants. The sum of each participant's allocated share of these forfeitures of nonvested participants, employee contributions, and any employer contributions may not exceed an annual limit. In 2011, the sum of employee and employer contributions and reallocations of nonvested forfeitures to any participant's account may be no more than the lesser of the participant's pay or $49,000. The aggregate dollar limit increases annually in $1,000 increments when warranted by future increases in the cost of living.

For most 401(k) plans, annual nondiscrimination testing is performed to ensure that employees of different pay levels are participating. Annual nondiscrimination testing limits the extent to which highly paid employees can participate in a 401(k) plan based on the participation of other (nonhighly paid) employees. One corrective method cited previously allows an employer to make additional employer contributions to nonhighly paid employees' accounts to the extent necessary to satisfy the nondiscrimination standards. Alternatively, the employer could recharacterize highly paid employees' contributions (such as from pretax to after-tax contributions). A third (less desirable) method to correct a nondiscrimination testing problem would limit or refund highly paid employees' contributions to the extent they are excessive.

Finally, contributions by employers and employees to individual 401(k) accounts may recognize only up to a certain amount of pay for each year. In other words, contribution formulas based on pay can take into account *only* the first $245,000 of a participant's pay for 2011. (This limit increases in $5,000 increments when warranted by future increases in the cost of living.) Technically, an employee earning $300,000 per year who elects to contribute 6 percent of pay would be limited to contributing $14,700 (= 0.06 × lesser of $245,000 pay limit or $300,000 actual pay) due to the pay cap limit of $245,000 during 2011.

Vesting

Vesting refers to entitlement upon termination of employment to different types of plan money that may be dependent on a participant's service with an employer. Your vested status in an employer-provided benefit is generally based on all service up until termination of employment, regardless of whether you were participating in the plan during that time. Service is generally measured as the time spent working for an employer. Once you become vested under a plan, you are entitled to your plan benefits when you leave your employment, regardless of the reason. By law, a plan may not include a "bad boy" clause that would preclude payment of statutorily vested 401(k) plan benefits for employee malfeasance or otherwise withhold statutorily vested 401(k) plan benefits for any other reason. Often a participant's vested status will vary with respect to plan funds attributable to employee and employer contributions.

Vesting of Employee Contributions   All money deposited by an employee into a 401(k) plan account and any resultant investment earnings are irrevocably the employee's. This full and immediate vesting applies to both employee contributions and investment earnings thereon. Certain employer contributions made to satisfy discrimination testing standards are also fully vested.

Vesting of Employer Contributions   Many 401(k) plans require their employees to work a certain period of time before they become entitled to, or vested in, the portion of their accounts attributable to employer contributions. Depending on the plan, the vesting schedule may gradually or abruptly grant an employee the right to keep the employer-derived portion of his or her account upon termination based on the employee's service up until that time. A vesting schedule often may serve as a retention device or incentive to remain with a company to attain the full employer-provided benefit under the plan.

There are two alternative minimum vesting standards that may apply to the portion of a participant's account attributable to employer contributions. A 401(k) plan must vest the employer-derived portion of a participant's account, composed of employer contributions and associated investment earnings, at least as rapidly as under one of the two following schedules.

Cliff Vesting   One minimum alternative vesting schedule is a three-year cliff vesting schedule, which provides full vesting after three years of service and none prior to that.

TABLE 3.1 2-To-6 Year Graded Vesting Schedule	
Years of Service	**Vesting Percentage**
0 to 1	0%
2	20
3	40
4	60
5	80
6 or more	100

Graded Vesting The other alternative vesting schedule is a two- to six-year graded vesting schedule, where an employee is 20 percent vested after two years of service and gains 20 percent additional vesting for each additional year of service, until fully vested after six years of service. This two- to six-year graded vesting schedule is shown in Table 3.1.

Of course, a plan may always provide more generous vesting that vests plan benefits more rapidly than provided under either of the two alternative minimum vesting standards described here. For example, a plan may offer full and immediate vesting on employer-provided as well as employee-provided benefits. In such case, a participant is immediately entitled to all plan benefits regardless of service upon termination of employment. The particular vesting schedule applied to plan benefits is up to the employer sponsoring the plan.

Vesting upon Retirement Note that a plan's vesting schedule applies to employer-provided benefits upon termination of employment before retirement. A participant will always be entitled to his or her full account balance upon qualifying for retirement under the conditions defined in the plan.

Vesting and You Vesting does not affect your ability to manage your 401(k) account assets. Even if you are not fully vested, you may direct the investment of your entire account. Whether you, your employer, or your fellow workers ultimately reap the rewards of your clever investment management of the employer-provided portion of your 401(k) account upon your termination of employment is determined by the extent to which you become vested under the terms of the plan. If you had worked the requisite years of service or attained the retirement age in order to become fully vested under the plan, you earned a nonforfeitable right to your entire account. By law, you are generally entitled to your full vested account balance, and it cannot be kept from you once you terminate employment.

Whenever you consider leaving an employer, you may want to at least be aware of any step-up in vesting of your retirement benefit for the service level that you may be close to attaining. Although vesting is designed to be a retention device, it should not be more than a reference point in influencing an employment termination decision. However, if you are nearing a vesting milestone upon an impending termination, you may want to delay your departure to reach the stepped-up vesting.

Investment Funds

All 401(k) plan contributions made by employees and their employers are generally deposited into a trust, custodial account, or insurance company account. By law, the plan assets are segregated from the employer's assets and can be used only to pay plan benefits.

A retirement savings plan sponsor typically hires a fund manager to invest plan funds and a record keeper to administer the plan. The fund manager invests the underlying plan assets for the benefit of participants. The plan record keeper tracks the contributions, investment earnings and losses, benefits, and expenses for individual accounts maintained for participants. These fund management and record-keeping services can be performed by separate entities or bundled together by companies with both investment management and record-keeping capabilities.

Participant at Risk   For a defined benefit pension plan, it is the plan sponsor who assumes all of the risk of investing plan assets to meet promised pension benefits. If investment results are unfavorable, the employer steps in to make up any shortfall to pay a pension plan's promised benefits. In other words, the employer steps in to fill up the asset tank when it gets too low to pay promised plan benefits.

One of the primary benefits to employers sponsoring 401(k) plans is the ability to shift the investment management, and associated risk, to employees. The employee is left to the task of monitoring the level of his or her own asset tank for its sufficiency to provide retirement income.

In managing a retirement savings account, a participant needs to make two decisions with respect to the allocation of new and old money among available fund options:

1. Where will the new money of ongoing contributions be invested?
2. How will the old money of the existing plan balance be invested?

Each participant bears the responsibility for directing the allocation of new contribution deposits and redirecting, if necessary, the investment of assets already held in the participant's individual account.

Fund Options   Most 401(k) plans offer a variety of fund options into which participants may elect to invest their plan accounts. Each plan sponsor establishes a menu of alternative fund options for their participants' investment of their account assets from among the mutual funds, institutional funds, and insurance company accounts available in the market. General information about a particular 401(k) plan's alternative fund offerings is usually included in the plan's Summary Plan Description. Specific information on a fund's objectives, historical returns, and expenses is available in a mutual fund prospectus or may be otherwise available upon request for other types of funds.

The assets within a retirement savings plan's alternative fund options can generally be classified as cash, bonds, or stocks, or combinations thereof. These fund options can run the gamut from secure money market funds to international emerging growth equity funds.

Other fund options offered by 401(k) plans include employer stock, funds of funds, loan accounts, and self-directed brokerage accounts. Many plans include employer stock as the default option for employer contributions and as one of the available options for employee contributions.

For plans automatically enrolling new employees, a fund of funds, such as a target-date fund, may be designated as the default investment option for employee contributions. This increasingly popular type of fund of funds allows a participant to put plan investments on autopilot by investing in a shifting composition of funds holding stocks, bonds, and cash in predetermined proportions depending on the participant's investment horizon until retirement.

A participant taking out a loan under the plan will, in effect, have the loan account as an investment option. This loan account tracks the participant's repayment of loan principal.

A *self-directed brokerage account* allows adventurous participants the opportunity to independently direct, usually at their own cost, the investment of their account balances among acceptable investments within the investment universe other than the standard fare offered under the plan.

Fund Features   In selecting an investment fund worthy of your hard-earned savings, it is important to consider the fund's risk, liquidity, management style, and expenses.

Risk   One way to classify funds is based on a fund's inherent risk. A fund's composition determines its risk level. Funds heavily invested in stocks carry more risk and more potential return than those with more bonds and cash. An investor's age and propensity for risk play a big role in determining how much risk the investor can bear within an investment portfolio.

Liquidity   Ease of access to account funds also plays a part in determining the appropriateness of a fund's inclusion in a retirement savings portfolio. A participant nearing retirement or one using a 401(k) account as a quasi-savings account may want to hold the account in liquid fund options allowing for quick redemption without any loss in principal.

Fund Management Style   Another way to classify funds is based on the management style of the fund. The mutual funds, institutional funds, and insurance company accounts offered as fund options under a 401(k) plan are composed of securities selected by the fund's investment manager under an active management strategy or as components of a market index under a passive management strategy. A passively managed fund tracks a market index, such as the Standard & Poor's 500 index. Whereas a passively managed fund requires minimal trading and oversight, an actively managed fund employs investment professionals to pick, buy, and sell securities in accordance with a specified strategy with the intent of beating a market index. Due to the extra oversight and trading involved in managing an actively (as compared to a passively) managed fund, its returns are burdened with additional direct and indirect costs that are passed along to shareholders as a reduction in net return.

Fund Expenses   Although a plan's investment management fees are borne by participants through a reduction in fund returns, plan sponsors usually pick up the costs associated with the record keeping for a 401(k) plan. A fund's trading costs for net security purchases or sales associated with all fund exchanges are also passed along as a reduction in fund returns for all shareholders in the fund. **Yet an individual directing a fund exchange is not directly charged for such an exchange in that the resultant trading cost is generally shared among all fund holders.**

     This avoidance of direct trading costs for a fund exchange under a 401(k) plan represents a big advantage over the charges an individual would incur for trading in a regular brokerage account. Since an exchange typically involves a sale of one security and the purchase of another, an individual would incur trading fees for both the purchase and the sale transactions in a brokerage account. Such direct fees are not charged for an exchange under a 401(k) plan. However, there are some exceptions that diminish this advantage in the event of excessive trading in a 401(k) account, which are addressed in Chapter 8.

Account Valuation   A 401(k) plan record keeper tracks the plan assets attributable to each individual participant account for the record-keeping purposes of allocating plan cash flows and determining each individual's tax basis upon eventual distribution. Within each participant's account, an accounting is maintained for the holdings in each of the fund options selected by the participant. In addition, subaccounts are established to track different sources of money, such as employee and employer contributions.

With the sophisticated plan administrative systems available these days, most 401(k) plans offer a daily valuation of individual plan accounts. According to a 2008 survey, 93 percent of 401(k) plans offer daily valuation and record keeping to their participants.[6] At the end of each business day, an accounting is made of the inflows and outflows affecting each participant's holdings in each fund option. Inflows, such as contributions, investment earnings, and exchanges into a fund, are netted against outflows, such as benefits, expenses, investment losses, and exchanges out of that same fund for each participant's account on a daily basis. This daily valuation feature is what makes it possible to enable and track daily fund exchanges directed by participants in the management of their accounts.

Stay tuned for a more thorough discussion of the diversity of investment funds used in 401(k) and other retirement savings plans in Chapter 4.

Access to Funds

As a retirement savings plan, a 401(k) plan allows participants to receive a distribution of the vested portion of their accumulated account balances on termination of employment. A 401(k) plan may also offer participants access to their vested account balances while still employed as well as after termination of employment. Such access is usually subject to restrictions, depending on the nature of the payment as a withdrawal, loan, or distribution. The taxation of funds received by the participant also depends on the type of payment.

Many plan sponsors allow loans or withdrawals from 401(k) plans so as to encourage participation among employees who may otherwise hesitate to save under their plans lest they be prevented from getting access to those funds when needed. For these employees needing the flexibility to access savings now (while employed) rather than later (upon termination), their 401(k) accounts serve as sort of a rainy-day fund.

Withdrawals   A 401(k) plan may allow participants to withdraw funds from their own individual account balances while still employed under limited conditions. Any employee after-tax contributions and associated investment earnings are generally available for withdrawal upon request. Just over four out of five plans offer employees the opportunity to make withdrawals on or after attainment of age $59^1/_2$. Likewise, 81 percent of plans offer employees hardship withdrawals for legitimate reasons usually specified in the plan.[7]

The IRS has suggested certain safe-harbor rules for plan sponsors to follow in administering in-service hardship withdrawals. These rules prescribe that a hardship withdrawal may be made only from employee pretax contributions to satisfy an immediate and heavy financial need. Investment earnings (except for those earned prior to 1989) on an employee's pretax contributions are generally not available for a hardship withdrawal.

Under these safe-harbor rules, participants availing themselves of a hardship withdrawal must have exhausted all other means from other employer-sponsored plans. In addition, the withdrawal is limited to only the amount needed. As a deterrent, a participant taking a hardship withdrawal is subject to restrictions on the amount of pretax contributions that may be made in the year following the withdrawal and is suspended from participating for a period of at least six months following the withdrawal. During such a suspension period, the employee may not make any plan contributions or receive any associated employer contributions.

In general, a hardship withdrawal may be obtained for the purpose of meeting an immediate and heavy financial need arising from:

- Payment of medical expenses for the employee, spouse, and certain dependents.
- Purchase of a principal residence for the employee.
- Payment of educational expenses for the employee, spouse, and dependents.
- Need to prevent eviction or foreclosure on the employee's primary residence.

Although most 401(k) plans follow the IRS safe-harbor rules, there are some 401(k) plans that offer hardship withdrawals for other legitimate reasons as well.

Withdrawals subject the recipient to some potentially onerous tax consequences. All taxable withdrawals are taxed as ordinary income in the year withdrawn. If the withdrawal is made before attainment of age $59^1/_2$, it is generally also subject to a 10 percent federal excise tax and possibly an additional state excise tax, unless an exemption applies. Exceptions apply in the case of a withdrawal upon disability, death, or retirement at or after age 55; payment as a life annuity; distribution of dividends; distribution used to pay certain medical expenses, divorce settlements, educational expenses, first-home purchase expenses up to $10,000, or IRS levies or adjustments; or payments to certain beneficiaries of governmental plans and tax-exempt organizations, public safety employees, or reservists.[8]

Loans Access to a plan loan is fairly prevalent, with three out of four defined contribution plans allowing plan loans.[9] Under 401(k) plans offering loans, current employees may take out a loan up to certain limits from their own accounts. Some plans limit the number of outstanding loans that a participant may have at any one time. Once the loan is granted, you simply repay it, along with a reasonable rate of interest defined under the plan, usually through payroll withholding directly back into your 401(k) account. The loan amount is generally limited to no more than the lesser of $50,000 or half of your vested account balance. However, a small loan of your entire vested balance up to $10,000 may also be allowed.

When a loan is initiated, its proceeds are generally drawn from, and then repaid proportionately into, the fund options held in the participant's 401(k) account, unless otherwise specified by the plan or the participant taking out the loan. Many plans charge a one-time loan initiation fee as well as ongoing loan maintenance fees to cover the loan administration costs.

An outstanding loan balance is separately tracked as a quasi-fund option during the life of the loan. This loan account is reduced by loan principal repayments as the loan is repaid. As such, the outstanding loan balance becomes insulated from the market conditions and associated investment results affecting the fund options from which the loan was drawn. Depending on the direction of the market, losing out on the forgone earnings (or losses) from such lapse in participating in the market while the loan is outstanding could have a dramatic effect on the accumulation of retirement savings under the plan.

Unlike a loan from your neighborhood loan shark, a 401(k) plan loan can be obtained for any reason regardless of your creditworthiness at a reasonable cost. If you have a legitimate need (or not) that is worthy of drawing upon your retirement savings, a 401(k) plan loan may be your answer. Best of all, a plan loan represents the most tax-effective way to access your 401(k) account funds while still employed. Any loan proceeds received by a participant are tax-free as long as the loan is repaid on a timely basis.

This 401(k) plan loan privilege typically disappears once a participant terminates employment. Once an employer can no longer automatically collect loan repayments through payroll withholding from a terminated participant no longer receiving a paycheck, a loan becomes a bit more difficult to administer. You typically lose your right to initiate a loan once you become eligible for a plan distribution (which would be taxable). Also, if you terminate employment before the loan is repaid, it usually becomes payable in full within a specified period, such as 30 or 90 days following your termination. This payment-in-full loan demand may deter loan-carrying employees from terminating employment. In the event your loan is not repaid when due, it becomes treated as a distribution subject to taxes.

Distributions   Typically, 401(k) plans allow for a full distribution of a participant's account balance upon the participant's retirement or death or in the event of plan termination. The participant's vested account balance would be payable upon termination of employment. In the event of a loan default, the outstanding loan balance would be treated as a plan distribution. Some plans also provide for distributions upon other events, such as disability or divorce.

Distribution Options   Once a 401(k) plan benefit is payable in the event of termination, retirement, death, disability, or divorce, you (or your beneficiary) may elect to receive your plan benefit immediately or defer its payment into the future if it is at least $5,000. If your final plan benefit is less than $5,000, a 401(k) plan may automatically distribute it immediately as a lump sum distribution to you or your IRA without your consent. For larger account balances, the plan may provide for the eventual payment of your vested account balance in the form of a lump sum distribution at your direction as to the timing of receipt. However, some plans also allow you (or your beneficiary) to select from optional annuity payment forms defined in the plan.

A distribution resulting from a loan default will result in the outstanding loan amount being treated as a distribution subject to immediate taxation. A distribution upon plan termination may allow for immediate payment in the form of a lump sum distribution or possibly other optional annuity forms.

Taxation of Distributions   A plan distribution may be composed of taxable and nontaxable portions. The taxable portion of a distribution comprises employee pretax contributions, any employer contributions, and any investment earnings attributable to pretax and after-tax employee contributions and employer contributions. The portion of a distribution representing a return of after-tax contributions or Roth contributions is not taxed upon distribution. Also, any investment earnings attributable to Roth contributions, as well as the Roth contributions themselves, are not taxed upon a qualified distribution.

Just like plan withdrawals, taxable plan distributions are generally subject to immediate taxation as ordinary income when received. They are also subject to excise taxes if the distribution is made too early or too late. A too-early distribution made before age $59^1/_2$ is generally subject to a 10 percent federal excise tax and any applicable state excise tax, with the same exceptions as noted previously for withdrawals.

A terminated employee must generally commence distribution of the taxable portion of a 401(k) account by age $70^1/_2$. Such a minimum distribution requirement does not apply to accumulated Roth contributions. In order to avoid an excise tax on a too-late distribution, a payment of at least a minimum required amount (tax-deferred savings divided by life expectancy) from tax-deferred savings accounts is generally required by April 1 of the calendar year following an individual's attainment of age $70^1/_2$. Otherwise, the deficiency in such distribution is subject to a 50 percent excise tax for a too-late distribution. Even Goldilocks might have a hard time finding a distribution that was timed just right (for purposes of avoiding an excise tax).

In order to defer income taxes on a plan distribution before age $70^1/_2$, a participant or beneficiary may generally roll it over into an IRA or another qualified plan, such as a 401(k) plan, that accepts rollovers. If a lump sum is paid directly to the recipient, the taxable portion of the distribution is subject to withholding of federal income tax at a 20 percent rate and any required state income tax withholding as well. The participant may take up to 60 days to roll the distribution over into an IRA or another qualified plan to defer taxation of the distribution. If he or she completes a qualifying rollover of the entire taxable distribution (including the portion that had been withheld for income taxes) within that 60-day period, then the recipient avoids immediate taxation of the distribution.

In order to altogether avoid tax withholding from a lump sum distribution, the recipient may elect to have the entire distribution directly rolled over to an IRA or another qualified plan. In this case, the participant avoids tax withholding and immediate taxation of the benefit that bypasses the participant and gets transferred directly from one plan to another plan or IRA.

Another way to defer taxes on a plan distribution would be to retain your account balance under your former employer's 401(k) plan. Keeping an old account in place is easy—you simply do nothing. Upon your departure, your former employer or its plan administrator will solicit your election as to the disposition of your plan account balance. This solicitation is required by law and for the convenience of your former employer, which may very well prefer not to keep track of the whereabouts of former participants with account balances who are entitled to continue receiving required plan disclosures. The plan fund manager will be only too happy to assist your employer in soliciting your distribution election, in hopes that you will roll over your plan account to an IRA with the fund manager.

Unless your account balance is less than $5,000, you are generally not required to receive a distribution of your 401(k) account upon termination before age $70^1/_2$. Despite the persistent solicitations, you should consider the advantages of leaving your money in your former employer's 401(k) plan instead of rolling it over into an IRA. First, you may continue to manage your account assets in the professionally managed funds prudently selected by your former employer and its advisers. Second, your former employer may continue to pick up the tab for plan administrative costs that it covered while you were an employee. Third, you may enjoy cost savings associated with the preferred pricing in investment management fees charged under the plan's investment options that are available only to larger clients. Fourth, you may need this extra account for day trading (to be discussed further in Chapter 8). Only you can decide whether these advantages warrant retaining an account balance under your former employer's plan.

Nevertheless, once you leave an employer, you lose some of the rights you had as an employee participating in your former employer's 401(k) plan. For example, you can no longer save in a tax-preferred manner, receive employer contributions, or take out a loan under the old plan. Since these lost opportunities also apply if you were to roll over your distribution into an IRA, they may serve more as points of fact than factors in your decision as to the disposition of an old 401(k) account.

RULES ARE IMPORTANT

The foregoing discussion is just a very brief summary of 401(k) plan rules—it is not intended to cover the vast body of law relating to 401(k) plans. You will have to follow these types of governmental rules, as well as those prescribed in your particular 401(k) plan, to get the most out of participating in your 401(k) plan. The plan's Summary Plan Description available to you from the plan sponsor should come in handy here.

The Summary Plan Description document should have been given or made available to you around the time you first started to participate in the plan. If you have trouble locating a copy of the Summary Plan Description on your own, it should be readily available to you from the plan sponsor or may be online at your employer's web site. Many employers spend a great deal of time promoting their plan to make sure employees appreciate it as an important part of their pay package. Therefore, they usually also have staff or outside plan administrators available to answer questions about the plan and how it applies in your particular case. You would be wise to take advantage of these resources as well.

Now that the framework for navigating 401(k) plans has been established, it becomes necessary to get more familiar with the assets underlying 401(k) fund options.

CHAPTER 4

Tools of
the Trade

A Look at Your Assets

Nobody goes there anymore—it's too crowded.
—Yogi Berra

The new Yankee Stadium has a short right-field porch and a favorable wind, apparently. As a result, left-handed pull hitters are having a heyday banging the ball out of the yard. This surge in home runs comes from professional baseball players selecting the right lumber to ply their skills within the confines of the dimensions of a particular ballpark. A hitter needs to choose from bats of different weights, lengths, and wood types. To pull the ball down the right-field foul line with power, a left-handed batter might want a bat that is lighter—for the necessary bat speed; longer—to reach those outside pitches; and made of maple—for some extra pop. Yankee Stadium is but one ballpark. A good hitter knows the tools of his trade so that he can perform in many different venues and situations.

You are the ballplayer. Your goal is to hit a home run in managing your retirement savings portfolio. The 401(k) plan rules are your ballpark, and different types of assets are your bat selection alternatives. You are the one who needs to know how to select from among a myriad of fund options to successfully manage your retirement savings within the confines of a 401(k) plan. You might say that by comparison a baseball player has it easy in selecting from among a few different bat options when you consider the wide range of choices available to you in managing your retirement savings portfolio.

Crowds draw people, as if the location were not crowded enough already. Such is the case with the investment management business. As more and more people save through their employers' retirement savings plans, fund companies have pitched in to offer more and more investment funds in which to park these retirement savings assets.

Investment options have gone the way of television programming. When did watching television become so complicated? There used to be three major network television stations, and that was it. Picking a show to watch was easy with the limited offerings available. Then cable arrived to bring an onslaught of new programming alternatives. Hundreds of stations sprang up to produce shows to suit almost any taste, mood, intellect, or instinct.

The trend toward offering consumers more choices has also hit the investment industry hard. The number of investment options has grown exponentially to fill almost every niche. There is a difference, however. Although there may be no accounting for good taste in television viewing, you can usually tell good investment management from its performance posted over the long run.

The number and complexity of investment products available today are astounding. In addition to thousands of individual stocks, there were about 7,600 mutual funds in the United States at the end of 2010.[1] This number does not even count many other investment options, such as 9,400 hedge funds, as well as other closed funds, institutional funds, and direct placements, also available for investment.[2] The crowded market of investment choices makes asset selection daunting, even for professional investment managers. Fortunately, your plan sponsor has culled through investment options to prudently select the ones suitable for your 401(k) plan. But even then if your plan's menu of alternative investment options is average, you still have 25 fund options from which to choose.[3]

It is always a good idea to know what you are buying, especially when it comes to investing your hard-earned retirement savings. You probably want to get a feel for the quality of the component parts of your prospective purchase in order to assess its suitability for the purpose at hand. When it comes to retirement savings, you are looking for assets that will last a lifetime.

The securities that make up most 401(k) fund options can be broadly classified into asset classes with different characteristics. The way a particular fund manages investment characteristics, such as risk, liquidity, and taxation, should bear on an investor's decision as to the suitability for inclusion in a retirement portfolio. Other factors such as a fund's management style and associated fees are also of paramount importance in assessing a fund's potential success in the fund-filled marketplace.

A 401(k) investor is generally limited to investing plan account balances among the fund options offered under the plan. Whereas Chapter 1 offered a bird's-eye view of fund options, this chapter looks more at the underlying components—the securities themselves within these fund options—before going into how they are used to construct the fund options. Accordingly, the following discussion focuses primarily on some useful concepts relating to the construction of retirement savings plan fund options from their component securities that can be translated into successful 401(k) investing and trading.

INVESTMENT CHARACTERISTICS

In theory, the true price of a security is measured as the present value of its anticipated cash flow that is payable to its owner. This cash flow is composed of payment of any dividends or income, return of the original invested capital, and realized gains or losses upon sale. To derive such present value, each payment in the cash flow is discounted back to the present at an assumed interest rate. The sum of these discounted payments in the cash flow is what the security is worth to a particular investor. When investors disagree on assumptions relating to the appropriate discount rate and the likelihood and amount of future cash flow payments to be made, they come up with different values for what the same security is worth to them. The actual price of the security is then determined through some sort of reconciliation of these differences between buyers and sellers.

The characteristics affecting the true worth of a security include its risk, liquidity, and taxation. Whereas investors expect to be compensated with higher investment returns for assuming risk, they are also willing to pay a price for liquidity and tax preferences through lower returns.

Risk

The likelihood of an interruption in a security's anticipated cash flow or decrease in its inherent value is where risk comes into play. Any real or perceived threat to the issuer's ability to generate earnings for use in paying dividends or building capital poses a risk. The price of a security at any point in time reflects that perceived risk of default investors may harbor as to the receipt of future payments. It also reflects investors' nagging doubt as to what the future payments will be worth upon receipt. A security's price varies as broad or specific conditions affecting its risk change.

Risk Types In a broad sense, *risk* is defined as "exposure to the chance of injury or loss."[4] In your gut, you know that risk represents a potential for getting hurt. From a financial perspective, risk is measured in terms of the volatility of an investment's periodic returns relative to the market. Technically, a security's risk can be broken down into the following components:

- Purchasing power risk.
- Credit risk.
- Interest rate risk.
- Market risk.
- Specific risk.

Purchasing power risk inherent in a security derives from the uncertainty of whether the value of the security can keep pace with inflation. Credit risk relates to the viability of the security issuer's business as it affects the issuer's ability to pay the security's anticipated cash flow payments when due. Interest rate risk relates to the degree to which credit markets affect the price of a given security, such as an interest-sensitive product like a bond. Market risk corresponds to the degree to which the overall market for similar securities affects the given security's price. Specific risk comes from the likelihood that business-specific events will impact the security issuer's future profitability and the underlying value of the security.[5]

Relative Risk Beyond that, the risk of holding a security of a particular company also varies by the nature of the guarantee provided for different asset classes. Securities in different asset classes offer different levels of guarantees and expectations relating to the return of the original invested capital, payment of income, and potential for realized gain upon sale. The risk associated with an asset class corresponds to the strength of the payment guarantee afforded such asset class under a preset *absolute priority order* established for satisfying obligations and interests in the event of bankruptcy. Each asset class's standing under this priority order affects its overall risk of default. Asset classes with lower priority for payment represent riskier holdings.

The securities underlying funds used in 401(k) plans can generally be broken down into three basic asset classes: stocks, bonds, and cash. A *stock* is an ownership interest in a company; a *bond* is a long-term loan to a company or government; and *cash* is more of a short-term loan or other liquid holding readily convertible to cash.

As the most liquid asset class, cash instruments typically offer little risk other than interest rate risk of having to reinvest matured funds at uncertain prevailing rates. Next highest on the risk scale are bonds, whose owners are entitled to payment before stockholders in the event of a company's bankruptcy. Stocks are the highest-risk asset class, as their owners are last in line for payment under the absolute priority order. Figure 4.1

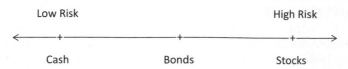

FIGURE 4.1 Risk Spectrum

depicts the relative level of risk generally associated with each of the basic asset classes.

Investors expect to be compensated according to the amount of risk undertaken in making an investment. The greater the degree of risk inherent in an investment, the more return an investor expects to earn over the long run. However, risk translates into greater short-term fluctuations in a given security's investment returns. Although risky investments may experience higher returns over the long term, they tend to have a higher possibility of losing value in the short term. In theory, a higher-risk investment with a possibility of generating losses as well as gains in the near term attracts investors by offering a higher long-term return as compensation for the additional risk.

Consistent with this risk-return relationship, stock, as the asset class with the most risk, has generated the highest long-term returns. The next highest returns over the long term have been generated by bonds, the asset class with the next highest risk level. Finally, the lowest returns have been generated by the cash asset class, which presents the least risk.

Risk Reduction Unless you are a skydiver, risk is a four-letter word. Even skydivers know how to minimize their risk, though. They pack a neatly folded parachute, carry a reserve parachute, maybe equip themselves with a device that opens the reserve parachute automatically upon reaching a certain speed at a certain altitude, and like to land in open areas with few trees. The favorable result of a safe landing is more likely to occur when a jumper has options to back up any potential failure in one area. You could say the jumper has diversified by investing in more than one option.

The fund options in 401(k) plans hold collections of underlying securities from which they derive their risk. The extent to which any given 401(k) fund option takes on the risk of the fund's underlying securities depends on the mix of the securities. Funds composed of securities in asset classes with more risk will naturally have more risk than other funds made up of of securities in less risky asset classes. However, through portfolio diversification, a fund's risk can be lessened by mixing in more securities of different asset classes or even, to some extent, other securities within the same asset class.

Synergy happens when a group's collective efforts bring forth a product that exceeds the sum of what each member of the group could have accomplished independently. Risk is the opposite of synergy, as the whole is not as great as the sum of the parts. The sum of the risk of individual securities in a portfolio is more than the risk of the entire portfolio. Certain types of risk can be diversified away to some extent by holding a variety of securities of different risk levels within a portfolio.

Fund managers as well as investors manage the risk in their portfolios. There must be something to that old adage warning you not to put too many eggs in one basket. Holding just one security is far more risky than holding a market basket of securities. If the stock price goes down, the entire portfolio composed of that single stock goes down proportionately. In a diverse portfolio of many stocks, a decline in price of a single stock will more than likely be offset by the price movements of other stocks within the portfolio. Hence a diverse portfolio of many stocks may experience less dramatic price changes than a one-stock portfolio. Using this philosophy, mutual funds and individual investors mitigate risk by pooling securities instead of betting the farm on just one security. Chapter 5 explores asset diversification a bit more.

Risk Comfort Level   As a measure heavily influenced by perception, risk gets a bad rap. Most people avoid risk like the plague. One study showed that people do not experience the same level of emotion from a gain as they do from a loss. Instead, they suffer more remorse from a loss than joy from a gain of the same size. The amount of their remorse from a loss is about two to two and one-half times the amount of pleasure derived from a gain of equal magnitude.[6]

The process of investing involves some introspection as to an individual's tolerance for risk, as any investment involves an assumption of risk. Since people prefer certainty over risk, investors expect to be compensated in the form of a higher return on investment for assuming risk. How much risk is tolerable comes down to personal preference. Each individual must settle on a balance of risk and return that will personally allow him or her to sleep at night.

Liquidity

Liquidity refers to the ease with which a security may be sold for cash on short notice at minimal cost. Since the liquidity of a security depends on the ready availability of a market to facilitate its sale, securities traded in large volumes on public stock exchanges are more liquid than others. Therefore, a stock traded on the New York Stock Exchange would be more liquid than a limited partnership with few ready buyers.

Liquidity is also enhanced by the absence of trading barriers, such as trading costs. Consequently, securities that can be sold at close to full market value with minimal offset for trading expenses tend to be more liquid than those that are more costly to sell.

Liquidity provides flexibility to investors and day traders needing easy access to cash. Unless the payoff is expected to be huge, it is usually advisable to invest in fairly liquid securities.

Taxation

The tax treatment afforded different types of securities is another factor that affects a security's value and, consequently, its yield. A tax preference may also determine a security's suitability for inclusion in a 401(k) or other retirement savings account.

Municipal Bonds' Tax Preference   Federal law grants a tax preference to municipal bonds issued by state and local governments. Whereas income payable as dividends from a corporate bond is taxed as ordinary income, municipal bond dividends are generally exempt from federal income taxation. Therefore, a municipal bond need only pay a lower (tax-free) dividend rate to match a corporate bond's after-tax return, the amount left over after paying the taxes due on the corporate bond dividends.

For example, an investor subject to a 28 percent marginal tax rate would derive the same after-tax return on a $10,000 taxable corporate bond dividend of $500 as from a municipal bond of the same face amount paying a tax-free dividend of $360 [= $500 dividend − (0.28 tax rate × $500 dividend)]. In this case, the holder of a municipal bond may be willing to accept dividends at the lower rate of 3.6 percent (= $360 dividend/$10,000 face amount), rather than 5 percent, as a result of the tax preference afforded holders of municipal bonds.

This tax preference afforded municipal bond dividend income makes municipal bonds attractive holdings for a higher-income investor seeking to shield dividend income from taxation. However, the advantage of tax-free municipal bond dividend income is wasted in a 401(k) account, where taxation of all investment earnings is deferred until distribution. First, all dividends, taxable or not, are not subject to immediate taxation in a 401(k) account. Second, municipal bond dividends that would have entirely escaped taxation eventually become taxable as part of a 401(k) plan distribution. Finally, the lower dividends typically paid by a municipal bond compared to a corporate bond would be a drag on the returns of a 401(k) account. For these reasons, a municipal bond is not an appropriate investment in a 401(k) account.

Stocks' Tax Preference   As noted earlier, tax preferences are given to stock investments. Qualified stock dividends and long-term capital gains realized upon a stock's sale are currently taxed at lower rates than are applicable to ordinary income (as of early 2011). Granted, short-term capital gains on stock held less than a year are still taxed upon sale at ordinary income tax rates. However, the tax preferences granted stocks' qualified dividends and long-term capital gains enhance the value of stock ownership in relation to other asset classes without such advantage.

However, the taxation of stock held in a 401(k) or other retirement savings account offers more of a mixed bag of blessings and curses. The general tax rate preference afforded long-term capital gains and qualified dividends does not carry over to stock held in a 401(k) or other retirement savings account. Instead, dividends and realized capital gains are generally taxed upon distribution in cash from a retirement savings account at the higher rate applicable to ordinary income. The tax advantage comes in the form of the deferral of taxes until distribution, offset by the potentially higher tax rates applicable to being taxed as ordinary income upon distribution.

The balance of the mixed tax treatment afforded a stock investment under a retirement savings plan may influence your consideration as to which types of stocks to include in your 401(k) or other retirement savings accounts. You need to determine whether the favorable opportunity to defer taxation of a stock's dividends and capital gains outweighs the unfavorable, potentially higher tax rates applicable at distribution of a retirement savings account. Based on your assessment of the tax consequences, you may decide to hold growth stocks with no dividends in your taxable brokerage account and stocks you intend to hold less than a year in your retirement savings account.

An investment in a tax-preferred financial instrument may lose some or all of its luster to avoid taxes within a 401(k) or other retirement savings plan. Therefore, it is important to consider with your tax adviser whether a tax-advantaged security's opportunity for potential returns more than offsets its loss of tax preferences enough to warrant its inclusion within a retirement savings account.

ASSET CLASSES

It is all very simple, or at least it should be. You saw how the blending of three features (weight, length, and wood type) distinguishes one baseball bat from another. Three also represents a magic number when it comes to the number of basic asset classes into which securities are generally classified. Focusing on composition rather than characteristics, fund options comprise securities from up to three different asset classes. Although sometimes sliced and diced into more refined categories, the assets used in 401(k) plans may generally be classified as stocks, bonds, or cash. Other more exotic asset classes usually do not make the cut in 401(k) plans, as plan *fiduciaries* responsible for selecting a 401(k) plan's menu of fund options may not consider such options to be prudent investments for retirement savings. Stocks, bonds, and cash constitute the building blocks of retirement savings plan fund options.

Each asset class has its own risk, liquidity, and taxation characteristics that differentiate one from another.

Stocks

Stock represents equity ownership in a company. Shares of stock represent units of ownership issued by a company to raise capital (or cash) to conduct its business. After issuance, shares may be bought or sold. An entity's ownership of a company is measured in terms of the number of shares of stock held.

Stock Types   Stock basically comes in two varieties: preferred and common. An owner of *preferred stock* usually receives a fixed dividend but has no voting rights on company business. Depending on the terms, preferred stock may be converted to common stock.

Owning a share of *common stock* entitles a shareholder to a portion of the issuing company's future earnings and voting rights. Profits or earnings are generated when a company's revenues exceed its expenses. After all other obligations are paid, the earnings are left to common stockholders to be paid as dividends or kept within the company as retained earnings. As noted earlier, a preset pecking order known as the absolute priority order puts common stock shareholders last in line behind senior creditors (like banks), bondholders, and preferred shareholders to receive payments in the event of the company's bankruptcy.

Common stock gets a good deal of attention from investors. As the more prevalent (or commonly held) form of stock, it is what general references to stock usually refer to.

Stock Issuers   Whereas the stock of publicly held companies listed on major stock exchanges may be fairly easily traded, the market for shares of privately held companies is less liquid. Thinly traded by design, the stock of a privately held company tends to be closely held by its founders, family, executives, employees (perhaps through an employee stock ownership plan—a defined contribution plan invested primarily in company stock), or an investment firm. Executives and employees leaving the firm are typically required to sell their shares back at fair value usually determined on an infrequent basis, such as once per year.

By contrast, the existence of stock exchanges facilitates regular trading of publicly held companies' stock, potentially resulting in its widespread ownership by unrelated parties. Whether a company's ownership is privately or publicly held, a party holding a share of stock has certain ownership rights.

Stock Pricing Stock ownership is like diamonds in one respect—it lasts forever. Yet companies issuing stock do not always last forever. Although the life of a company issuing stock may be finite, the ownership rights granted by its stock do last forever; it is just that these rights may take on a different form in the case of a merger or may not be worth much of anything if the company's fortunes sour or collapse.

Owning a company's common stock allows you to participate in its future as well as the overall growth of the U.S. economy. At any point in time, a company's stock price reflects the market's current perception of how future conditions will affect the company's ability to earn a profit.

The value of a share of common stock comes from the right granted stockholders to receive future earnings into perpetuity. These future earnings take the form of capital appreciation and any dividends paid by the company. *Capital appreciation* is the increase in the value of a share of stock over its original purchase price due to the market's perception of the company's increased earnings potential. *Dividends* are periodic (or special) payments of a portion of earnings to shareholders to the extent approved by a company's board of directors.

A company's future earnings potential is reflected in its share price as well as its dividends. Going back to the formulaic theory for valuing a security, the price of a company's common stock is the present value of its future earnings into perpetuity. To the extent a company's earnings are distributed as dividends, the share price would be equal to the present value of the anticipated dividend stream.

Otherwise, a shareholder intending to own a stock for a fixed term may value its current share price as the present value of any anticipated dividends and its sale proceeds, including any capital appreciation at the planned sale date (which is still the present value of future earnings beyond the planned sale date). When all is said and done, it is a company's *future* earnings potential that determines its common stock share price.

Stock prices should be more a story about the future than the past. Yet investors cannot quite help dwelling on the past as their only reference point in assessing a company's future. The market's collective assessment of a company's future earnings determines its common stock price.

This concept works on an overall basis as well, inasmuch as corporate and government activity drive the economy. Just as one company's stock price reflects its prospects, the aggregation of stock prices of companies constituting the total stock market is a harbinger of the aggregate earnings of the market's component companies. In turn, the valuation of the total stock market is often viewed as a barometer of the condition of the economy about six months down the road.

Stock Classification   With thousands of stocks publicly traded on stock exchanges, it makes sense to organize these stocks in a manner that will facilitate the selection of ones to fit an investor's particular taste.

You have already seen how assets can be broken down into three general asset classes. It turns out that stocks can be further classified into subcategories. These refined stock classifications are useful not only for picking winners, but also for measuring their suitability for investment in terms of risk exposure, liquidity, and tax treatment.

As clearly the most popular asset class, stocks have drawn the most attention. Fund managers, in particular, spend an inordinate amount of time classifying stocks and studying market trends to find the companies whose stock will outperform all others. Although there seem to be as many ways to classify stocks as there are fund managers, stocks can generally be broken down by the issuing company's size, relative stock price (indicating its growth/value bent), and place of business.

Market Capitalization   A company's size is measured in terms of its *market capitalization* (market cap), or total market value of common stock shares. As with soft drinks served by fast-food establishments, all companies come in a small, medium, or large size. Conveniently they are called small-cap, mid-cap, and large-cap companies, respectively. Under the current convention, a small-cap company has a market value of under $1 billion, a mid-cap company has a market capitalization between $1 billion and $5 billion, and a large-cap company has a market cap of over $5 billion.

Although there are exceptions, larger companies are generally viewed as more stable than smaller ones. The stocks of these well-established companies generally carry less risk. Since these large-cap company stocks are frequently traded on major stock exchanges, their shares are more liquid.

Growth versus Value Stocks   Perception plays a role in distinguishing between a growth stock and a value stock. Whereas a growth stock has higher than normal earnings potential, a value stock has more of a solid track record of consistent earnings over time.

Different objective measures are also used to distinguish between growth and value stocks. One basis, known as the price-to-book ratio, compares a company's price (market capitalization) with the book value of its assets reported in company financial statements.

$$\text{Price-to-Book Ratio} = \frac{\text{Market Capitalization}}{\text{Book Value of Assets}}$$

The stock of a company with a high price relative to its assets is deemed a growth stock with higher earnings potential. Conversely, a value stock is more of a bargain with its lower price-to-book ratio.

Another measure used to distinguish growth from value stocks is the price-earnings (P/E) ratio. It can be calculated as a company's current stock price divided by its annual (trailing or estimated future) earnings.

$$\text{Price/Earnings Ratio} = \frac{\text{Stock Price}}{\text{Annual Earnings}}$$

The price-earnings ratio gets complicated by the different types of earnings—such as past or future, pro forma, generally accepted accounting principles (GAAP), or operating—that can be used, and the overall market sentiment (bullish or bearish). It can also be meaningless or a little misleading for companies that have no earnings or are in a loss position.

Nonetheless, growth stocks typically have higher price-earnings ratios than value stocks. The higher expectations for a growth stock company that go along with its higher price-earnings ratio represent a risk that its earnings and stock price may not pan out. Thus an investment in a growth stock carries more risk than one in a value stock.

Many growth stock companies do not pay any dividends at all and instead reinvest (retained) earnings back into the company's operations. Common stock shareholders of these companies seek their return through share price appreciation rather than dividends.

Value stocks provide a steady return through the regular payment of dividends. Unlike growth stocks, which tend to exhibit exaggerated market swings, value stocks' share prices are less sensitive to the overall market.

The tax preferences granted stock ownership under U.S. law affect the desirability of holding different types of stocks. Whereas the deferral until sale of taxation at lower long-term capital gains tax rates may favor holding growth stocks, the equally low tax rates applicable to qualified dividends and long-term capital gains presents a case for holding value stocks.

Domestic versus Foreign Stocks Most large companies do business on a global scale these days. Local securities laws, tax structures, government oversight, and accounting standards affect a company's business operations and the trading of its stock. Another way to classify a company's stock is based on the domicile of its operations.

The stock of a company based in the United States is considered a domestic stock, and that of a company based outside the United States is— you guessed it—a foreign stock. Foreign company stocks may be broken down even further by geographic region, such as Asia-Pacific, Latin America, or Europe. Alternatively, foreign stocks can be classified based on the perceived state of the local economy, such as emerging or developed. Due to the strength and business standards of the U.S. economy, domestic company stocks generally carry less risk than those of foreign companies.

Bonds

A bond is a loan at a set interest rate by a bondholder, such as you, to a company or a government as the bond issuer. The loan (or note) is to be repaid over a specified term, which can range from one year to 30 years or more. In return for the loan, the bond issuer (as borrower) pays the bondholder (as lender) periodic interest payments in the form of dividends during the term of the bond (or loan) and full repayment of the bond's face amount (or initial loan principal) at maturity of the bond (or loan term). Dividends are typically paid on a quarterly, semiannual, or annual basis.

Consider the case in which you purchase a government bond at issuance and hold it until maturity. At the issuance of a government bond, you as the bondholder pay the government as the bond issuer the face amount of the bond. In return, the government contractually commits to repay you the original face amount of the loan with interest. The government's interest payments on the loan take the form of periodic dividends paid to you over the term of the loan. The government also pays you the entire face amount of the original loan in full at the end of the loan term (or maturity). Since the repayment at maturity equals the initial face amount of the bond, the annual (absolute) yield on the bond held from issuance to maturity is equal to the annual dividend payments.

Bond Issuers Corporations and governments, in the United States and abroad, issue bonds to finance ongoing operations and special projects. As noted earlier, dividend income from municipal bonds issued by state and local governments generally receives a tax preference. Whereas dividends from corporate and federal government bonds are taxed as ordinary income, dividend income from municipal bonds is generally not taxed at the federal level. In addition, dividends paid under municipal bonds issued by the state in which you live may also be exempt from state income tax.

Bond Pricing   Bonds differ from stocks in a number of key ways. Unlike stock, where a shareholder shares in the fortunes of the issuing company, a bond offers a fixed income stream over a finite term and full repayment at maturity. Because of its set terms, a bond held from issuance to maturity provides the yield that was promised at the outset. Also, a bondholder has no ownership rights in the issuer and, consequently, does not share in its earnings or get any voting rights.

However, bonds can be bought and sold like stocks. In the event of a sale, a bond's yield depends on any appreciation or depreciation in the price, as well as the future dividend stream. Then it becomes necessary to establish an interim price for a bond prior to its maturity.

The price of a bond at any point in time is the present value of its defined future cash flow. In the case of a *noncallable* bond (where the issuer has no right to prepay the loan), its current price is determined as the present value of future periodic dividend payments and of the final repayment of the face amount of the bond. Therefore, the bond's price is heavily influenced by its term to maturity and the yield rate used to discount the bond's cash flow in determining its present value. The yield rate assumption used to value a bond takes into account many risks, such as current interest conditions, the creditworthiness of the bond issuer, and collateral, if any, for securing the loan.

Bond Risk   Among other risks, bond prices are particularly sensitive to interest rate risk. Bond prices have an inverse relationship with prevailing interest rates. That is, bond prices tend to go in the opposite direction of prevailing interest rates. When interest rates rise, bond prices go down. This results from prospective bond purchasers demanding a discount on a bond's price to produce a higher yield commensurate with the higher current interest rates available in the marketplace. When this higher yield rate is used to discount the fixed stream of bond payments, the resulting lower present value is what prospective buyers expect to pay for the bond. Conversely, when interest rates decline, the use of a lower yield rate to discount a bond's cash flow stream results in a higher bond price. The longer the term of the bond, the greater the impact a change in the discount rate has on the value of a bond.

Credit risk also affects bond yields and prices. Bond rating agencies assign credit ratings to bonds based on the bond issuer's creditworthiness and collateral backing the loan. Bonds issued by the U.S. federal government are considered to have no risk of default. (Perhaps the federal government's ability to print money has something to do with its unblemished credit record.) With no credit risk, a U.S. Treasury bond will yield less than a corporate bond of the same duration.

Municipal bonds issued by local governments are only as secure as the local governments standing behind them. Investment grade bonds are backed by well-established companies with solid earnings track records and prospects perceived to be capable of repaying their bond obligations. Even then, certain types of bondholders stand before others when it comes time for a bond issuer to pony up. In the event of a bond issuer's bankruptcy, bondholders of debt secured by specific collateral get paid before unsecured debt holders. Therefore, unsecured debt carries more risk and yields a potentially higher return than debt secured by specific collateral.

Also more risky are high yield or junk bonds used to raise capital for unproven or struggling companies. In order to attract investors, junk bonds offer higher yields than investment grade bonds to compensate for the additional credit risk undertaken by the bondholder.

According to the standard yield curve (which plots bond yields by duration to maturity), bond yields tend to increase with time to maturity. All other things being equal, a bond with a shorter time to maturity, such as five years, normally yields less than a bond with a longer term, such as 30 years. It turns out that prospective bond purchasers expect to get higher yields on bonds with longer terms, due to their lengthened exposure to an issuer's credit risk and the market's interest rate risk. There is a bigger risk of an issuer's potential for default and the market's changing interest conditions when there is a long time between the promise to repay a loan at a bond's issuance and the fulfillment of that promise by its repayment at maturity.

The risk of stuff possibly happening to get in the way of repaying a loan grows over time. Changes in general economic or specific business conditions could happen at any time so as to present challenges to a bond issuer's ability to pay off its loan on a timely basis under the terms of the bond. As a result, bond investors expect to be compensated for the length of time—between the promise to pay and the fulfillment of that promise—during which they are exposed to the issuer's credit risk.

Market interest rates and inflation may change during the term of the bond so as to make prospective dividend payments more or less attractive than when the bond was first issued. A decline in interest rates would make the bond's current dividend stream (that had not changed since its issuance) more attractive and easier to sell at a premium from its original face amount. Conversely, a rise in interest rates, possibly due to inflation, would make the original bond dividend payments appear stingy, requiring its price to be discounted if it were to be sold. These bond price adjustments act to ensure that the bond's future cash flow generates a return comparable to rates currently available in the marketplace at the time of a bond's potential sale.

As noted, a bondholder's interest takes precedence over that of a stockholder in the event of a company's bankruptcy. Accordingly, the lesser risk associated with holding bonds has historically translated into lower long-term returns for bonds than for stocks. Then there is cash, an even lower-risk asset class that generates an even lower return than bonds.

Cash

Cash is legal tender, or a short-term loan readily convertible to it. You will not find cash-stuffed-in-a-mattress as a fund option in a 401(k) plan. Instead, the cash asset class, as used in a retirement savings plan, is ultimately composed of secure short-term loans to governments and corporations. Each such loan is repayable with interest and may or may not be *callable* before maturity, depending on its terms. In short, the cash asset class provides a liquid source of funds from readily marketable, short-term loans with little risk of default.

The collective cash funds typically found in a 401(k) plan are essentially either money market funds or stable value funds. Both of these types of funds are collections of loans with shorter maturities. Money market funds invest primarily in money market instruments with maturities of less than one year, whereas stable value funds invest more in short- to medium-term insurance contracts and bonds.

About one-third of 401(k) plans offer money market funds, and most of the rest offer stable value funds.[7] You may also find other variations of labels for a cash fund, such as a short-term investment fund. Whatever their name, they all provide a secure, liquid source of funds invested in shorter-term securities.

Money Market Instruments   Registered investment companies bundle money market instruments into mutual funds for use as investment options under retirement savings plans. These highly regulated money market mutual funds, as well as other institutional funds, offer minimal risk through the pooling of already low-risk money market instruments like U.S. Treasury bills, other federal agency issues, certificates of deposit, bankers' acceptances, and commercial paper.

U.S. Treasury Bills   U.S. Treasury bills, which have maturities of one year or less, sell at government auctions in denominations of at least $10,000. As a zero coupon security, a Treasury bill pays no periodic interest. Instead it sells at a discount and can be redeemed for the full face amount, including interest, at maturity. There is no risk of default, due to its backing by the full faith of the U.S. government.

Other Federal Agency Issues A related money market instrument included in the cash asset class is a short-term obligation resulting from a loan to other federal agencies, which typically offers a slightly higher interest rate than a Treasury bill of the same duration.

Certificates of Deposit Money market instruments also include bank certificates of deposit (CDs) with maturities of less than one year. A certificate of deposit is a bank account promising the payment of predefined interest and a return of principal at the end of a fixed term. CDs are currently insured by the Federal Deposit Insurance Corporation (FDIC) for up to $250,000 per depositor through 2013, after which the $250,000 limit is scheduled to revert to $100,000 for nonretirement accounts. CDs typically pay a slightly higher interest rate than government-backed issues of the same duration.

Bankers' Acceptances A bankers' acceptance is a short-term draft (or loan) made by a bank to finance a customer's purchase from a vendor unwilling to accept the customer's credit without the bank's guarantee. It works sort of like that bank cashier's check you may have used to place a deposit on your first apartment, except it applies to business transactions of a larger magnitude.

Commercial Paper Commercial paper is an unsecured loan made to a large company with a maturity of under one year. Since repayment is not guaranteed by the federal government, its return is usually higher and depends on the creditworthiness of the borrower.

Stable Value Funds Stable value funds include collections of loans with slightly longer maturities (from two to four years) than money market instruments. Historically, they have been primarily invested in guaranteed investment contracts (GICs) and bank investment contracts (BICs) with staggered maturities. Like overgrown CDs, these guaranteed contracts provide that a deposit made during a one-day window will earn a set interest rate if held until maturity, upon which it is available for redemption or reinvestment. Liquidity comes in the form of the contract's redemption at maturity and an allowance for withdrawals at book value to provide plan benefits. GICs and BICs are offered by insurance companies and banks, respectively.

Cash as a Parking Spot   The modest returns on cash holdings are not highly correlated with those of the market. Accordingly, a cash fund attracts the investment of individuals seeking liquidity and safety of principal above all else with the understanding that securing a return of the original invested capital on short-term notice has its price in the lower returns to be received on the investment. As a result, cash assets tend to pay the lowest returns of the three asset classes over the long term. On top of that, interest income, modest as it may be, derived from a cash fund in a taxable account is generally subject to income taxation at ordinary income rates.

In short, cash is a low-risk, liquid investment with a fairly feeble but generally positive return. **Individuals place money in a cash instrument when it is of paramount importance that their entire original investment or capital will be available when needed**.

Cash should be viewed as a short-term parking spot. You drive to that spot as an interim stop on your way to something more important; that parking spot is not your destination (unless you are with someone special). You leave your car in that well-lit parking spot in a good neighborhood with no worries about whether you will be able to return to pick it up later at a moment's notice. In a 401(k) plan, you may park your account assets temporarily in cash when you close in on your destination, such as an imminent retirement or an investment or trading opportunity. When the time is right, you will draw on those secure cash account assets for the big event. Parking account assets in cash should be treated as only a temporary stop on your way to something better.

History has proven that the risk-return relationships noted previously apply to the different types of securities under normal conditions. Of course, this basic discussion of risk does not attempt to cover all possible scenarios that may generate a different result. No matter how you cut it, though, the market determines a security's yield commensurate with its perception of the level of risk to which it exposes its holders.

RETIREMENT SAVINGS ACCOUNT MANAGEMENT

Most 401(k) plans allow participants to manage the investment of the assets within their individual accounts. Under these plans, participants direct how their contributions and individual account assets are to be allocated among the alternative investment (or fund) options selected by the plan sponsor. Each of the alternative fund options offered in 401(k) plans is essentially a different collection of securities composed of assets in one or more of the asset classes just described.

By law, plan sponsors must exercise due diligence to offer a diversified menu of investment options that can run the gamut from professionally managed collective funds to self-directed brokerage accounts. By design, the plan leaves the account management responsibility to participants. Then it comes down to how well individuals manage their retirement savings portfolio that determines their retirement destiny.

Participant Investment Decisions

Whether taken on by choice or by accident, participants bear the responsibility for making two separate decisions as to the investment of new and old money among available investment options in managing a retirement savings account. As noted in Chapter 3, these decisions deal with the investment of: (1) new money in the form of ongoing plan contributions and (2) old money accumulated in an account balance from prior plan contributions and investment earnings.

The first decision as to the investment of your own and any employer contributions is initially addressed upon enrollment in the plan by either the election you make or the default election made for you by your employer. All plans offering investment options allow new participants an opportunity to direct how their contributions will be allocated among the plan's fund options at the time of their enrollment. Any participant-directed election is typically made online, by telephone, or on an election form as part of the enrollment process. However, many plans now provide for automatic enrollment of employees to participate in their 401(k) plans when first eligible. In this event, a participant not making an investment election will have his contributions automatically invested in the plan's designated default fund option, such as a target-date fund or conservative fund. In either case, a participant may modify an election regarding the investment of future contributions by following plan procedures.

The second decision as to how a participant's existing account balance is to be invested among the plan's fund options may also be addressed in two alternative ways. One way is to ignore it. You may figure the election pertaining to the investment of your contributions was good enough when you made it so as not to warrant any further tinkering with the balances that resulted. The other way is to actively or selectively make changes to the allocation of your existing account balance among alternative fund options in accordance with plan procedures. This is where investment strategy and day trading will come into play (but more on that later).

In a typical investment transaction, an individual buying a security draws upon cash reserves (or a loan facility) to purchase the security. On the other end, the security owner receives cash upon sale of the security. Under a 401(k) plan, purchases and sales of fund option shares are handled through fund exchanges, deposits, and withdrawals. A deposit or exchange into a fund represents a purchase, and a withdrawal or exchange out of a fund represents a sale. So a 401(k) plan participant wishing to realign existing account holdings will make a fund exchange pulling money out of one fund option and depositing it into another.

Plan Sponsor Responsibility

Leaving these important investment decisions to participants also presents a risk to a plan sponsor, which may have employee relations or legal problems if the plan's funds perform poorly. Just because a plan sponsor allows its employees to manage their own 401(k) accounts does not mean it will not be blamed for a disgruntled employee's bad investment decisions. These days people can sue anybody for just about anything, and they do.

Along with the sponsorship of a 401(k) plan comes a fiduciary responsibility to act solely in the interest of plan participants and beneficiaries in providing plan benefits and paying administrative expenses. Furthermore, plan fiduciaries are held to the standard of executing their duties as a prudent expert would. To mitigate its fiduciary risk, a plan sponsor may often employ outside experts to assist in carrying out its duties.

An employer sponsoring a 401(k) plan allowing participants individual control over the investment of their accounts can also limit its fiduciary risk by meeting certain standards. First, the plan must offer participants at least three diversified categories of investments other than employer stock, with different risk and return characteristics. Second, the plan must allow an employee to exchange account assets among alternative plan fund options no less than quarterly. Third, the plan sponsor must provide sufficient information for participants to make informed decisions in allocating their account assets among the available investment options.[8]

Against this backdrop, you may be able to better appreciate what employers and their advisers face when designing a 401(k) plan and its investment options.

FUND OPTIONS

It all comes down to deciding how to invest your hard-earned retirement savings among the fund options offered under the plan. Part of the fund selection process has already been done for you by your 401(k) plan sponsor or its investment committee. From the fund universe, your plan sponsor and its advisers have selected a menu of fund options under the 401(k) plan in a prudent manner and in the best interest of plan participants like you.

After your plan sponsor's narrowing of potential investment choices, the chances are high that you still have quite a few fund options to consider for the investment of your contributions and plan account balance. It seems that 401(k) plan sponsors tend to favor a wide range of choices when it comes to investment options. If your plan is average, you may wish the investment alternatives were limited even more. Although the typical defined contribution plan offers an average of 25 fund options, it turns out that the average participant divvies up his or her account balance only among three to four funds.[9]

Your fund choices generally come in the form of collective funds, target-date funds, employer stock, self-directed brokerage accounts, and loan accounts.

Collective Funds

Plan sponsors commonly offer as investment options professionally managed collective funds that pool securities. Each collective fund is an investment vehicle comprising securities in one or more of the three asset classes (stocks, bonds, and cash). A fund holding a mix of more than one asset class in significant amounts is considered a *balanced fund*. Each fund generally follows a predetermined investment policy guiding the allocation of fund assets among different asset classes. The variety of funds available in the marketplace derives not only from the blending (or balance) of the asset classes but also from the specialization of stock funds within certain sectors of domestic and world economies. The pooling of investments within these funds offers advantages in reduced risk due to asset diversification, lower expenses through economies of scale in managing a large asset base, and presumably better investment oversight (but not necessarily better performance) resulting from professional management.

Fund Types The types of collective funds typically found in 401(k) plans are:

- Mutual funds.
- Commingled institutional funds.
- Insured funding instruments.
- Exchange-traded funds.

Mutual Funds The fund options commonly offered in many 401(k) plans are mutual funds managed by registered investment companies. At the end of 2010, almost 60 percent of 401(k) assets were held in mutual funds.[10]

Mutual funds offer 401(k) investors an inexpensive way to invest in a professionally managed collection of securities. Depending on a fund's objectives as to risk, liquidity, and taxation, its underlying investments may range from secure cash to speculative emerging market stocks.

Widely marketed to retail as well as institutional customers like 401(k) plans, mutual funds are highly regulated funds under the purview of the Securities and Exchange Commission (SEC). Investors may obtain general and specific information about a mutual fund in its prospectus. This document summarizes the fund's investment objectives, strategy, management philosophy, security types, risk, historical investment performance, expenses, valuation method, and trading policies.

The popularity of mutual fund investment alternatives in a retirement savings plan derives from its advantages of liquidity, diversification, variety (of objectives), availability, and ease in tracking current and historical pricing information. The pervasive accessibility of pricing information and the liquidity of mutual funds especially facilitate trading of its shares. **Mutual fund shares may be bought and sold at the fund share's *net asset value* (NAV) in effect at the close of the market on each business day.** Daily closing NAV fund prices are posted online and in financial publications.

Commingled Institutional Funds   Large 401(k) plans may offer commingled institutional funds managed by banks and other investment managers within their menu of fund options. These commingled institutional funds invest in a variety of securities in accordance with a set investment policy. These securities may include bank and insurance products as well as other financial instruments.

These institutional funds resemble mutual funds but are subject to less regulation. Like mutual funds, institutional funds offer liquidity, diversification, and a variety of objectives, to some extent. However, as these funds are available only to large institutional clients like retirement plans, they are not quite as available or accessible as mutual funds. Since they are not offered directly to the public, their share prices may not be published. Yet the resulting lower marketing and regulatory compliance costs can enable institutional funds to charge lower expenses.

Insured Funding Instruments   Insurance companies offer separate accounts and guaranteed investment contracts (GICs), among other products, for use in 401(k) plans. These products are generally segregated from an insurance company's general account in order to avoid the strict regulatory restrictions applicable to an insurer's investment in stocks. A plan sponsor may engage an insurance company to manage separate accounts for inclusion as fund options in its 401(k) plan. Each such separate account may be invested in accordance with a plan-sponsor-defined investment strategy to serve as a fund option for one or more plans. It functions like a privately managed account tailored to the investment policy laid out by the plan sponsor.

Alternatively, a sponsor may include a stable value fund composed of GICs with staggered maturities, each providing a fixed return over a set duration. These GICs are like an insurance company's version of a certificate of deposit, but offered in larger denominations. The stable value funds usually stagger the maturities of the different GICs over time to enhance liquidity and reduce the reinvestment risk associated with the uncertainty of reinvesting the proceeds of matured contracts at rates then currently available on maturity of each GIC.

Exchange-Traded Funds The future is coming but is not quite here yet. Just as anyone with a brokerage account can buy and sell stocks at any time throughout the day, he or she can also trade or invest in *exchange-traded funds (ETFs)* on a real-time basis. As with a mutual fund, an ETF is a collection of securities under professional management. Although ETFs do not offer nearly the variety available through mutual funds, they do share the advantages of liquidity and diversification. An ETF is priced on a real-time basis throughout the trading day rather than priced like a mutual fund once per day at the day's closing price. Whereas regular investors can capitalize on intraday price swings through opportunistic buying and selling of ETFs, most 401(k) investors do not have such an opportunity, as very few 401(k) plans offer an ETF as an investment option.

Fund Management Style Funds can be classified according to their management style. The distinction between whether a fund is passively managed or actively managed comes down to the fund manager's role in meeting the fund's defined objectives.

Passive Management A market index is an average of the prices or values of certain securities, usually of the same type, for a specified group of companies. The weighting of each company's security price within a market index is defined by the terms of the index. The companies reflected in a market index remain relatively constant over time unless the index's sponsor deems that changes in a company's business conditions or ownership structure warrant a replacement.

Various market indexes have been established to track the performance of different types and blends of securities. One prominent example of a stock market index is the Standard & Poor's 500 index (S&P 500 index). As a composite average of the market value of 500 of the largest U.S. companies, the S&P 500 index is a universally accepted benchmark index widely considered to reflect the condition of the stock market. Other major stock indexes are the *Dow Jones Industrial Average* (DJIA), reflecting a price-weighted average of 30 of the largest publicly owned companies in the United States, and the *NASDAQ Composite index*, reflecting a composite average of the stock prices of all companies listed on the NASDAQ stock exchange.

A fund holding a collection of securities that attempts to replicate the performance of a market index is a passively managed fund, or otherwise known as a *market index fund*. The role of a passively managed fund manager is to match, or come as close as possible to matching, the performance of a certain index's market basket of securities. The fund manager accomplishes this through the investment in a sample of the index's securities, large enough to replicate the overall performance of all securities within the index.

A passively managed fund requires less fund manager oversight than an actively managed fund, because strict adherence to investment in the securities included in the market index virtually eliminates the security selection process required for an actively managed fund. The passively managed fund requires just enough trades to balance its holdings to match the weightings of the securities within the index it is intended to replicate. The fund manager's primary responsibility is to adjust the holdings in accordance with the net trades in and out of the fund and any index rejiggering. He or she is not making any strategic decisions on the weighting and timing of investments. As a result, fund expenses for investment management and trading are typically low.

Conceivably a fund manager could establish a fund to track any one or a combination of market indexes. Most ETFs fall into the passively managed style of investing and track a market index. Other collective funds do not share that penchant for passive management. As of the end of 2010, 365 index mutual funds held about $1 trillion in assets. These holdings in passively managed index funds represent about 8 percent of all U.S. mutual fund assets. About 37 percent of the assets in index mutual funds were invested in funds that tracked the S&P 500 index.[11]

Active Management An actively managed fund comprises an array of securities that the fund manager assembles and adjusts continuously with the intent of beating the market. Active fund managers select the securities and decide when to buy and sell them. They make any strategic decisions on the weighting and timing of fund investments. They employ an active trading strategy that is intended to pick the best securities within the given universe defined by the fund's investment policy and time their security purchases and sales to produce the highest returns. An actively managed fund's performance is usually judged relative to a market index.

As compared to a passively managed fund, the security trading in an actively managed fund usually translates into a higher portfolio turnover and associated trading costs. These higher trading costs, along with the additional costs required for the investment manager's involvement in picking and timing security purchases and sales, are passed along to shareholders as a reduction in the fund's returns. These higher expenses directly reduce an actively managed fund's net returns, which puts it at a disadvantage from the outset just to stay even with a passively managed fund.

Even though study after study has concluded that, after fees, actively managed funds do not outperform passively managed funds on a consistent basis over the long term, hope springs eternal. Despite their overall less-than-stellar long-term performance, there is no lack of investor confidence in actively managed stock funds. From 2009 to 2010, the portion of all U.S. mutual fund assets invested in actively managed funds still rose from 90 to 92 percent.[12]

Target-Date Funds

A target-date fund, or life cycle fund, is essentially a balanced fund of funds with a mix of stocks, bonds, and cash that shifts over time to a more conservative blend. Mutual fund companies offer target-date funds to take the personal decision making (or fun, depending on your perspective) out of investing in a 401(k) plan. Target-date funds appeal to participants with little time, inclination, training, or interest in managing their own accounts. These participants are willing to pay for the convenience of placing account management responsibilities on autopilot by enlisting an investment manager to fill this role.

A target-date fund typically operates as a fund of funds that bundles underlying, stand-alone funds within an investment management wrapper. The additional layer of investment management provides for the automatic transfer of target-date fund assets from underlying funds with higher risk to more secure funds as the investment time horizon of shareholders in the fund shortens with the approach of retirement. For the dual layers of investment management, the fund manager charges the shareholder fees at both the underlying fund level and the wrapper level.

Young investors tend to have a longer time to save and invest than older investors before they will need to draw on their retirement savings after they stop working. This longer investment horizon of a young investor translates into a presumed capacity to assume more short-term risk than an older investor can afford to bear as he or she approaches retirement. Taking this into account, a target-date fund holds more aggressive investments for younger investors with a longer investment horizon (and later projected retirement date) and gradually shifts into more conservative investments as investors age and close in on retirement.

Stocks have historically provided the highest returns over the long term, although they may be subject to the highest risk of losing value in the short term (as many investors have learned all too well). Bonds and cash have historically provided lower but stable returns due to their lower risk. Because the unforgiving market does not allow do-overs for untimely losses, you want to make sure your savings are secure and intact when you are ready to retire. To avoid getting caught in a stock market downdraft when retirement nears, you should be investing in more conservative holdings like bonds and cash that are less impacted by market swoons as you approach retirement. The philosophy behind target-date funds takes into account these historical market trends and an investor's need to reduce risk with age by calling for a gradual shift out of stocks into bonds and cash over time. Consequently, a target-date fund for a young investor would be weighted more toward stocks than bonds and cash. As the investor ages and gets closer to retirement, the target-date fund asset mix shifts to a more conservative balance with a greater portion of the fund moving out of stocks into bonds and cash.

At any point in time, the mix of stocks, bonds, and cash in a particular target-date fund depends on how much time the fund's assets are to be invested. In a retirement savings plan, this investment time horizon depends not only on a participant's age, but also on his or her health, means, desire, and ability to work. Therefore, the investment time horizon for a target-date fund is defined in terms of a range of years in which an individual's retirement is projected to occur rather than the current age of the individual for whom the target-date fund is intended. For a given retirement year, a target-date fund's asset mix follows a policy dictating a gradual shift over time to a portfolio of less risk. In order to accommodate as many participants as possible, plans typically offer several target-date funds, each targeted toward participants within a certain range of projected retirement dates.

Each target-date fund is labeled with respect to the time frame in which potential investors would be expected to retire, and the fund is invested accordingly. For example, a 401(k) plan might offer a menu of different target-date funds, each based on a participant's potential year of retirement within a five-year range. One fund would be for participants already retired, another for participants retiring around 2015, yet another for participants retiring around 2020, still another for participants retiring around 2025, and so on. In such a plan, for a participant age 40 in 2010 intending to retire at age 65, the appropriate target-date fund would be the one applicable to individuals intending to retire around 2035 ($= 2010 + 65 - 40$). The current mix of assets in 2010 for this target-date 2035 fund might be 80 to 90 percent in stocks and 10 to 20 percent in bonds and cash. This composition would shift gradually so that by retirement, the fund might be invested 20 to 30 percent in stocks and 70 to 80 percent in bonds and cash.

Target-date funds have been around for more than a decade. They are becoming more and more popular as 401(k) participants leave the management of their accounts to investment professionals, whether by conscious election or by default upon automatic enrollment in a plan. Investing 401(k) contributions in target-date funds especially picked up after a 2006 law change and subsequent ruling that enabled employers to direct the contributions of participants automatically enrolled in their plans toward funds such as target-date funds. About 42 percent of participants in 401(k) plans with target-date funds had invested in such funds by the end of 2009.[13]

Employer Stock

Almost one-half of 401(k) plans offer employer stock as an investment option in which ongoing contributions and accumulated account balances may be invested.[14] Many of these plans initially direct that all employer contributions to participants' individual accounts be invested in the employer stock fund. It is different for employee contributions, though, as participants may elect to invest their own employee contributions in the employer stock fund as well or, for that matter, in any other available fund options.

A 401(k) plan offering company stock as an investment option can limit its fiduciary liability by also offering at least three other diversified investment options, no less than quarterly exchange privileges, and employee education. Additionally, to be eligible for fiduciary liability protection, the company's stock must be publicly traded, and ownership activities must be executed on a confidential basis. In the wake of lessons learned from retirees and near-retirees devastated by the loss of their retirement savings primarily invested in Enron stock following its collapse, laws were enacted to allow participants with at least three years of service to divest their interest in company stock and direct such divested amounts into other fund options.

Whenever considering an investment in employer stock, you need to recognize the level of your personal financial exposure to the fate of your employer. Your livelihood from continued employment and savings invested in stock through 401(k) and other company plans may depend on the continuing viability of your employer. In view of this risk, it is always advisable to consider all of your employer stock holdings in deciding how much of your 401(k) account to invest in employer stock or other fund options.

Self-Directed Brokerage Accounts

Some employees will just never be happy no matter how many investment options an employer gives them in a retirement savings plan. In response to this concern, some 401(k) plans offer participants the flexibility to independently manage the investment of their accounts through *self-directed brokerage accounts*. In such a plan, a participant may direct contributions or redeem some or all of his or her shares in other fund options for deposit into a personal brokerage account embedded within the plan. The typical self-directed brokerage account then allows a participant to use the funds within the brokerage account to trade most securities available on the market, with some exceptions. This added investment flexibility comes at a cost, though, as the participant's account is usually subject to additional direct trading costs and fees that would not otherwise be charged under other plan fund options.

Loan Accounts

Another type of investment—or quasi-fund option—found in 401(k) plans that offer loans is a separate loan account for those participants borrowing from their own plan accounts. A 401(k) plan loan represents a liability to be repaid by the participant but an asset in the participant's plan account. The fact that a loan occupies plan account money that would otherwise be invested in other plan fund options warrants its treatment as a separate fund option. Any plan assets devoted to a loan are not participating in the market's gains and losses during the term of the loan. Instead the participant's account derives income on the outstanding amount of the loan only from loan interest paid by the participant.

As noted in Chapter 3, if you take out a personal loan from your own 401(k) account, you are required to repay the loan with interest and any associated fees on at least a quarterly basis at a reasonable rate of interest back into your account. The initial loan amount paid to you is drawn proportionately from your fund options, unless you specify otherwise.

If you took out a $10,000 loan from a $100,000 total account composed of $80,000 in an S&P 500 index fund and $20,000 in a money market fund, $8,000 (= $10,000 loan × $80,000 S&P 500 index fund balance/$100,000 total account balance) would be drawn from the S&P 500 index fund and $2,000 (= $10,000 loan × $20,000 money market fund balance/$100,000 total account balance) would be drawn from the money market fund. Your account balance after the loan would be made up of $72,000 (= $80,000 S&P 500 index fund balance − $8,000 loan portion) in the S&P 500 index fund, $18,000 (= $20,000 money market fund balance − $2,000 loan portion) in the money market fund, and $10,000 in the loan account.

TABLE 4.1 Impact of Loan on Fund Balances

Fund Option	Before Loan	After Loan
S&P 500 index fund	$ 80,000	$ 72,000
Money market fund	20,000	18,000
Loan account	0	10,000
Total	$100,000	$100,000

Table 4.1 illustrates the composition of your account balance before and after the loan.

Once you initiate a loan from a 401(k) plan, a loan account is established as a quasi-fund option to track the repayment of your loan. The loan account's initial balance is the original amount that you borrowed. Each loan repayment you make is composed of interest on the outstanding loan balance and a repayment toward the outstanding principal balance of the loan. At the same time that your loan account's balance diminishes over time with each repayment of loan principal, the rest of your account balance under the plan grows by the amount of your entire loan repayment of both interest and principal (as well as by any contributions and investment earnings). The principal portion of each loan repayment reduces the outstanding principal in your loan account, while your entire loan repayment is added to the alternative investment fund balances in your account, typically in accordance with your investment directions as to the allocation of your ongoing plan contributions. Along the way, the principal repayments added to your fund option balances are canceled out by the reduction in your loan account. In short, the net growth in your total account balance attributable to repaying your loan comes from the interest you pay.

Of the investments available in a plan, a loan is the only one that can provide you with a predictable return. Sure, a loan may remove assets that might have otherwise participated in the performance of the fund options in which the loan proceeds would have been invested, but the return a loan provides is steady.

For the previously mentioned $10,000 loan, repayable monthly at 5 percent annual interest over five years, you would pay $189 each month. If you invest plan contributions 80 percent in the S&P 500 index fund and 20 percent in the money market fund, each payment of $189 increases your S&P 500 index fund balance by $151 (= 0.80 × $189 loan payment) and your money market fund balance by $38 (= 0.20 × $189 loan payment).

Your first payment of $189 breaks down into $147 in principal and $42 in interest. At the same time it increases your S&P 500 index fund to $72,151 (= $72,000 S&P index fund balance + $151 portion of loan repayment) and money market fund to $18,038 (= $18,000 money market fund balance + $38 portion of loan repayment), the first payment reduces your loan account balance to $9,853 (= $10,000 initial loan account balance − $147 principal repayment). Absent any other account activity, your total account balance has increased from $100,000 to $100,042 (= $72,151 in S&P 500 index fund + $18,038 in money market fund + $9,853 in loan account) after one payment. Eventually the principal portion of each of your loan repayments will pay down your loan until it is completely repaid and the outstanding balance of the loan account is eliminated as a quasi-fund option (that is, until you take out another loan).

PLAN EXPENSES

Are you the kind of person who stops dead in his or her tracks in order to pick up a penny off the ground? How about a nickel? Is it worth the time and trouble and potential embarrassment? Admit it—doesn't it depend on who's watching? Why were you looking at the ground in the first place when so much life is out there in front of (not under) you? Are you tempted by a Benjamin or C-note ($100 bill), then? You bet, and who cares who's watching?

If you are not out there looking for money, you may very well be paying too much for participating in your 401(k) plan. Mutual fund companies, insurance companies, and other investment managers offer different types of funds for use in retirement savings plans such as 401(k) plans for a fee, of course. Those fund managers to whom you have entrusted your 401(k) accounts are collecting investment management and other fees day in and day out from you, regardless of whether they make you money. The fees you pay to fund managers holding your 401(k) account balances come right off the top, never to be seen again. Fund fees can have a dramatic impact on wealth accumulation. If you are not paying attention to the types and amounts of fees being deducted from your 401(k) account, you may very well be wasting your hard-earned retirement savings. Paying excessive fees is like giving money away but without the good feeling a charitable act brings. It would not be so bad if the fund manager of your 401(k) accounts were your favorite charity.

Participating in a 401(k) plan has its price, but there are ways to manage the costs you are charged. The three general types of fees that your 401(k) account may be charged cover plan administration, transaction, and fund management expenses. Although plan administration fees are not within your control, you may be able to cut your transaction and fund management costs by the way you use and invest your 401(k) account.

Plan Administration Fees

A plan administrator may charge fees based on the number of participants to cover the cost of ongoing administrative services involved in operating the plan. The fees for such services cover the costs of record-keeping, accounting, and other services. The amount of plan administration fees charged for a plan generally depends on the vendor, size of the plan, and fee arrangement with the plan sponsor. Larger plans tend to get a break on administration fees due to economies of scale and potential revenue from providing bundled investment management services for the plan. If your employer does not cover these fees, your account, as well as those of your fellow participants, will be directly charged the same flat fee on an ongoing basis.

Transaction Fees

Transaction costs may be charged to participants engaging in plan transactions or needing special services from the plan administrator. The amounts of these transaction fees are usually set forth in a flat fee schedule for each transaction or service established by the plan administrator. If your employer does not pick up these fees, the accounts of participants availing themselves of these services and transactions are charged directly for the scheduled fee amounts. As an example, the account of a participant taking out a plan loan would usually be charged fees at the initiation of the loan for its establishment and then on an ongoing basis for the maintenance of the loan. Also, the account of a participant executing a trade through a self-directed brokerage account would be directly charged for the brokerage commissions involved in the transaction. If only the participant had instead executed a fund exchange between the standard plan fund options, he or she could have avoided any direct charges for the exchange.

Fund Management Fees

There are two general types of fund management fees: those you can see and those that you can't. Both are skimmed off the top before any earnings are passed along as fund returns to shareholders. Explicit fees are limited to those disclosed in a mutual fund's prospectus, and implicit fees are not as well disclosed or limited.

Explicit Fees   Explicit fund fees come in the following variety of forms: operating expenses, sales and redemption loads, and short-term trading fees.

Operating Expenses   Fund managers charge fund operating expenses, comprised mostly of investment management fees, directly to your 401(k) plan account. Mutual funds' operating expenses also include distribution (12b-1) fees and other expenses. Expressed as an expense ratio, operating expenses are collected as a percentage of fund assets under management. The fund manager deducts these operating expenses from fund assets on a daily basis, regardless of whether shareholders made money.

Unlike flat plan administration and transaction fees that may appear as a direct charge on your account statement, operating expenses are discreetly passed through as a reduction in your gross returns from the plan funds in which you invest. Your net return from a fund comes after the fund's expense ratio of operating expenses expressed as a percentage of assets is deducted from its gross return. For a mutual fund, this expense ratio, disclosed in its prospectus, is applied to your fund assets under management to cover the operating expenses charged your account in a year. Under a fund with an expense ratio of 1 percent, an investor with a flat $100,000 balance in the fund would pay $1,000 (= 0.01 expense ratio × $100,000 balance) in operating expenses each year as a deduction from the gross return from the fund. If the fund had earned a 5 percent gross annual return before fees, the investor's net annual return would be 4 percent (= 5 percent gross return − 1 percent expense ratio) before any other fees like trading costs were considered.

One size does not fit all when it comes to the fund returns credited to participant accounts under retirement savings plans. Although all participant accounts within the same plan are generally subject to the same fee structure, the expense ratio for operating expenses reflected in a particular fund's net returns can vary by fund class based on the size of the retirement savings plan's investment in the fund. As with many products, volume discounts apply to operating expenses charged to fund options held in larger retirement savings plans. Plans with more assets meeting certain fund threshold levels generally get preferential expense ratios reflected in their funds' net returns. Many fund companies offer institutional, retail, and sometimes midsize versions of their most popular funds, in which the fund's expense ratio netted out of its fund returns goes down as the size of the investment in a fund option goes up. Thus the larger a plan's investment in a fund, the less a shareholder's fund returns are impacted by operating expenses within that fund.

Actively managed funds generally have higher operating expenses and trading costs passed along to shareholders than passively managed funds. With investment management fees generally constituting the largest component of operating expenses, active fund managers will tell you these higher investment management costs result from the additional level of professional expertise involved in security selection and market timing for an actively managed fund. Regardless of the explanation, these higher investment management costs translate into a higher expense ratio for actively managed funds than for passively managed funds.

The expense ratio charged for operating expenses as a percentage of the assets under management can typically run from a few basis points (hundredths of a percentage point) for index or passively managed funds to 2 percent or more per year for some actively managed funds. On average, a passively managed mutual fund has an expense ratio of 0.8 percent, whereas an actively managed mutual fund has an expense ratio of 1.26 percent. For exchange-traded funds, most of which are passively managed, their average expense ratio is only 0.58 percent.[15] However, an active trader's ability to trade ETFs at any time may very well translate into higher trading costs.

With an added layer of investment management over and above that provided to its underlying funds, the average asset-weighted expense ratio of a target-date fund in 2009 varied by fund manager from just under 0.2 percent to over 1.7 percent.[16]

Service firms generally get paid by the hour, by the project, or by commission for their work. A lawyer may get paid based on the number of hours he or she works on a case. A dentist gets paid for a project such as filling a cavity. Fund managers get paid a commission of a percentage of the assets under management. In the first two cases, you receive the lawyer's or dentist's bill, review it, and cut a check if it is right. In the third case, you feel no pain, as the operating expenses are collected before any of the fund's net returns are paid to shareholders—there is no detailed charge showing up on your account statement. If these fund operating expenses were more transparent and you had to cut a check to pay for them, you might very well wish you were under the influence of the dentist's anesthesia to ease the pain.

Sales and Redemption Charges   Some funds charge a front-end or back-end load upon the purchase or redemption of a fund, although 401(k) plans generally do not charge such loads. As a sales commission, a front-end load is determined as a percentage of the money invested in the fund and is added to its purchase price. A redemption charge in the form of a back-end load is determined as a percentage of the fund redemption and is deducted from the proceeds of the sale. This back-end-load percentage may decrease over time or disappear after a period of six to eight years.

Short-Term Trading Fees   Short-term trading fees are charged by some stock mutual funds to discourage individuals from rapidly trading in and out of a fund. A short-term trading fee is charged to shareholders upon redemption of fund shares within a period of their initial investment, such as 60 or 90 days. An exception usually applies for fund investments resulting from contributions made into a 401(k) plan. The amount of the fee is typically in the range of 1 to 1.5 percent of the amount redeemed. When investing or trading in a 401(k) plan, it is necessary to avoid incurring any short-term trading fees.

More trading into and out of a fund increases its turnover and associated trading costs passed on as an implicit fee that reduces the returns to all remaining shareholders. Also, short-term trading may disrupt a fund's investment strategy. Therefore, a short-term trading fee is assessed an individual for frequent trades, which gets invested back in the fund, thereby compensating the remaining shareholders for the trading costs incurred by the redeeming shareholder during his or her brief investment in the fund.

Implicit Fees Fund managers also charge shareholders another form of fees known as implicit fees. They are separate from, and in addition to, explicit fees that are passed along to all fund shareholders as a reduction in fund returns. Implicit fees are composed of trading costs and bid-ask spreads.

Trading Costs Fund managers pay brokerage commissions to trade securities that support their fund objectives and changes in cash flow. Fund turnover, whether made for strategic reasons or to accommodate cash flow requirements, results in trading costs that are passed along to all shareholders as a reduction in net fund returns.

Efforts to meet fund objectives entail strategic as well as required trading of securities to stay within fund investment guidelines. Actively managed funds employ trading strategies in executing their market timing bets that result in higher portfolio turnover than that of a passively managed fund. The additional trading costs resulting from an active fund's higher portfolio turnover are passed along to shareholders as a reduction in fund returns. Consequently, an actively managed fund with high turnover of its underlying securities will incur more trading costs that reduce fund returns than would a passively managed fund.

Cash flow needs resulting from participants' fund exchanges may also affect a fund's trading costs. In the context of a 401(k) plan, a fund exchange involves the use of the proceeds from the redemption of one fund to purchase another fund. To the extent redemptions and purchases within a particular fund do not offset each other, a trade of the fund's underlying securities would be required to maintain its holdings in accordance with the fund's asset allocation guidelines laid out in its investment policy. These trades resulting from an imbalance in a fund's purchase and redemption instructions submitted by shareholders increase the trading costs associated with the turnover of the fund's underlying securities.

Such indirect sharing of trading costs among all fund shareholders is comparable to the way most health clubs charge for their services. Because members generally pay the same monthly dues regardless of their individual usage patterns, the buff guy or gal enjoying a daily workout pays the same monthly dues as the weekend warrior. Never mind that their usage is many times more than that of the guy using the club only on weekends. The direct costs of an individual's usage are not charged to the individual but are spread evenly among all users. **Likewise, an individual shareholder does not directly bear the trading costs resulting from his or her own fund purchases or redemptions. Instead a fund's trading costs are passed along as a reduction in fund returns to all shareholders.**

Bid-Ask Spreads The sale of a security results when a buyer and seller agree on its price. The difference between a seller's ask price and a buyer's bid price is the bid-ask spread for a security. The amount a fund manager pays over its bid price to complete a purchase and the amount a fund manager receives below its ask price to complete a sale represent additional trading costs that are passed along as a reduction from fund returns. The amount of these spreads absorbed by a fund depends on the fund's turnover and the trading volume of its underlying securities. Funds whose underlying securities are actively traded and funds dealing with thinly traded securities with wider bid-ask spreads generate more trading costs in the form of spreads.

One indication of the level of a fund's implicit fees is its turnover. The increased amount of trading associated with a fund's higher turnover results in higher trading costs and bid-ask spreads. A mutual fund's portfolio turnover is described in its prospectus. One study shows that implicit fees amount on average to about 0.78 percent.[17]

Look Out for Fees!

Many plan sponsors pay for the administrative expenses associated with the operation of a 401(k) plan. Participants usually bear any transactional or special service fees directly. Participants also bear operating expenses through a reduction in the net returns posted to their accounts. A participant is not generally directly charged for redirecting the investment of his or her individual account through a fund exchange, unless a self-directed brokerage account is used. Instead a fund's trading costs are levied as implicit expenses deducted from the returns of all fundholders.

The extent to which you will be affected by the different types of fees levied on a retirement savings account depends on an awareness of how they are imposed. No big surprise here, but you need to monitor, control, and manage your investment expenses lest they eat into your retirement savings.

FUND VALUATION AND EXCHANGE

The price of a security at any point in time is determined by the *law of supply and demand*. In an *efficient market* where buyers and sellers have access to all available information, a sale will occur at a price point where the demand for a security is equal to the supply of the security. As conditions change, a security's price may change moment by moment throughout the course of a day.

Investors can trade securities on a real-time basis continuously throughout the day. When an investor places a *market order* with a broker to buy or sell a block of common stock shares at the current market price, the trade can be completed within seconds at a price close to the current bid or asking price when the order is placed. The share price usually does not change much in the very brief time it takes to execute the order. Obviously, what you pay up front in a stock purchase ultimately affects the amount of your gain when it is time to sell. On the other end of the transaction, how much you obtain upon the sale of the stock also affects the amount of your realized gain from holding the security. Therefore, the amount of time between the placement and execution of a market order during which a security's price could change is critical to a trade's profitability.

Generally, 401(k) and other retirement savings plans offer a variety of investment options composed of mutual funds, collective institutional funds, and insurance company accounts that are valued at the end of each business day. Not that many plans offer ETF and self-directed brokerage account fund options that can be traded continuously throughout the day. With the widespread availability of sophisticated record-keeping systems, most 401(k) plans update participant accounts daily to reflect any account activity. At the end of each business day, the daily refresh of participant account balances updates participant holdings in each plan fund option for any deposits, withdrawals, and investment gains or losses.

The daily update, or valuation, of accounts facilitates the offering of a common retirement savings plan feature that allows participants to make daily exchanges of account assets from one fund option to another. Such 401(k) plans with daily valuation of accounts almost universally allow participants to make daily fund exchanges based on the funds' closing prices at the end of a day. For mutual funds and other funds that are valued daily, exchanges submitted before the close of the market (generally 4 P.M.

eastern time except for holidays) are executed each business day based on the funds' net asset values (NAVs) at market close.

Buy and sell orders submitted throughout a day for daily valued funds are generally batched together and executed at the end of each business day on the basis of the fund's closing price. Institutional funds and insurance company accounts used as fund options in 401(k) plans are also valued on a daily basis. Therefore, any exchange order submitted by the market's close, whether made in the morning or the afternoon, will be executed at the same closing price at day's end. Also, any exchange order made after the close of the market on a given day will be made at the closing price for the following business day.

Any lapse in time between the submission of exchange directions and its execution creates uncertainty in an investor's mind as to the actual closing fund prices on which the exchange will be based. So why not submit the exchange as close to the end of the trading day as possible when you have a pretty good idea as to the fund values at which the transaction will occur? In the case of an index fund based on the S&P 500 index, the corresponding S&P 500 index is published continuously throughout the day. Absent an untimely "flash crash" (or "flash bolt," for that matter), the timing of an exchange order just before the market close would give the investor some degree of price assurance similar to the extent offered in a market order transaction for a stock. **An index fund exchange submitted just prior to the market close will be executed at a closing fund price, which is likely to be very near the level of its associated real-time index at the time the exchange order is submitted.**

Although participants could conceivably make daily fund exchanges under almost all 401(k) plans, most do not avail themselves of the opportunity to make any fund exchanges. According to one study involving over three million employees of 1,700 plan sponsors, about 13 percent of participants made a fund transfer in their defined contribution plan accounts during 2009.[18] With the remaining 87 percent making no trades or fund exchanges at all during 2009, it turns out that the daily fund exchange feature appears to be like a security blanket that provides more in comfort than in actual utility. The use of a day trading strategy would take advantage of this daily fund exchange privilege in ways not seen before.

COVER YOUR ASSETS

You already did—cover your assets, that is. The prior discussion touched on asset issues relating to the construction of retirement savings portfolios. There is so much more that could be included about assets, and much of it has already been published by others. The asset primer in this chapter is intended merely to acquaint you with background information on fund options so as to familiarize you with the setting in which retirement savings account asset management operates.

The challenge before you is to successfully manage your retirement savings account assets. Doing this requires knowledge of the use of the fund options available in your 401(k) and other retirement savings accounts. Your familiarity with your fund options' holdings, investment characteristics, expenses, and exchange privileges will put you in a position to better manage your 401(k) portfolio. For further information on your particular plan's fund options, terms of participation, and procedures, you may want to check your plan literature, such as a Summary Plan Description and mutual fund prospectuses.

Now that you know your choices for a bat, you will need to turn your attention to pulling the ball down the right-field foul line to have a chance at hitting a homer in Yankee Stadium. Likewise, you must manage your 401(k) portfolio to increase your odds of reaching your retirement income goal. Deal with it—the quality of your life in retirement depends not only on how much you save but also on your ability to manage your personal retirement portfolio. An individual who saves a level annual amount in an account earning 5 percent per year for 40 years prior to retirement would accumulate an account that comprises 32 percent from actual savings and 68 percent from investment earnings. Such is the power of investing over the long term. You must not also underestimate the power of saving, without which there would be no investment earnings.

The strategic use of day trading with your 401(k) accounts will enable you to improve your 401(k) portfolio returns in an uncertain market through timely fund exchange orders involving the least expensive fund options of different risk levels. Before turning to day trading, though, first you need to consider the various market forces that fuel the day trading strategy.

CHAPTER 5

Uneven Playing Field

Volatility in a Sideways Market

History doesn't repeat itself—but it rhymes.
—Mark Twain

Their future was uncertain. After a long day at a girls' volleyball tournament, an exhausted daughter and her father were headed back to their hotel room late that night. Much to their displeasure, it looked like a large crowd in the ground floor elevator lobby would surely delay them as they waited their turn for a lift up to their room. After all, the father (and maybe his daughter, too) needed rest before heading back for more volleyball early the next morning.

Drawing upon experience as a subway commuter, the father summoned an old trick—sometimes you need to go backward before you can go forward. When subway lines were long for trains headed in his direction, he would catch the first train going in the opposite direction, get off at the first stop, and switch over to the next train headed in his intended direction. Once on the train, he knew he was on his way home, as he had already secured a spot on what was becoming an overcrowded subway car while others at his original embarkation point are left behind to wait for another train.

Although the father and daughter simply wanted to retire to their room on the 22nd floor, the father led his daughter to get on the first elevator, which was heading down, not up. The throngs waiting to go up had no problem allowing the father and daughter through in order to board the elevator going down one floor to the basement arcade level. Once aboard the downward elevator, the father pushed the button for the 22nd floor, and his daughter rolled her eyes, wondering why she was accompanying this dork of a father. The father also endured the ridicule leveled by the few passengers already on board the downward elevator. To that, the father coolly responded in a twist on Newton: "What goes down must come up."

The stars must have been shining on the father that night. As expected, the elevator emptied all but the father and his daughter at the basement arcade level. Then, without further ado (or any other action by the father and daughter), the elevator inexplicably headed straight up to the 22nd floor, without stopping for the throngs in the lobby or at what would have been their many stops along the way. Yes, they felt guilty for about a minute as they retired to their room. Whoever said Father does not know best?

History has shown us that, like the father and daughter's elevator trip that evening, the U.S. stock market goes both ways, before eventually heading up. By all indications, history will repeat itself on the count of continued market volatility. As long as there is a stock market, there will inevitably be ups and downs in traders' sentiment and how it relates to stock prices. However, like an elevator once it drops off its passengers, the U.S. stock market appears headed in the near term toward where it started.

Day trading relies on both the daily ups and downs of the stock market on its way to settling at a level at or near where it started. Since day trading involves timing fund exchanges involving domestic stock funds within retirement savings plans, the discussion hereafter will primarily focus on U.S. market conditions. The rocky, but ultimately flat, performance of the broad stock market during the first decade of the new millennium provided pretty close to optimal conditions for day trading. This chapter touches on the forces expected to bring about the continued volatility and sideways direction of the stock market through at least 2020.

MARKET VOLATILITY

Prepare for market mayhem, or at least some volatility. The uncertainty in the U.S. economy is prone to drive the stock market wild at times. With the right approach, you can turn stock market fluctuations into your friend. Slick promoters routinely tout the incredible returns generated from activities ranging from trading commodities and options to investing in asset-backed securities and leveraged hedge funds. As a retirement savings plan participant, you too can profit from the market's volatility, although your choices may be somewhat limited from what may otherwise be available in the broader marketplace. If simpler is better, you are lucky in that you will mostly find 401(k) fund options composed of stocks, bonds, cash, and mixtures thereof, rather than of more exotic investment vehicles. However, even with a somewhat limited selection of fund options, you will be able to take advantage of market volatility by exchanging into and out of stock funds on a daily basis. As you will see, the key to your success in day trading your retirement savings accounts lies in the stock market's volatility.

Market volatility can be measured in terms of swings in price and direction. Rather than using volatility indexes such as the Chicago Board Options Exchange Market Volatility Index (VIX) or the Treasury bill/Eurodollar futures contract (TED) spread, day trading relies on the straightforward concepts of stock price changes and directional swings. Showing that the U.S. stock market can be quite volatile and is getting moreso over time, the S&P 500 index commonly used to track the broad stock market has experienced dramatic swings in price and direction over the course of its history. Although individual stock share prices and broad stock market index levels fluctuate continuously throughout a day, market volatility shows up only once per day when each retirement savings plan fund option is valued as the aggregate value for its component stock prices at the market close.

Back and forth, market participants continuously overshoot the market price of a stock or a fund before it settles at an equilibrium point. Day trading takes advantage of daily market volatility through its reliance on the basic underlying premise of buying low and selling high. Each day you need to buy on every dip and sell on every rise. Each daily market gyration presents an opportunity for gain through day trading a retirement savings portfolio.

Historical Perspective

The stock market *rose* more than ever during 2008. Really. In absolute terms, the cumulative daily increases in the S&P 500 index amounted to 2,167 points, or almost 150 percent from where it started in 2008. Of course, this cockeyed basis for deriving stocks' outlandish performance during 2008 considers only the days that the S&P 500 index rose. To the dismay of many, the market's rise during 2008 was decimated by cumulative daily point decreases of 2,732 on days that the S&P 500 index declined. The net result of the market's up and down days was a crushing loss of 38.5 percent [= (2,167-point increase – 2,732-point decrease)/1,468 S&P 500 index level at beginning of 2008] in the level of the S&P 500 index for 2008. Even after adding in dividends, the S&P 500 index suffered its largest single calendar year loss in over 50 years.

The stock market goes up some days and down others. You just do not know when until it is all (or almost) over. It is these daily market fluctuations that day trading uses to set up and capture gains with timely stock trades based on the direction and size of the market's daily price fluctuations. Day trading relies on stock market volatility, and the more the better.

Annual Market Volatility To get a feel for the magnitude of the market's volatility, consider a brief history of the cumulative daily point changes in the S&P 500 index during each year. Each day the change in the S&P 500 index is measured as the difference between its opening and closing values. If the S&P 500 index opens at 1,000 and closes at 1,010 for a day, its daily point increase is 10 points. On the next day, if it opens at 1,010 and closes at 1,000, the 10-point change for the day is its daily point decrease.

This personal journey for gaining an appreciation of the magnitude of market volatility starts with separately deriving the cumulative daily point increases and decreases in the S&P 500 index. To do this, you would first calculate each daily point change in the S&P 500 index. After segregating between up and down market days, separately take the sum of the point increases on days the market advanced during each year. Similarly, sum the point changes on days the market declined. Then for perspective, relate these cumulative daily point increases and decreases in the S&P 500 index as a percentage of the S&P 500 index value at the beginning of the year. Finally, offset these cumulative daily percentage increases from the decreases to derive the net annual percentage changes in the S&P 500 index. The cumulative daily percentage increase represents the aggregate sum of the daily increases for all days the S&P 500 index went up over the course of a year. Likewise, the cumulative daily percentage decrease represents the aggregate sum of the daily decreases for all days the S&P 500 index went down for a year. The sum of these two percentages is simply the net annual percentage change in the level of the S&P 500 index for the year. What you get from these resulting cumulative measures of increases, decreases, and net changes are aggregate measures of daily market volatility for each calendar year.

Figure 5.1 presents the cumulative upward, downward, and net daily point changes in the S&P 500 index as a percentage of its beginning value for each of the 10 years ended December 31, 2010.

The aggregate annual sum of the S&P 500 index daily increases has ranged from 65.9 percent in 2005 to 166.9 percent in 2009. The aggregate annual sum of the S&P 500 index daily decreases has ranged from –55.0 percent in 2006 to –186.1 percent in 2008. By these measures, market volatility in some years ranges up to three times or more of the volatility in other years. More important, the magnitude of the daily changes presents opportunities to take advantage of market volatility through day trading.

The changes in the stock market can be pretty dramatic, on both an absolute and a relative basis. If you could figure out a way to be invested in stocks only on days when the market rises and out of stocks and in cash when it falls, you could make a bundle riding the market up and staying out as the market went down. Unfortunately, you need to make other plans, as

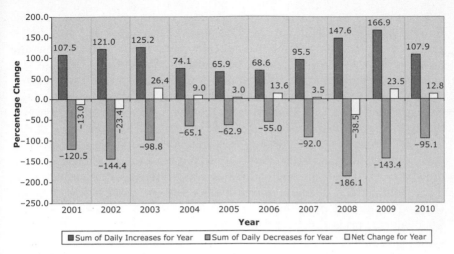

FIGURE 5.1 Cumulative Daily Change in S&P 500 Index as Percentage of Value at Beginning of Year for Years 2001–2010

this type of clairvoyance does not exist. This is where day trading comes into play.

In a given year, each daily stock market advance represents an opportunity to capture past stock gains and forgo potential losses by cashing out of stocks. Conversely, each daily market decline represents an opportunity to set up potential future gains by investing in stocks. You want to be more invested in stocks when the market advances but less so when the market declines. By gradually shifting your portfolio's exposure to stocks based on prior market movements, day trading gets you more invested in stocks after the market declines and less invested in stocks after the market rises. This daily shift in your portfolio's exposure to stocks sets you up for realizing gains when you are more invested in stocks in time for the next market advance and for avoiding losses when you are more invested in cash and less in stocks before the next market decline.

Daily Market Volatility The separation of cumulative daily market changes into gains and losses lends perspective to the potential size of gains set up and captured through day trading. Yet the magnitude of each daily change dictates the rate at which day trading's gains will accumulate. It follows that larger daily changes in stock prices trump slow and steady changes of equal magnitude in impact on returns from day trading.

The stock market can be quite volatile at times with large jumps and drops on a daily basis. The dual forces of daily changes and directional swings in the market fuel day trading. As you will see, day trading thrives in an environment with more market volatility in the form of larger daily changes and more directional swings in stock prices, because day trading's gains over time rely on retirement savings account fund exchanges that are based on the size and direction of the market's daily dips and rises.

A measure of the size of daily changes in the stock market is the average daily percentage change in the S&P 500 index. Each daily percentage change is derived as the absolute daily change of the difference between the opening and closing values, divided by the day's opening value of the S&P 500 index. In the prior example, if the S&P 500 index opens at 1,000 and closes at 1,010 for a day, its daily percentage increase for the day is 1 percent [= (1,010 closing price − 1,000 opening price)/1,000 opening price]. If instead the S&P 500 index opens at 1,000 and closes at 990 that day, its daily percentage decrease for the day is 1 percent [= (990 closing price − 1,000 opening price)/1,000 opening price].

The average daily percentage change for a year represents the average of (the absolute value of) each daily increase or decrease in the S&P 500 index as a percentage of its daily opening price. The size of the average daily percentage changes, whether up or down, can be viewed as a measure of the degree of daily stock market volatility of the type on which day trading relies.

As measured by the S&P 500 index, the stock market has experienced a dramatic increase in daily volatility over the past 20 years. In the decade from 2001 through 2010, the average daily percentage change in the S&P 500 index ranged from 0.47 percent in 2006 to 1.74 percent in 2008, with an average for the decade of 0.91 percent. By comparison, the average daily percentage change in the S&P 500 index ranged from 0.37 percent in 1995 to 1.06 percent in 2000, with an average of 0.67 percent for the preceding decade. These dramatic increases in daily stock market movements over the two most recent decades demonstrate the type of increased daily volatility that is quite useful in day trading.

By definition, the average daily percentage changes in the market are fairly representative of the absolute size of the average daily increases, as well as decreases. From all this, the realization comes that the most recent 10-year average stock market change of 0.94 percent *for one day* (as long as it is in the right direction—positive) exceeds the current (as of September 2010) average return offered under interest-bearing bank accounts of 0.92 percent *for a whole year*.[1] That is, the stock market can give you in one day what it would take a whole year to earn in a bank account. This volatility makes a compelling argument to stay invested in the stock market to earn these types of returns when they are positive.

Market Directional Changes   Just when you think you have a handle on the general direction of the market, things can change in a hurry. You know the market will not go straight up or down forever without retracing some steps once in a while. Yet nobody knows where the market is headed on a given day.

Market swings change the course of stock prices on a fairly regular basis. A directional change in the stock market occurs when stock prices turn in the opposite direction from the previous day, such as when a market advance one day follows a market decline the previous day, or a decline follows an advance on successive days. When looking at market prices over time, each spike and valley in a chart of market index daily prices, such as the one for the S&P 500 index in Figure 1.1, represents a directional change.

From 2001 through 2010, the annual number of directional changes in the daily closing price of the S&P 500 index ranged from 128 to 145. Its average of 136.2 directional changes out of 252 or so trading days each year means that the stock market changed direction more than every other day from 2001 through 2010. Think about it—the market changed direction 54 percent of the time. With the odds of a market swing better than 50 percent on any given day, you win more than you lose by betting on directional changes in the market. So a daily bet on a market swing in this type of environment makes sense (and dollars, too).

By this standard, the bull market of the 1990s was not as volatile. The annual number of directional changes in the S&P 500 index ranged from 113 to 133, with an average of 123.3, from 1991 through 2000. The increase in the average annual number of directional changes in the S&P 500 index from 123.3 directional changes in the 1990s to 136.2 in the succeeding decade represented a 10 percent increase. Perhaps this sustained trend of a significant and increasing number of market directional changes over two decades, as well as some economic uncertainty, suggests market volatility for years to come.

More directional swings in the market, along with the larger daily share price changes, may make for one heck of a bumpy ride for long-term stock market investors. Yet day traders recognize that along with every directional change in the market comes an opportunity to set up or capture gains through day trading. The size of the gains from day trading then depends on the magnitude of each daily change following a directional swing in the market.

What the Future Holds

So the stock market is volatile and is expected to remain that way in the future. As a pool of all publicly traded stocks, the market gets its volatility from share price fluctuations of individual stocks of which it is composed. Each stock's share price is determined by the convergence of what a buyer will pay and what a seller will accept. In an efficient market, the buyer and seller complete a stock sale transaction by agreeing on a share price reflecting all available information. This price is established at the *equilibrium* price point where the supply of the stock equals the demand for the stock. Anything that disturbs the equilibrium affects the stock's price. If a stock's previous share price reflected a balance of supply and demand for the stock, any event, or perception thereof, causing an imbalance as to the supply of available stock for sale or demand to purchase a stock causes a change in the stock's price. When supply exceeds demand, the price will decline. When the demand exceeds supply, the price will increase. Or so the theory goes.

Then there are those who subscribe to the notion that the true price of any security is not really known at any point in time. Instead a security's current price somehow reflects the market's reaction to relevant news using its previous price as the starting point for any adjustment.

However a stock's price is determined, its price movements along with those of the rest of the market's stocks affect the volatility of the market as a whole. Yet the diversification inherent in the entire market reduces the effect of any one stock's price change on the market as a whole. On any given day, with some stocks rising and others falling, some more so than others, the market's diversification reduces its volatility to the extent that some stocks' share price gains will offset other stocks' share price losses.

Still, the increasing magnitude of the S&P 500 index's cumulative annual price changes, daily price changes, and number of directional swings all point toward continued volatility in the stock market in the future. The stock market is constantly subject to all types of outside influences, many of which pose continual threats to stock price stability. There are many reasons to believe that the increasing daily volatility of the stock market witnessed in the past will only continue its course into the future.

Cash Needs   Investors are real people with lives. They need cash to live, but hopefully not all drawn from their stock accounts at the same time. In addition to handling financial responsibilities, such as paying taxes, answering margin calls, and covering options, they also cover personal expenses to support families, buy homes and cars, and put their kids through school. Fund managers are no different to the extent they need to cover the net fund withdrawals of individual investors with their individual needs. These financial and personal responsibilities require cash to settle. As a relatively liquid asset openly traded on public exchanges, stocks usually stand as a ready source of cash to meet their owners' obligations (although they should not necessarily be viewed that way). Any need to sell stock increases the supply of the affected stock's shares available for sale. If the intended or actual sale is significant enough in size, the increased supply of the stock available for sale could potentially lower the stock's share price as well as the level of the overall stock market.

On the other hand, an individual receiving a windfall in the form of a bonus or inheritance may stand ready to invest his or her new found fortune and consequently spur demand for investable securities like stocks. Depending on its timing within a market cycle, a stock sale or purchase may also affect an investor's overall financial position. Selling at a low point in the stock market cycle can do irreversible damage to a portfolio through elimination of the potential for future appreciation on the cash proceeds drawn from the stock sale that are no longer invested in the stock market. Likewise, buying at a market peak can also hurt a portfolio in the event of a subsequent market decline.

Information Flow   The media bombard investors almost continuously with ideas and information useful (or not so useful) in managing their portfolios. It seems every news story, even a sports story, has an angle applicable to investing. Many people have heard about the theory that a Super Bowl winner from the original American Football League portends stock market losses for the year, whereas a winner from the original National Football League is good news for the stock market. It turns out that a reverse corollary was developed to predict the Super Bowl champion based on stock market performance: If the market rises from the end of November through game day, the team whose full name falls later in the alphabet wins the Super Bowl. Like most random indicators, these theories' effectiveness has faded somewhat with time. Yet there is no shortage of market pundits who stand ready to step in and offer their views of how current events will shape the markets, or vice versa.

The news streaming continuously from all directions may be hard for anyone to digest but still affects the markets. Depending on the circumstances, the ubiquity, transmission speed, content, and accuracy of all of this news have the potential to create market imbalances that could lead to more volatility.

Media Coverage   Stocks get all the fanfare. Whoever is doing their public relations work is doing one heck of a job. Investing has become a form of entertainment. Colorful characters bring to life the effect of the day's events on the markets as if they were sportscasters covering the twists and turns of the latest season-defining game. A sudden recovery in the market is no longer just a recovery, but instead a snap-back reflex or a dead cat bounce. The attention alone these personalities and their lively metaphors bring to the market effectively advertises trading and spurs action on the part of their audience.

You can catch the market "score" through most media sources on an almost continuous basis. Unlike the relatively scanty coverage available for bonds and cash, following the stock market is easy with the latest updates on your favorite company continually streaming online, on television, and at your local brokerage house. You can still get less frequent updates through the written press, which used to be the primary form of stock coverage. Now more information theoretically enables investors to make more informed investment decisions, or at least quicker and more numerous investment decisions. With every trade having a potential impact in setting a stock's share price, this media blitz only adds to the stock market's volatility.

Speed of Transmission   These days information travels at unprecedented speeds through all the electronic gizmos that are out there. Not only can people get news faster, but they can also react and trade on it instantaneously. This wireless culture fueled by portable devices, such as personal digital assistants (PDAs) and smart phones, has greatly increased the amount of available information and the speed at which it travels today. No longer are investors relying just on newspapers and teletype machines to get business news these days.

When a news story breaks, it reports on an event that is happening right now or has just happened or been discovered to have happened. That's why they call it news. Breaking stories about new technologies, experimental drug trials, new products, proposed law changes, company acquisitions, stock buybacks, dividend changes, and other such game-changing events get reported every day. Professional investment managers with instant access to these breaking news stories can capitalize on the news by trading securities ahead of everyone else.

By comparison, the casual, or lunch pail, investor does not have access to (or is not paying attention to) such information on a basis current enough to profit like a professional trader. What was true yesterday is probably still true today, but may not be of as much use for trading today as it was yesterday. By the time a lunch pail investor catches on to a story—during lunch, of course—it is too late to get in on the early action. So he or she may become a momentum trader who makes stock trades that continue the trend until its price overshoots its true target. Think of overshooting as being like a golfer who hits a shot long to the green only to have the backspin on the ball carry it below the hole. If news is good, momentum traders buy stock, making its share price go too far up before adjusting downward to an equilibrium price. If news is not so good or does not meet expectations, momentum traders oversell the stock so that its price goes too far down before adjusting upward. Eventually these price fluctuations subside at an equilibrium price point for the stock, which in turn gets reflected in the market's overall volatility. The more rapid pace at which breaking news stories hit the streets and people can react to the news through the wonders of modern information technology increases the market's overall volatility.

Content Many news outlets publicize major economic reports coming out each day. These government, research organization, industry trade group, and company reports cover topics such as national and local jobs data; inflation and credit conditions; public sentiment; industry sales and inventories; and company earnings, revenues, acquisitions, and new products. Although all of these reports have the potential to affect segments of the market, you need to be careful in your analysis of the breaking news, as the impact may not be immediately clear. For example, you need to know whether a company's announcement of a new product spells doom for the rest of the industry or could possibly bolster the entire industry by bringing more attention to it.

So much information is out there, and when presented in all its complexity it may be hard to digest. With money to be made, you are competing with legions of investment professionals specializing in certain products and industry sectors standing ready to assimilate and process all this information into profitable trades.

Other times it just may be hard to distinguish whether information is really relevant to an investment decision with all of the other noise going on. You need to filter out unreliable information. A trading mistake is blamed for the flash crash of May 6, 2010, when the market and many blue-chip stocks declined precipitously and recovered somewhat within 15 minutes. Also, many a rumor has started a run on a stock. In September 2008, news broke that a major airline had filed for bankruptcy. Granted, the airline had emerged from bankruptcy only two years earlier. Its share price plummeted 76 percent from $12 to $3 within 15 minutes of the news report. Then the airline hastily issued a statement claiming the story to be untrue, and trading in its stock was temporarily suspended. It turned out that a news agency had reported an old news story it had uncovered that related to that airline's actual bankruptcy filing back in 2002. Once the air was cleared for takeoff, so to speak, trading of the stock resumed that same day. The airline's stock bounced back somewhat but still ended 11 percent lower for the day, and most other major airline stocks also suffered losses on the day as well.[2] Even unfounded rumors cause market volatility.

Human Nature The transition from pension plans to defined contribution plans has put more investment decisions in the hands of individuals rather than professional pension fund managers. Whereas fund managers stick to a policy to meet fund objectives, individual investors are complex human beings with emotions who exhibit irrational behavior at times when it comes to investing. As a result, individual investors tend to be less grounded than the pros. Rather than staying the course, the skittish individual investor may pull in and out of stocks.

The field of behavioral finance studies the patterns emerging from people's emotional behavior in investing. Behavioral finance specialists have coined the terms *herding* and *anchoring* to refer to common human reactions to news or trends. Anchoring refers to the reluctance investors have to change their position, regardless of the news. In a way, their inertia anchors them to their original convictions. Only gradually will stock share prices respond to new information. Especially when news is positive, a full response to such good news comes gradually over time.

Herding—otherwise known as momentum investing—is a term used to refer to gradually buying into a rally or selling into a decline.[3] On the upward side, the additional buying associated with herding reinforces advances in stock prices until the high valuations it creates can no longer be sustained, causing prices to drop back. Recent examples include the tech bubble in the late 1990s and the housing bubble of 2007. Once herding on the upside caused these bubbles to burst, in came herding on the downward side to bring about excessive stock selling, sending share prices down to the point where they became too cheap to ignore. These depressed stock prices then attracted investors, causing the market to recover and the cycle to begin all over again.

Both anchoring and herding play a part in the volatility of the stock market. Whereas investors' underreactions to news involved in anchoring may slow stock price movements, their overreactions to trends in herding carry stock price movements to extremes. Their balance plays out with other aspects of human nature that affect trading volume as volatility in the market.

Short Attention Span   That the good things in life take time is sometimes lost in today's warp-speed culture. People are getting more impatient, and they change their minds all the time. Speed dating, video on demand, and easy credit have created a culture of instant gratification. A stock trade can be executed online within seconds of placement of an order. Ever briefer response times have transcended all aspects of life and only serve to accommodate and encourage the human being's already short attention span.

This short attention span has affected investors' patience with stocks. The average holding period for a stock listed on the New York Stock Exchange has decreased from about five years in 1980 to about six months in 2009.[4] Investors have turned into gamblers in a climate where mood has replaced research. This collective bias toward market churning profoundly affects the stock market's volatility.

Winds of Change   People frequently change their tastes toward what constitutes a suitable investment, as moods, perceptions, circumstances, economic conditions, and age dictate. What may be good today is different from what is good tomorrow. Over the years, really hot commodities have come in and out of favor—from tulip bulbs in Holland in the 1630s to dotcom stocks coming into the new millennium, and back to most things green in 2011.

What was fashionable yesterday does not make the grade today, but may still be on the menu at a reduced price. The new greasers are goths; pedal pushers came back as capri pants; audiovisual geeks are technowizards; and coffee is, well, coffee, except if you want one of the other 87,000 variations of drinks available from one major coffeehouse.[5]

Too Many Choices   The number of choices available to consumers these days is staggering. With so many varieties of investment products and more on the way, confused investors are left to make some difficult investment decisions. Those who accept the task should periodically review their choices, but in the process may sometimes find themselves doubting their choices and chasing the latest investment fads. This type of behavior usually results in more trades and increased market volatility.

Market Products   The world is filled with stock-based financial instruments known as derivatives that cause market volatility. Unlike stock, which grants an ownership claim on a company's earnings into perpetuity, other financial instruments, such as stock options, include a time restriction that forces the holder to act within a certain duration.

Triple Witching Hour   A stock option gives its owner the right, but not the obligation, to buy or sell a stock at a certain strike price within a limited time period. Options to buy or sell market indexes within a certain duration also exist as index options. Therefore, an option holder may need to exercise an option prior to its expiration to realize any value from the option. Such exercise may involve the purchase or sale of underlying stock to complete the transaction.

A futures contract obligates its owner to deliver a security at a predefined price on a specified future date. In order to deliver the security, a futures contract holder may need to buy the security before it can be delivered.

When stock options, index options, and futures contracts all expire at the same time, traders needing to cover or offset their positions just before their expiration can increase trading volume and create havoc for the share price of the underlying stock. As a result, the stock market can be quite volatile in the final hour of trading on the third Friday of the final month of each calendar quarter (March, June, September, and December) when these options contracts all expire at the same time, known as the *triple witching hour.*

Margin Call An investor taking out a loan from a broker to buy stock is said to be buying stock on *margin.* The lending broker typically requires the borrowing investor to maintain assets in his or her account equal to a certain percentage of the outstanding loan. In the event that a decline in the value of a borrowing investor's securities causes the account assets to dip below a specified percentage of the loan balance, the lending broker would require the borrowing investor to deposit cash into the account. In order to come up with this required deposit, known as a *margin call,* an investor might have to sell already depressed stock, sending the share price even lower.

Automated Program Trades Cautious investors seeking to protect stock gains and minimize losses direct their brokers to sell stock at certain market price limits above and below the current share price. Such a stop loss order calls for a stock sale when its market price declines to a certain level in order to protect gains or avoid any further losses. Opportunistic investors instruct their brokers to buy stock through limit orders. Automated systems allow brokers to track share prices and carry out these trading instructions. Any automated program trading of this form only tends to exaggerate market movements. For example, when the market suffers a sudden decline, carrying out the automated stock sales instructions may dramatically increase shares available for sale and therefore depress share prices even further.

Although these types of transactions and features typically will not be available under a retirement savings plan, it is important to recognize some of the other types of market forces that cause volatility. The proliferation of these types of financial instruments and market mechanisms will only continue to add to the stock market's trading volume and volatility.

Power Brokers Money is power in the financial world, and institutional investors have it. Institutional investors rule the stock markets with advantages in knowledge, data, technology, capacity, speed, leverage, and costs at their disposal for executing trades. Their bulk trades can create the very imbalances in a stock's supply and demand that move its market price.

It was not always that way, as individual investors owned about 90 percent of the shares of U.S. stocks in the 1950s. Over time, as individuals sought help in managing their stocks, professionally managed funds prolif-erated to meet that need. This transition from individuals' outright owner-ship to indirect control of their investments resulted in the dramatic growth of mutual funds, pension funds, hedge funds, insurance company accounts, endowments, and other institutional funds. Now institutional investors, such as mutual funds, pension funds, and endowments, own 75 percent of stocks.[6] With so much stock ownership concentrated in so few hands, the greater potential for uneven trading makes the market bound to be more volatile.

Legislation   For all its good intentions, the government is a major con-tributor to market volatility. Operating through various federal, state, and local agencies, the government regulates commerce to promote free trade within a capitalist society. The various agencies wield power to control credit through monetary policy, subsidize industries for the common good through tax policy and other support, ensure fair trade, protect domestic industry, secure national interests, ensure product safety (such as pre-scription drugs) for use in the marketplace, rule on business and other conduct through the judicial branch, promote education, and run welfare agencies. Investors analyze federal, state, and local government reports, deliberations, actions, and rulings to align their portfolios to capitalize on current and anticipated policy shifts that may affect segments of the market. Their collective analysis plays out as trades or investments in the marketplace.

Trading Volume   Years ago, a security trade was processed manually by those yelling guys on the stock exchange floors that you used to see on television. Now electronic technology that executes trades almost in-stantaneously has replaced the former paper-based systems and some of the yelling guys. Faster trading processes facilitate higher trading volume, meaning more trades executed in a shorter period of time. The increased number of price resets resulting from the higher trading volume translates into increased market volatility.

Each publicly traded company has a relatively fixed number of shares outstanding on a given day. So when a large number of a particular stock's shares is traded within a short period, its price swings may become exag-gerated if the supply level of shares put up for sale and demand for shares to be purchased is tilted in one direction before it eventually reaches equi-librium. Unlike the higher volume of rush hour traffic that clogs freeways to a crawl, increased trading volume usually causes the type of market mo-mentum that accelerates the movement of security prices.

While investors' personal cash needs and human nature affect the tim-ing and frequency of their investment decisions, technology has enabled investors to have easy access to more choices, news, and trading. To the extent these market forces increase trading volume and affect stock prices, they will continue to cause the type of daily volatility in the stock market that will enhance the value of day trading with your retirement savings accounts.

SIDEWAYS STOCK MARKET OVER NEAR TERM

After a good night's rest, father and daughter awoke ready for another day of volleyball. Craving some nourishment from the bagel shop in the hotel lobby, they strolled down the hall from their room to catch an uneventful elevator ride from the 22nd floor back to the first floor. They ended up just where they had started the night before.

Parsing Historical Market Performance

History has shown that the stock market generally goes up over time. Yet a closer look at recent history reveals that the upward trend of the market can be attributed to some relatively brief periods of dramatic growth interspersed among longer durations of sideways movement where the market ends up where it started.

In the 50 years ended in 2010, the S&P 500 index went sideways for 11 extended periods of varying durations, covering a total of between 37 and 38 years.[7] Put another way, the stock market ended right where it had started about three-quarters of the time and advanced the remaining one-quarter of the time. During the extended periods when it moved in a sideways direction, the stock market continued to fluctuate up and down (sometimes quite a bit) before settling back to where it had all started, or close to it. Along the way, the market's movement may not have felt sideways due to the turbulence encountered before it ended back at the level from which it all started. In the end, the day-to-day changes of good and not-so-good days canceled each other out during these extended periods of sideways movement, while the dramatic advances that have propelled market advances occurred over relatively shorter periods. Market volatility resulted from scattered market bursts, driving stock prices to extremes in both advancing and sideways markets.

Analysts measure the stock market's performance over different durations, such as decades, years, months, weeks, and even days. These measures provide a forensic perspective on the volatility, as well as source, of the market's performance. When viewed from this forensic perspective, it

TABLE 5.1 Number of Days of Most Extreme Daily Returns Needed to Achieve S&P 500 Index's Annual Return

Year	Annual Change in S&P 500 Index*	Number of Days to Generate Annual Return
2001	−13.0%	4
2002	−23.4	7
2003	26.4	11
2004	9.0	6
2005	3.0	2
2006	13.6	9
2007	3.5	2
2008	−38.5	5
2009	23.5	5
2010	12.8	4

*Excluding dividends.

turns out that the market derives its annual performance from the returns of just a few days each year. In good years, a year's worth of positive investment performance comes from the days with the highest daily gains; in other years, its negative performance comes from the days with the largest daily losses. That means the stock market's net return for the rest of the year is neutral, with all of the annual return having been generated in just a few days.

Table 5.1 shows how many days of each year's most extreme daily returns it took to generate the full year's change in the S&P 500 index from 2001 through 2010.

Table 5.1 shows that a year's worth of the stock market's investment return is made in a matter of days. Out of the 252 or so days investors trade stocks each year, it took an average of only five days to generate the annual returns experienced during the first decade of the new millennium. For a buy-and-hold investor, the rest of the year was a wash. As long as they were fully invested in the market on the right days, investors looking to match the market may as well have buried their money in a hole to get the same result of no net return for the remaining 247 or so trading days of the year.

Of course, the problem with this approach is you do not know ahead of time which of the few days during the year are going to generate the year's worth of investment returns. Because no one can predict the future of the stock market, it is essential to remain invested in stocks over the long term to have an opportunity to realize the gains when they happen. What you really need, though, is a way to time your trading to be in the market when it advances and out when it declines so that you can set up and capture the market's gains. Day trading provides a gradual way to opportunistically be more invested in stocks in anticipation of a market advance and more invested in cash before a market decline.

Where Is the United States Now?

The most widely used indicator of the condition of a nation's economy relates to its output of goods and services, otherwise known as its *gross domestic product* (GDP). It measures the value paid for goods and services produced by work or property in the country. It may have some faults—such as how it would count the wages paid a guy to dig and fill a hole repetitively (or, for that matter, rebuild a house in a flood plain after a hurricane), yet would not count the unpaid services rendered by a homemaker—but it is still a pretty effective overall indicator of the current state of an economy.

News flash! The United States is a superpower with the most robust economy in the world. In terms of goods and services produced, its GDP of $14.3 trillion represented nearly one-quarter of the gross world product (GWP) of $58.1 trillion for the entire world during 2009. The United States' GDP was almost three times the GDP of its nearest competitor, Japan. Figure 5.2 presents the annual GDP for each of the world's five largest countries during 2009.[8]

The U.S. Bureau of Economic Analysis issues quarterly GDP estimates that are used by the investment community to gauge whether the U.S. economy is expanding or contracting. An increase in the GDP from the

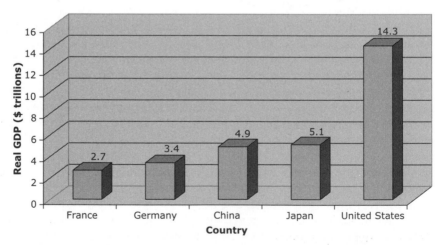

FIGURE 5.2 2009 Real Gross Domestic Products of the World's Five Largest Economies

prior quarter to the current quarter indicates the U.S. economy is in an expansionary mode, whereas a decrease for at least two consecutive quarters indicates the economy is in a recession.

In a period of economic recovery, some consider the stock market to serve as a leading indicator of the condition of the economy six or so months down the road. Other leading indicators like consumer confidence, length of the manufacturing workweek, and interest rate spreads also provide a preview to the economy's health.[9] Yet strict reliance on a stock market advance or other leading indicator for presaging expansionary economic conditions may turn out something like predicting 11 of the next four recoveries. Yes, that makes no sense. So be careful with any indicator, as it could be off a bit.

Sideways Forecast

No one knows exactly what the future holds for the stock market or, for that matter, where the economy is headed. Yet that does not stop economists from taking a shot at predicting economic and stock market conditions down the road. For a variety of reasons, many market prognosticators warn that the stock market may head sideways over the near term in anticipation of sluggish economic activity.

Current economic conditions in 2011 indicate that the market is in the midst of an extended sideways period that got started in the new millennium. Two massive stock market meltdowns later, the U.S. stock market has shown some signs of recovery due to the resilient nature of the economy and some massive government aid. Yet as the markets struggle to regain their prior glory, many obstacles remain.

Going back to the law of supply and demand, a nation's economy depends on the worldwide demand for the supply of goods and services produced by that country. Simply put, the supply side of a nation's economy is primarily a function of its workforce and resources. A large, motivated, well-trained workforce working with the right tools and enough resources is capable of producing loads of economical goods and services available for the world's consumption. Then all it takes is for the world to crave these goods and services enough to buy them.

Although volumes could be, and have been, written and spoken about the future course of the market, the reasoning behind its projected sideways direction over the near term comes down to a few noteworthy trends affecting the future supply and demand for U.S. goods and services.

Supply The continuation of the United States' dominance in the world economy depends just as much on its access to resources as on the demographics, training, and passion of its skilled workforce.

Resources   The United States has led the way into the twenty-first century with its technology and innovation, giving it the tools needed to
efficiently produce goods and services demanded by the world. Yet its continuing dependence on diminishing natural resources will continue to drag
on its economy.

Judging from all the battles fought over it, you might consider the availability of energy as the principal driver of economic expansion. Besides
polluting the environment, the fossil fuels generated by increasingly sophisticated extraction methods will not be enough to keep up with the
world's demand for energy forever. By necessity (and government sub-
sidy), alternative clean energy sources will eventually become more readily available once it just becomes too difficult and expensive to extract the
level of fossil fuels needed to meet the world's energy demands. Still, with
oil reserves sufficient to cover worldwide demand into the twenty-second
century, the depletion of oil and other energy sources is not perceived to
be as much of an immediate problem as the political balance of the nations
controlling these reserves.[10] Yet challenges remain to get through this transition from traditional to alternative energy resources while supporting the
world's growing industrialized population.

Although energy remains very important for sustaining a vibrant world
economy, the impact of increasing industrialization on the environment
and of the limited supply of other natural resources could also curtail what
the United States can supply the world. Naturally any political or environmental forces threatening the ready availability of needed resources would
threaten the United States' production capability as well as service sector
output, thus potentially stalling economic growth and the stock market.

Skilled Workforce   The level of a nation's gross domestic product relies
on a ready supply of able-bodied and skilled workers effectively using resources to produce the goods and services demanded by a modern society.
The size of a nation's available workforce depends on demographic patterns, and its productivity derives from how effectively skilled workers use
available resources and tools to perform their jobs.

Labor supply is a function of the number of people willing and able
to work in the areas needed. Since U.S. employment law restricts child labor but encourages senior labor, potential workers are generally age 16
or over. Early teenage babysitters and newspaper boys do not count. Due
to the steady growth of women's participation in the workforce over the
years, they constitute about half the U.S. workforce as of mid-2009. Now
that women and men are equally represented in the U.S. workforce, the
size of the pool of potential workers becomes more a matter of the number of its native-born citizens and immigrants of working age. Therefore,
any working population growth potentially comes on a deferred basis from

more births than deaths and more immediately from more immigrants than emigrants. Another embedded factor that does not diminish labor force growth comes from inclusion in the workforce of an increasing number of older Americans who cannot afford to retire. The combination of these forces resulted in an increase in the U.S. civilian workforce of less than 1 percent per year in the past decade, from 141 million as of August 2000 to 154 million as of August 2010.[11]

Not all of these potential workers are continuously employed, for various reasons ranging from a slow economy to a mismatch of job requirements and available talent. In the first decade of the new millennium, the unemployment rate of those seeking work as a percentage of the labor force has ranged from 4.0 percent in 2000 to 9.8 percent in September 2009.[12] Even higher are underemployment rates, which also count people who have stopped looking for work or work part-time instead of full-time as well as those unemployed. Such an economy perennially running at less than full employment (historically defined as a 4 percent unemployment rate) speaks to an adequate number of potential workers, but not to their skills or qualifications. Different jobs require different physical capabilities, training, and commitment.

Physical Requirements

The average American's life expectancy at birth increased 30 years, from 48 to 78, from 1900 to 2000.[13] The resultant aging of the American population has prompted many changes in the way work is done. As a result, modern-day workers generally have less physically demanding jobs.

Increases in longevity have both allowed and forced cash-strapped workers to lengthen their working careers. As the U.S. workforce lost some muscle with age, its economy adapted by transforming from a manufacturing economy led by heavy industry (cars, steel, rubber) to more of a service economy (banks, restaurants) offering less physically demanding work. Due largely to the outsourcing of many heavy manufacturing jobs to younger and cheaper labor forces overseas, about 75 percent of Americans work in the service industry as of 2009.[14]

Advances in automation have reduced the physical requirements of both manufacturing and service jobs. If the Great Pyramids in Egypt were built today, there would likely be more cranes and trucks involved than thousands of manual laborers using brute strength to move large boulders into place. Likewise, more American jobs now require more brains than brawn.

Training

Education transforms intelligence into skills. The good news is that the U.S. workforce is among the most intelligent in the world. Americans' raw

IQ scores have increased by three points per decade since World War II.[15] Furthermore, more young people are putting their intelligence to good use by enrolling in college, as the percentage of young adults enrolling in college rose sharply from 1970 to 2003.

Yet the U.S. educational achievement level is slipping by comparison with other developed countries. Due to the huge numbers of high school dropouts, the average 15-year-old ranks in the bottom third in math and in the middle in science when compared with peers in other developed countries.[16] Without education, individuals find it increasingly difficult to adapt to the continually changing skill requirements of the modern workplace. Since 2000, this inability to adapt has resulted in the displacement of many workers.

Despite the growth of the American labor pool, workers' inability to adapt to industry's changing skill requirements has caused the number of qualified workers to decline. As a result, what used to be American jobs are being outsourced to other countries with trained workforces at a lower cost.

Commitment

Commitment is a function of an individual's personality and motivation. Some people are hardwired to achieve. You have seen some kids naturally hit the floor to go for a loose ball, while others couldn't be bothered. Then you have the adults who get their motivation to work from the obligation of a family or mortgage. Yet others draw inspiration from peers or leaders or on their own from their work.

All of these individuals with their different physical skills, educational backgrounds, and motivations inhabit the working world to produce goods and services that keep an economy humming along. The qualified labor pool then depends on the interplay of workforce demographics with workers' physical, educational, and commitment attributes demanded by a cyclical economy of booms and busts.

As of early 2011, the U.S. economy appears headed toward another jobless recovery. Despite moderate increases in GDP, the persistently high unemployment rates suggest a large labor pool with a weak demand for workers' current skill sets. A continuing area of uncertainty relating to the size of the qualified labor pool depends in large part on how American workers adapt to changing skill requirements demanded by an evolving economy.

Demand   It is all very well and good to have the available resources and qualified workforce for producing a ready supply of goods and services, but then people have to buy them to support an economy. The demand side of an economy comes from worldwide personal, business, and government consumption of goods and services produced by a nation. In recent times, personal consumption has accounted for about 70 percent of the U.S. gross domestic product. Related business consumption anticipates personal consumption with advance purchases of goods and services needed to enable personal consumption. Government spending provides a steady backdrop of spending to support national interests, while taking on increasing significance with stopgap measures to assist a flagging economy when needed.

The condition of a nation's economy basically depends on its ability to efficiently produce, sell, and deliver goods and services that the world wants and can afford to buy. The primary forces driving demand are wealth and demographics (again). If that is not enough, then there is government spending.

Wealth Personal consumption has historically been the primary driver of the U.S. economy. As long as Americans have good-paying jobs, they will continue to be able to afford, and be the primary consumers of, the products and services made in the United States as well as elsewhere. With the United States producing about one-quarter of the world's output of goods and services, it only makes sense that they would prefer the familiarity and ease of consuming those home-grown goods and services. Many less developed countries cannot afford to consume the relatively expensive goods and services offered by the United States. As a result of the low foreign demand for American-made goods and services, the U.S. exports less as a percentage of output than any other developed nation.[17]

Americans have racked up total consumer debt at the staggering level of $11.7 trillion as of June 30, 2010.[18] Years of overspending have put consumers (and nations) in debt to the extent that previous levels of consumption may not be sustained. High unemployment and diminished housing values have also eroded Americans' wealth. During 2009, the percentage of Americans living in poverty hit a 15-year high of over 14 percent.[19] The overall decline in personal wealth affects people's confidence and ability to spend enough to prop up the U.S. economy. Even during the ensuing tentative economic recovery, former consumers are hunkering down to save and reduce debt instead of spending to support the economy.

Demographics Population changes, as well as shifts in the composition of the population, greatly influence the condition of the economy and the stock market.

Population Changes
Size matters when it comes to a population's consumption. It only makes sense that if there are fewer people, they will consume fewer goods and services; and if there are more people, they will want more goods and

services. So a growing population naturally supports growth in demand for goods and services, which, in turn, can lead to economic growth and stock market advances.

Projections indicate that the U.S. population will grow at a tepid rate of less than 1 percent per year for the next few decades. About 82 percent of this population growth is expected to come from net immigration, and the rest is to come from the number of babies born exceeding the number of people who die.[20] As a result, weak population growth is not expected to generate much personal consumption or contribute to future economic growth.

Not all Americans spend equally, as marketers surely know. Aggregate personal consumption is driven by a number of factors, the most influential of which are the gender and age of the population.

Gender

No surprises here. On average, women control 65 percent of consumer spending.[21] Therefore, any shift in a population's ratio of women relative to men would affect consumer spending. A female population growing faster than the male population, whether from immigration or births, would increase the proportion of spenders in society. More females as a proportion of the population would generate higher consumer spending, spurring economic growth and the stock market. The extent of the shift toward a more feminine population bears further consideration as to its impact on the U.S. economy.

In the beginning, guys rule, but the gals come through at the end. The number of boy babies born into the world exceeds the number of girl babies. In the United States, boys make up 51.2 percent of the baby population, as compared to baby girls at 48.8 percent.[22] Yet females catch up with and surpass males in numbers as they travel further down the road of life. Since females live an average of slightly more than five years longer than males, these extra years of life translate into more women than men in the world.[23] In the end, the U.S. population is composed of 49.3 percent males and 50.7 percent females.[24]

Census data shows that the female population had increased faster than the male population every decade from 1910 to 1980. This turned around in 1980 when the male population of the United States started growing faster than the female population, resulting in the proportion of males increasing from 48.6 percent in 1980 to 49.3 percent in 2009.[25] One primary factor in this faster growth of the male population has been the relatively greater increases in males' life expectancy, as compared to females'. Males' increased life expectancy over that for females translates into more males hanging around longer and getting them closer to keeping the majority of the population into which they were born. Since women control more of the purse strings, any continuation of this gradual shift toward an increase in the male population relative to females could conceivably translate into less consumption, a weaker economy, and reduced stock market returns.

Age

The impact of an individual's age on his or her consumption pattern is a different matter entirely. Wealth permitting, individuals of certain age groups buy more goods and services than others and thereby grow the economy. People in their mid-40s to mid-50s tend to consume the most as they reach their career peaks while raising a full family household. Once the kids start moving out, those individuals nearing retirement tend to favor saving over spending. A generation reaching this period of peak consumption at the same time could increase demand, spur economic growth, and push stocks higher.

The U.S. population includes two outsized generations that have influenced and will influence personal consumption: About 77 million baby boomers were born between 1946 and 1964, and 81 million millennials were born between 1977 and 1997. The millennials currently making up 27 percent of the U.S. population now outnumber the baby boomers constituting 23 percent of the population. A smaller "gap" generation born in fewer numbers each year from 1965 to 1976 is sandwiched between the two larger generations.[26]

Starting in 2007, the U.S. economy began to show strains of less consumption, as half of the baby boomer generation had already reached and passed their years of peak consumption. Moving along as the consumption of the aging baby boomer generation wanes, personal consumption is expected to decrease as the smaller "gap" generation cannot sustain the baby boomer generation's former consumption levels and the economy awaits the lift of the massive millennial generation hitting its peak consumption years. With personal consumption continuing to play such a major part in the U.S. economy, it appears that a resurgence in personal spending awaits the arrival of the millennials' peak spending years, thus keeping the economy and stock prices in a sideways mode of little or no growth until at least 2020.

The demographic factors of negligible population growth outside of immigration, an increased proportion of the frugal gender (males) in the population, and a generation gap in spending all pose threats to consumer spending, the largest component of economic activity in the United States. Add to that the cost of paying off personal and national debt of unprecedented size, and you may have tepid, if any, economic growth in the near term.

Government Spending   The dependence of the modern economy on government spending to boost demand, whether it be in the name of public works projects, industry bailouts, education, welfare, or national security, cannot be overlooked. Fiscal policy generally calls for growth in government spending in recessionary times and restraint in expansionary times. When businesses can no longer afford to keep workers on their payrolls due to a flagging economy, the government temporarily steps in to hire displaced workers. These government stimulus programs are intended to get a nation through air pockets in its economy. Conversely, in expansionary times when inflation is threatening, there is no need for the government to compete for already scarce resources through its spending.

Following the near collapse of the financial markets in 2008, the U.S. government pumped trillions of dollars into the revival of the economy. In fiscal year 2009, government expenditures approached $4 trillion, or about 28 percent of the GDP of about $14 trillion. This level greatly exceeded (by 40 percent) average government expenditures of 20 percent of GDP for the prior 50 years.

These expenditures led to a U.S. federal budget deficit of $1.4 trillion for fiscal year 2009. Mounting another $1.3 trillion deficit the following year, the total U.S. federal debt weighed in at around $14 trillion through fiscal year 2010. As a percentage of GDP, the U.S. federal deficits of 10.0 percent for 2009 and 8.9 percent for 2010 were the highest on record since the end of World War II in 1945.[27] Each of these repeated levels of deficit spending represents about three times the maximum 3 percent limit recommended by most economists.[28] With the continuation of U.S. annual budget deficits projected not to get below the 3 percent of GDP threshold for some time, the national debt will continue to reach unprecedented levels.

Government spending usually increases the competition and corresponding cost for securing capital, thereby having the inflationary effect of raising interest rates for those trying to secure credit. The additional inflationary effect of government spending's diversion of resources away from private enterprise also drives up the costs of goods and services. Eventually, Americans, the largest consumers in the world, may no longer be able to afford their own goods and services that they produce. Furthermore, inflationary pressure may reduce foreign investment in U.S. government bonds. As the federal government increases the money supply (i.e., prints money) to repay the huge deficits, the U.S. dollar is devalued against other currencies. A weakened currency makes foreign investments in U.S. government bonds less attractive. So the United States cannot count on the rest of the world continuing to prop up its economy with investments in government bonds.

Government spending in the form of stimulus packages and bailouts preserves wealth and jobs in the short term, only to be paid off later. The short term impact of temporarily propping up the economy with borrowed money will be felt years down the road as payments are made to reduce the massive debt. Retirement of growing U.S. debt can be expected to slow economic recovery and continue to be quite a drag on the economy for years to come.

FORECAST: CLOUDY WITH A CHANCE OF SUN AND RAIN

If you believe what you hear, the economy runs in cycles, going from boom to bust and back again and again. If the economy literally did run in cycles, everyone would know what to expect and when. In reality, it is often the timing of the stages of the cycles that does not quite go according to plan.

Demographics, human nature, and other factors suggest the immediate future is marred with uncertainty and potential limits on economic growth. These are the types of conditions that cause the stock market to fluctuate both up and down without any clear sense of direction. This roller coaster of a ride in the market can be nerve-racking if you do not expect it or are not equipped to deal with it. Therefore, you need to see this volatility coming and develop a way to harness it to your advantage.

As in navigating crowded elevators (and subways), you can manage your retirement savings portfolio using a strategy to take advantage of both instances when the stock market goes up and down, or when it goes down, then up. Unsettling as it may seem to some, this type of environment combining uncertainty and sideways movement in the stock market is ideal for day trading retirement savings accounts.

Before you can day trade, you need to develop a systematic approach for managing your retirement portfolio. A sound investment strategy provides the framework from which day trading will operate to take advantage of a fluctuating market. Many of the same time-tested principles underlying a sound investment strategy also apply to day trading. That would make now a good time to walk you through the development of a sound investment strategy for managing your retirement portfolio before you run with day trading.

PART III

Rationale

CHAPTER 6

Playbook

*Retirement Savings
Investment Strategies*

*The safest way to double your money is to fold it over
once and put it in your pocket.*

—Kin Hubbard

I t was her turn at the podium. The high school graduating class had already taken their seats on a stage set on the campus softball field. The festive crowd awaited the words of the senior class president. With her cap and gown flowing in the wind, she stood there grounded with a foundation of a solid education that she had worked hard to build for herself. Yet today she discounted the sweat that went into earning her academic honors and instead shared the little things she had picked up along the way that she said gave her an edge in school. She entertained her audience with tales of managing time, accommodating teacher quirks, avoiding distractions, and distinguishing between student pratfalls and real trouble. For her role was to refresh her classmates on their way to the next stop rather than to pontificate with anything too deep or serious. Deep down, though, she knew these little things were just the finishing touches that added strength to an already sound foundation.

WEALTH

Your accumulated financial wealth represents your foundation. It is measured by the physical and financial assets, including retirement savings accounts, that you have accumulated over your lifetime. Spiritual wealth is a whole different thing that will not be explored here. Just as an education is nurtured at school, your financial wealth should be anchored by a sound investment strategy upon which a finishing touch of a trading strategy can be added.

Without inheritance or savings to begin with, there is no strategy. Inheritance and savings, along with sound management of it, beget wealth. Investment and trading strategies only add to the wealth.

Inheritance

In basketball, there is a saying that goes: "You can't coach height." You can teach kids how to shoot, dribble, pass, rebound, and defend, but you can't make them any taller. You just cannot grow a kid to a height not dictated by his or her own inherited traits.

Chris Wall stood a pudgy six feet four inches tall as a 13-year-old freshman in high school. A personable, but clumsy, kid who just grew too fast, he did not appear particularly athletic to an outside observer. Up to that point, Chris's exposure to basketball had been minimal. When Chris started public high school at New Trier East, Coach John Schneiter saw Chris's height as something special in need of development for his ambitious basketball program. Before he showed Chris a basketball, he had him working out and running endless laps on the school track to work off his baby fat. Chris worked hard and got in better shape, but was still a bit awkward. When basketball season came around, the coach generously awarded Chris a roster spot as a project on the freshman "B" team. Over the next few years, Chris continued to grow, work hard, and develop an inside game. By his junior year, his game had progressed to the point where he found himself starting at center for a very athletic team in the final game of the Illinois High School Championship game. Following his solid high school basketball career, he landed a scholarship to Northwestern University.

Most people are not as lucky as Chris "Too Tall" Wall to inherit the gift of size from their parents or get the special attention afforded that gift. Yet everyone has an opportunity to make the most of what they have. If you were not born into a wealthy family, you may very well be out of luck when it comes to building wealth through an inheritance. Even if you were, you probably have very little say as to the amount or timing of any inheritance distribution (outside of assisting with some estate planning). You just cannot plan for an inheritance. Therefore, it may be best not to count on any inheritance in your retirement planning. But just in case, it is always a good idea to be nice to your folks.

Savings

Unlike height and inheritance, you *can* coach savings. Savings is an area where individuals can directly influence the accumulation of their own personal wealth. As noted earlier, savings is the residual amount of an individual's disposable income that is not spent. When you earn more than you spend during your career, you have the resources to save for the time when you are no longer working and need to draw from your savings to cover living expenses. Whether saving under a retirement savings plan or otherwise, saving during your working career is important to the maintenance of your standard of living after retirement.

In theory, everyone believes in saving. It is no secret that you could save more by increasing your income and/or reducing personal expenditures. With more left over to save for retirement, these increased savings will add to your wealth. Because saving may not be all that easy for many, the question then becomes how much saving is enough.

Planning is essential when it comes to retirement savings. You need to define a retirement income goal in terms of a desired *replacement rate* (retirement income as a percentage of final earnings) at an anticipated retirement date. Deduct your other sources of retirement income, such as Social Security and employer-provided pensions, to come up with your savings goal. Then it becomes a matter of actually saving enough each year that, when accumulated with investment earnings, you will reach that savings goal at the desired retirement date.

Individual Savings Rate Guidelines   Saving may not be all that convenient for many people. However, what you give up by saving now affects how much will be available later to support you in retirement. Rather than worry about not saving enough, find peace of mind from knowing how much you need to save for retirement.

To determine your annual savings commitment necessary to meet your retirement savings goal, you first need to define your retirement income goal and desired retirement date. Then deduct other sources of retirement income, such as Social Security and employer retirement plans, to derive your net income needed from savings. After converting this net income from savings payable for the rest of your life into a single lump sum, you need to derive the amount of annual savings commitment required to meet this lump sum savings goal.

The duration of your savings period and that of your payout period affect the necessary commitment to reach your savings goal. The ages at which you begin and end your saving regimen determine how long you will have to save. Your life expectancy will determine how long you may be depending on your accumulated savings.

Assume you will have the good fortune to retire from an illustrious career, or just quit working, at age 65. Social Security projections show the average American male age 65 in 2010 can expect to live another 17 years. Meanwhile, the life expectancy of a female age 65 in 2010 is about 20 years.[1]

To be on the conservative side, the following savings rate projections use the longer female life expectancy to assume a payout of your savings over a 20-year retirement. That is all right if you are average. Because you know you are not average in so many ways, you may want to save more now than just to cover your life expectancy, lest you run out of savings later for living too long.

Taking the simple case where you expect no other sources of retirement income, you would first need to translate the income stream resulting from applying your desired replacement rate to your final earnings into a lump sum at the anticipated retirement date. Then you would determine the duration over which your savings would accumulate, marked by when you start saving in relation to when you retire. Finally, you can derive what percentage of pay to save each year from your current age until retirement to reach your goal. Otherwise you can check Table 6.1, where this has been done for you.

Table 6.1 projects an individual's savings rate (savings as a percentage of current pay) that would be necessary over different durations to provide a level retirement income payable starting at age 65 for 20 years of 70 percent of the individual's pay just prior to retirement. Viewed in a different way, Table 6.1 presents the savings rate that would be required of an individual from each designated age until retirement in order to reach the desired retirement income goal.

Personal preference will determine one's comfort with a retirement income of 70 percent of preretirement pay beginning at age 65 that is payable for 20 years certain. Otherwise, these savings rate projections in Table 6.1 rely on certain assumptions: personal savings, and nothing else (not even Social Security), make up an individual's retirement income; interest accumulates on savings at a level rate of 5 percent per year; and an individual receives 3 percent pay raises year in and year out while working. In view of the use of such broad assumptions, these savings rates in Table 6.1 should

TABLE 6.1 Savings Rate Necessary to Provide Level Retirement Income of 70 Percent of Preretirement Pay for 20 Years Starting at Age 65

Age (Years) at Which Savings Starts	Savings Period (Years)	Savings Rate*
25	40	14%
35	30	21%
45	20	35%
55	10	77%

*Assumes investment earnings of 5 percent per year, pay increases of 3 percent per year, retirement at age 65, and retirement income payout period of 20 years.

be used more as general guidance under certain situations rather than as the absolute answer for reaching your retirement goal.

Without any other sources of retirement income, you would need to save 21 percent of pay each year for 30 years starting at age 35 if you desired a retirement income starting at age 65 that would replace 70 percent of your final preretirement pay for 20 years. All the while, the absolute amount you would save each year increases with your pay by 3 percent per year, and your accumulated savings grow at 5 percent per year. For example, if your annual pay increased steadily at 3 percent per year from $42,435 at age 35 to $100,000 just prior to retirement at age 65, you would need to save $8,911 (= 0.21 savings rate × $42,435 pay) the first year and an amount 3 percent higher each succeeding year for 30 years until you reach $21,000 (= 0.21 savings rate × $100,000) in the thirtieth year to provide a retirement income of $70,000 per year for 20 years.

You may be able to save less and still reach your retirement income goal if you have other sources of retirement income from Social Security or company retirement plans. You may even get an employer matching contribution under your existing 401(k) or other retirement savings plan to help you in reaching your retirement goal. You may also be able to reduce your savings rate if you can muster up better investment returns. Other than counting on an early demise before age 85, your last resort may come down to modifying the timing of your retirement or desired retirement income.

Potential Impediments to Reaching Your Savings Goal   The individual savings rates needed to produce the desired retirement income in Table 6.1 apply under a certain set of assumptions relating to your investment returns, pay increases, retirement goal, retirement age, and payout period. Consequently, any variation from these assumptions could affect savings rates required to reach the desired retirement income. Additionally in the real world, uneven market returns, cash flow requirements, taxes, and savings habits may also influence your accumulated nest egg and how long it will last.

Market Conditions and Cash Flow   Varying market conditions that may not necessarily produce level annual returns each year would affect how much and how long your accumulated savings could support you. The interaction of varying investment returns with how fast you put money in and take money out affects your accumulated savings.

As an example of how market conditions can affect the accumulation of periodic savings, consider a fellow making two annual deposits of $1,000 each into a savings account at the beginning of each year. In his savings account, he earns a steady 5 percent interest per year. His balance after two years would be $2,153. Suppose he has a twin brother who also makes two annual deposits of $1,000 at the beginning of each year, but into a brokerage account. He loses 10 percent the first year and earns 22.5 percent the second year in his brokerage account. In this case, the twin brother's brokerage account balance after two years would be $2,328. In both scenarios, the effective annual return over the two-year period was 5 percent per year. Yet after two years, the first fellow with a steady annual 5 percent return has a balance of $2,153, and his twin brother experiencing a 10 percent loss followed by a 22.5 percent gain ends up with a bigger balance of $2,328.

Not only do variable investment returns from year to year affect your savings accumulation before retirement, but the interaction of market conditions with your actual drawdown of savings in retirement also affects your remaining accumulated savings. For example, consider twin sisters, each starting with $20,000 in savings under the exact same type of market conditions as the twin brothers. The first sister makes two annual withdrawals of $1,000 at the beginning of each year from an initial balance of $20,000 in her savings account that earns her a steady return of 5 percent per year. Her balance is $19,898 after two years.

Her twin sister also makes two annual withdrawals from a brokerage account at the beginning of each year, the first of which is $800 and the second of which is $1,200. As with the twin brother, the twin sister also loses 10 percent the first year and earns 22.5 percent the second year in her brokerage account. The twin sister's balance after two years is $19,698. Although both sisters withdrew the same sum of $2,000 and earned an effective annual return of 5 percent over the two-year period, the first sister ends up with a higher remaining balance of $19,898, compared with her twin sister, who is left with a balance of only $19,698.

These examples are intended to show that the interaction of market conditions with when and how much you deposit into or withdraw from your savings affects your savings balance and how long it will last.

Taxes   Not only do actual market conditions and cash flow in and out of your savings affect how much you need to save to reach your desired retirement income goal, but income taxes also need to be considered. In a tax-deferred retirement savings plan, your pretax savings grow tax-free until taxed as ordinary income upon distribution. Roth contributions get taxed before deposit and, along with their investment earnings, escape taxation upon a qualified distribution. Taxable personal savings get taxed before deposit and then each year on their investment earnings. Regardless of whether you pay taxes now, later, or in between, you need to save enough to cover income taxes as well as provide an adequate retirement income.

Delay Simply put, every day you delay saving for retirement, the more you will need to save over a shorter period to fund a certain retirement income goal. The older you get without saving, the less likely you may be able to meet the more burdensome saving commitment required to support an adequate retirement income at an age such as 65. Eventually the continued delay in the commencement of a retirement savings program may doom any plans to retire at a reasonable age.

Likewise, delaying participation in a formal retirement savings plan such as a 401(k) plan is even more costly in that you are shortchanging yourself from taking full advantage of the tax-deferred nature of employee savings, any employer matches, and investment earnings within the plan. In order to avoid irreparable harm to your plans for a long and active retirement, you need to recognize the urgency of your plan participation as much as your employer does.

Because employers recognize the importance of employees' saving for retirement, employers are increasingly stepping up, with the government's blessing, to encourage employee savings. One type of savings incentive comes in the form of employer matching contributions to a 401(k) plan, where an employer contributes a percentage of what the employee contributes to the plan. Another type of incentive allows employers to automatically enroll new employees in their 401(k) plan. Still another attractive plan feature inducing participation allows participants access to 401(k) funds through plan loans and withdrawals. Whether these efforts are enough for their employees to accumulate enough to support them in retirement remains to be seen.

Due to the challenging landscape affecting pensions and Social Security benefits as noted in Chapter 2, the accumulation of your savings over time is more important than ever as a source of retirement income. The tax preferences afforded accumulated savings, employer contributions, and earnings in retirement savings accounts should make them a primary component of your retirement savings. Your wealth at retirement depends on how you manage your retirement savings accounts through investing, trading, and expense management.

WEALTH MANAGEMENT PROCESS

There are a lot of lousy investors out there. By definition, half of investors experience portfolio returns below the market's median returns. If you are in the other half who experience market-beating returns in your portfolio, you are to be commended. Either way, you may be able to improve your portfolio's investment performance by following some basic principles of wealth management.

Instead of holding a steady course over time, some individual investors exhibit tendencies to jump on the momentum bandwagon, panic, or time the market. *Momentum investors* buy or sell securities depending on the whim of the market. Poor investment performance results when investors follow market momentum late into or out of an investment. By the time they are on or off the bandwagon (or train), it has already left the station. A late purchase after a stock's rise may cause the investor to miss out on a good portion of the gains, and a late sale after a stock's decline may lock in most of the loss, allowing little or no chance for recovery.

Panic selling occurs when an investor loses the intestinal fortitude required to hold steady in an investment that is losing money. In raising cash at the wrong time after a deep loss has already occurred, a panic sale also locks in realized losses and prevents any chance of experiencing a recovery in the stock's price.

Most *market timers* who buy and sell securities in an attempt to anticipate changes in the market are more often wrong than right. Extensive research, some luck, and pure guts serve the rare market timer who manages to stay in the game over the long term.

The types of individual investors characterized here are at a disadvantage to professional investment managers. Unlike professional investors managing large portfolios, individual investors generally pay higher investment expenses. They do not enjoy the economies of scale that professional investors managing large portfolios enjoy. Individual investors also tend not to keep as watchful an eye on how much of their returns goes toward paying investment management expenses. For these and other reasons, individual investors' returns generally fall short of those obtained by professional investment managers. This pattern is confirmed in a study comparing the returns of pension funds managed by professional investment managers with the returns of defined contribution plans managed by individual participants. This study found that the annual investment returns generated by pension funds exceeded such returns under defined contribution plans by an average of over 1 percent per year from 1995 through 2006.[2]

There are some things you as an individual investor can do to improve the investment performance of your retirement savings accounts. It all starts with making sure you have an investment strategy in place from the outset of your plan participation. For an investment strategy to work, you need assets. Your retirement savings account assets may already be allocated to fund options based on your investment instructions for your contributions and any previous allocations. The investment process involves monitoring and modifying the allocation of your retirement savings accounts to accommodate changes in the markets and your investment objectives.

You need to have an investment plan to harness the unpredictable markets and modify it over time as conditions change. For instance, you may very well find your risk tolerance mellowing with age from trying to make a killing in the market when you are young to just holding on to what you have as you get closer to retirement.

A sound financial plan employing investment and trading strategies can add value to a foundation of already accumulated wealth in retirement savings accounts. Recall the distinction between investing and trading. Whereas investing is characterized more as a buy-and-hold strategy that is intended to build wealth over the long term, trading involves more rapid-fire purchases and sales in a quest to capture short-term gains.

Judging by all the sales materials, the pyramid model seems to be quite popular in the world of financial planning. Perhaps there is something to the magical belief about a pyramid's spiritual and preservation powers that translates into wealth. You, too, can think of your retirement savings account wealth management plan as a pyramid. A sound wealth management plan includes an investment strategy that serves as the cornerstone to anchor the pyramid's asset foundation in place. The investment strategy provides a framework for the allocation of already existing assets among investment alternatives. Then the day trading strategy is overlaid on the investment foundation as a finishing touch. Day trading is just the tip of the pyramid built on an already solid investment foundation. Keep in mind that a sound investment strategy precedes all else, as the day trading strategy just adds to the party. Unlike the commencement speech from the beginning of the chapter that discounted the effort required for a solid educational foundation, any wealth management plan must begin with a sound investment strategy as a foundation before topping it off with a trading strategy.

FIGURE 6.1 Retirement Savings Account Management Pyramid

There are many ways to establish investment and day trading strategies. Certain functions are common to both, although the order may vary depending on your method. Whether investing or trading your already existing retirement savings accounts, you need to establish a target asset mix, select fund options, derive a plan to allocate account assets to fit fund options, and then perform any necessary fund exchanges to produce the desired asset allocation.

Establish Target Asset Mix

Based on your risk tolerance, objectives, and other criteria, you first need to set up a model asset class mix. This mix would define the portion of your portfolio to be initially allocated to each of the stocks, bonds, and cash asset classes. For example, you may simply want to allocate your account balances so as to have 60 percent in stocks, 30 percent in bonds, and 10 percent in cash.

Select Fund Options

You should select the best fund options from your retirement savings plan menus that fit into your target asset mix. If you swore off stocks (which is generally not a good idea), an international stock fund would not be one of your selections. In your selection process, you should review information on the available fund options, such as mutual fund prospectuses, from the plan's fund manager or your employer. Despite the warnings that a fund's past performance may not be an indication of its future performance, many investors rely on historical returns in selecting fund options into which they allocate their account balances. Although performance might give an indication of a fund manager's skills, other considerations in fund selection should include the fund's objectives, risk, holdings, and expense ratio.

Allocate Assets

The actual asset allocation process would be easy if each fund option fit nicely into only one asset class. However, fund options can include one or more of the asset classes. Then it becomes even more complicated if you go further to break down fund options into asset class subcategories based on criteria such as the industry, management type, company size, or geographic region of the issuers of the securities within the fund. You need to take these different criteria into account in allocating your account assets among available fund options.

Perform Fund Exchanges

On the basis of your review and selection of fund options, you need to make any necessary fund exchanges to bring your existing asset allocation within your accounts into line with your desired allocation among asset classes. It is usually advisable to make these transfers over an extended period rather than all at once to avoid any distortion in value due to unfavorable market conditions.

This cursory description of the asset allocation process merely summarizes the basic steps involved in managing your retirement savings accounts. This process requires some personal introspection as well as knowledge of the markets, fund options, and plan rules. It also requires continuous monitoring and repetition of some steps as conditions change.

When it comes to investing your retirement savings, you can do it yourself, get help, or farm it out completely. Your approach may depend on what is offered and whether any outside help is subsidized under your plan. If you do it yourself, you perform the functions of investing your account assets without any outside assistance. If you get help, you may access computer modeling software or an adviser for a fee to assist in allocating your account assets. Finally, you could just hand off your account management responsibility to an outside adviser for a fee. Regardless of your approach or involvement in your account management, you should be aware of the conventional wisdom of what drives the securities markets and alternative approaches used for investing retirement savings accounts.

MARKET ECONOMICS

The market acts like a worldwide opinion poll on security prices. It assigns a value, or price, to each security based on the collective opinion of the world's population at any given point in time. Everyone has a vote. Of course a lot of people do not cast a vote because they are underage, are otherwise uninformed, or do not care. Then there are traders who care too much and vote often. Finally, there are those somewhere in between.

Investors who are willing to take on risk for the potentially higher long-term returns offered by stocks vote for stocks. Others who value the steady income provided by bonds vote for bonds. Those who value capital preservation and liquidity inherent in cash vote for cash. Each vote for a particular security within one of these asset classes comes with a price assigned to it. The collective votes of buyers and sellers result in a price assigned to a security. As people's opinions change over time, the price for a given security traded on the open market changes moment by moment.

The prices of publicly held securities are driven by basic economic principles. They are exchanged in markets where, in theory, their prices are established on the basis of the supply of and the demand for them by profit-seeking market capitalists with access to all available information. Buyers and sellers establish a security's price by reaching a consensus that balances the worth of its acquisition to the buyer with the value received for its disposition by the seller.

Law of Supply and Demand

Introductory economics defines the price of a good or service as the equilibrium point where its supply at a given price equals the demand for it at that price. Supply represents the amount made available for sale at a given price point. The amount that companies are willing to supply is directly related to price, as a higher price generating more profit attracts more companies to increase the supply of a good or service. Conversely, suppliers shy away from offering goods and services that generate little profit.

Demand represents the aggregate intention of potential customers to buy a good or service. As well as being influenced by perception and quality, the amount of demand for something is inversely related to its price. If the price is set too high, the demand may not be as great as the available supply. Lowering the price may increase demand, but if the price becomes too low, demand will outstrip a scarce supply. Then suppliers react to a low inventory by raising prices to what the market will bear. Suppliers also eventually react to increase the supply of the now higher-priced good or service with plans to cash in on the profit generated at the higher price.

Even though sales transactions may occur at different prices along the way, each sales transaction occurs at the price where supply equals demand at a given point in time. In each instance, the price reflects the conditions present at the time of the transaction that led to the balance between sellers' supply and buyers' demand. So goes the *law of supply and demand*, in theory at least.

Have you ever noticed that you seem to get a better price for an airline ticket on a particular flight the earlier you buy your ticket before the flight's scheduled departure? Absent any price wars, airlines base their ticket prices on available seats. Although the supply of a given plane's seats is fixed, an airline may swap aircraft to accommodate demand for a particular flight. Meanwhile the demand for those seats increases as travel plans become firmed up and the departure date approaches. An airline ticket purchased six months in advance of your travel date is generally priced lower than one purchased just before takeoff. Those business travelers who make sudden plans pay full fare for the convenience of getting one of the limited number of seats still available on a moment's notice.

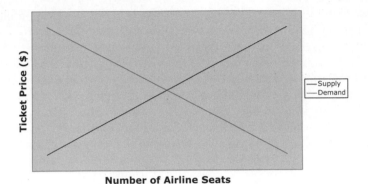

FIGURE 6.2 Supply-Demand Balance for Airline Seats

Airlines use sophisticated yield management systems in their reservation and booking systems to maximize ticket prices using the law of supply and demand. Since not that many travelers know their exact itineraries well enough to buy airline tickets six months in advance of their departure, airline seats are widely available (i.e., not in demand) and priced cheaply to sell. As the travel date approaches, seats fill up as more and more passengers book that same flight. This reduction in the number of a given plane's available seats can be met with airfare increases for the few remaining seats or a more spacious aircraft. With demand increasing for a dwindling supply of airplane seats as the travel date approaches, the airfare becomes pricier the closer the flight's departure gets. But then there is the pricing of standby seats for people with flexible travel plans, which is a totally different matter. See Figure 6.2.

Security pricing follows the law of supply and demand as well. Changes in broad or specific conditions affecting a security's supply and demand cause its price to be fluid over time. If it is not broad forces like the economy, taxes, or regulation, it could be specific forces (or even rumors of them) like a company's earnings, new products, leadership or ownership changes, or resource availability that have been known to move a company's stock price higher or lower throughout the trading day.

The supply of a security is relatively fixed depending on the quantity offered for sale at any given point in time. For a security such as a company's stock, the number of outstanding shares made available for sale determines its supply. A company's decision to issue more common stock increases its supply and consequently dilutes the value of all outstanding shares. Similarly, the supply of an entity's bonds is based on the amount of debt issued by a company or government.

Demand for a security depends on all investors' purchase intentions denoted by buy orders, which may vary over time. The amount of demand for a security, such as a particular company's stock, relies on public perception of the issuing company's reputation and the potential for its current and future lineup of products or services to generate future earnings. A company's reputation is built on its ability to supply what its customers demand. Whether a company reacts nimbly and appropriately to changes in its business—be it something as fickle as changing consumer tastes or as catastrophic as a product recall—affects the public's perception of its place in the market and the demand for its stock. Security prices adjust continually in reaction to the ever-changing market conditions affecting the balance of supply and demand.

Efficient Market

A number of media sources provide continuous coverage of breaking business news and continuous access to company financial data. In an *efficient market*, the price of a given security is based on investors having access to all available information. In theory, rational buyers and sellers use this information to strike a deal on the price of the security. In reality, how investors use all of the available information determines their success.

Nobody can predict the future, but parties to a transaction probably have different views, whether right or wrong, of how a certain trade would fare in their favor. Armed with the same information, it must be their independent analyses (that presumably they do not share with each other) of the available information, or disregard thereof, that cause one party to buy and another to sell a security in an arm's-length transaction. Each of them entered into the trade with a motive to profit from it. Presumably the trade would not have been executed otherwise.

If the market were all that efficient, it would be futile to entertain thoughts of beating the market, especially after paying trading costs and any taxes on a transaction. To the delight of active fund managers banking their reputations on outperforming the market, the markets may not be all that efficient.

As human beings, investors tend to overreact or misjudge the impact of breaking news stories on a stock's price. A game-changing event may cause a stock price to fluctuate like an oscillating rubber band until it settles at a price, only to change again when the next news story comes along. With some notable exceptions, the existing level of efficiency in the markets has managed to work quite well in determining security prices in a free market.

Yet oversight appears to be required at times to keep the human element in check. To limit the human dimension from disrupting the markets, government regulators and professional standards boards promote market efficiency by establishing and enforcing standards as to a company's disclosure of public information. Oversight relating to corporate governance, accounting standards, information dissemination, insider trading restrictions, and other corporate behavior levels the playing field for all investors, big and small. Among other things, government regulations require simultaneous disclosure of public information to all parties. They also restrict company insiders from profiting on inside information not available to the general public.

Although modern communication transmission methods have better facilitated information dissemination among all investors, some investors still have better access to information. Certain groups, such as professional investors and insiders, have an edge over individual investors in their use of tools, talent, and time dedicated to obtain useful company-specific information and act on it before everyone else. An individual investor operates at a great disadvantage to a professional fund manager continually trolling company reports and the news services for information. Even individual investors with access to the information may not see it or may ignore it for one reason or another. If this describes you as an individual investor, you may want to steer clear of individual stocks and instead stick to investing in collective funds with at least some professional oversight, especially low-cost market index funds.

Fear and Greed

The market is driven by fear and greed. Consider the typical momentum investor endowed with the emotions of fear and greed, whose trades follow the momentum or direction of the market. When the market is up, greed causes momentum investors to pile on, buying stock in the hope of making a fortune. When the market drops, fear haunts momentum investors, causing them to flee the market by selling stock out of fear that they are going to lose what they had worked so hard to accumulate in the first place. If they are late enough into and out of the game, these momentum investors will lose their shirts by buying and selling at precisely the wrong times. They take losses by selling after the market has already dropped and forgo gains when they stay out of the market while the market advances. Alternatively, they buy after the market has already run up, only to suffer losses when the market declines. This herd mentality behavior is a recipe for disaster. These momentum plays by investors also cause stock prices to fluctuate and add to their risk.

On the other side, *contrarian* investors, with the same constitution of fear and greed, are snapping up stock when the market is down and unloading stock when the market is up. Their success comes from purchasing stock at low prices to create opportunities for gain and selling at high prices to lock in already accumulated gains. These emotions of fear and greed can wreak havoc on stock market volatility.

What would happen if investors bought instead of sold when the market dropped, and sold when the market rose? Stay tuned, for, as noted in Chapter 7, this contrarian view is the underpinning of the day trading strategy.

CONVENTIONAL WISDOM

Securities have been exchanged on open markets for years. Historical studies of the markets have led to the identification of some basic principles and trends useful to investors in allocating their investment holdings among different asset classes. These principles apply to all investments, both inside and outside of retirement savings accounts. Of most importance are long-term trends relating to the risk-reward relationship and the long-term performance of stocks that affect your investment and trading decisions.

Risk and Reward

Firefighters earn a good living. Their responsiveness to an incident depends on extensive preparation, physical conditioning, astute decision making, and pure guts. Their service in performing a dangerous job for their communities is highly regarded. Because many firefighters routinely put their lives at risk on the job, they are paid handsomely for it. All other things being the same, an equally qualified individual pursuing a less risky line of work—say, an office worker—would most likely receive less compensation than a firefighter. The higher pay firefighters receive compensates them for the extra risk they face in their job.

Fortunately, an investor is not risking life and limb by plunging into the markets. Instead an investor puts his or her future livelihood at risk. Just as people expect to be compensated well for taking on risk in their line of work, investors expect to be rewarded with higher returns for bearing risk in their investments. In the investor's mind, he or she may be willing to bear the risk of experiencing short-term setbacks in exchange for potentially higher long-term returns. The greater the risk a given investment presents, the higher potential return an investor will demand. Then it is up to the investor to gauge how much risk he or she is willing to bear for that potentially extra long-term return.

Chapter 4 presented a breakdown of the overall risk of a security into its component parts. The risk associated with each asset class is judged by its relative exposure to its underlying purchasing power risk, credit risk, interest rate risk, market risk, and specific risk. With the most exposure to more of these underlying risk components than the other asset classes, stocks represent the asset class with the highest overall risk or chance of loss. Bonds generally carry less risk than stocks. **Cash has the least risk of any of the asset classes.**

History bears evidence to this direct relationship between risk and return among the asset classes. Whether expressed in terms of a beta, standard deviation, or some other measure, a security's risk is based on the volatility of its investment returns. Counting dividends, investors in stocks (as measured by the S&P 500 index) over the 50-year period ended December 31, 2009, have enjoyed the highest average absolute return of 9.4 percent per year for assuming the greatest volatility of returns, ranging from 37.2 percent in 1995 to a negative 36.6 percent in 2008. Over this same 50-year period, long-term bonds (as measured by 10-year U.S. Treasury bonds) yielded an average annual return of 6.6 percent, with annual returns varying from 32.8 percent in 1982 to negative 11.1 percent in 2009. Finally, cash (as measured by three-month U.S. Treasury bills) generated an annual average return of 5.3 percent over this 50-year period, with annual returns falling between 14.3 percent in 1981 and 0.1 percent in 2009.[3] **True to its nature as the riskiest asset class with the highest volatility of investment returns, stocks have generated the best long-term investment returns of the three asset classes.**

A fund reduces its overall risk by investing in more than one security, regardless of whether its holdings are all of the same asset class or of different asset classes. When securities of different asset classes are blended into a balanced fund, the securities themselves as well as the relative weightings of the fund's holdings in stocks, bonds, and cash determine a fund's overall risk level.

Stocks for the Long Haul

Not only do stocks manage to outperform the other asset classes over the long term, but money invested in stocks has more than managed to retain its purchasing power over time. In an inflationary environment, the amount of money needed now to buy a loaf of bread at its current price will not be enough to buy a fresh loaf years later. However, long-term investments in a market basket of stocks have historically retained their purchasing power by generating returns that exceed inflation, thus allowing for that purchase of a fresh loaf of bread and more from your earlier investment.

Stocks have rewarded its owners the most of any asset classes for more than two centuries. Although the returns of all three asset classes have more than kept pace with inflation, stocks have performed the best over the long term. After adjusting for inflation, stocks have had an average inflation-adjusted annual return of 6.6 percent from 1802 through 2009. By comparison, bonds have yielded 3.6 percent and cash 2.8 percent real annual returns over this same period.

Some broad assumptions were used to compute these real rates of return where historical data were sometimes scanty. In viewing these comparative real returns net of inflation, you may note that stock investment returns reflect dividends and capital gains on a diversified portfolio of stocks; bond yields are based on long-term U.S. Treasury bonds, or, if not available, high-grade municipal bonds; and cash returns are based on short-term U.S. Treasury bonds or bills.

Not only have stock returns outpaced other asset classes over the past 200 years, but their returns have exceeded those of other asset classes over every period of at least 30 years, but one, since 1802.[4]

During this time, the United States and the world weathered all types of economic conditions ranging from outright depression to unsustainable, bloated expansion; uneven market conditions ranging from devastating crashes to irrational exuberance; and tragic events like world, civil, and cold wars as well as man-made and natural disasters. Not even 11 recessions since World War II could stall the superior long-term returns generated by stocks.

Keep in mind, though, that an investment in stock brings along the possibility that its performance may tumble at times. Stocks have not and probably will not outperform bonds and cash every year, nor should they be relied on to do so. Risk works both ways. Stock's short-term performance has run through giddy times as well as hit some rough patches. Indeed there have been some short and even prolonged periods in history when stocks lost ground to bonds or cash. However, history has shown that patience with holding stocks has reaped the rewards of higher returns over time.

If history holds true again, stock investment returns will continue to fluctuate over the short term but generate wealth over the long term. You may very well have to endure some short-term volatility for holding stock in order to garner its superior long-term investment returns over other asset classes. In short, stock's long-term track record of outperformance and hedge against inflation makes it a necessary component of every patient investor's portfolio.

RULES OF THUMB

People need to recognize their place in the world. Individual investors should be mindful of the size of their stash, in relation to the magnitude of the world's financial assets. In 2008, the world's financial assets amounted to \$178 trillion.[5] Unless you are in an elite class of Americans with a first or last name beginning with a *W*, or even having a *w* in it (as in William Gates, Warren Buffett, the Walton family, or Lawrence Ellison), there is a good chance your lot in life may not have much pull with the financial markets. Even if you were in the *W* class, you would still be hard-pressed to move the markets with your holdings of less than 0.03 percent of worldwide financial assets.[6]

Institutional investors are in a little better position to wield some power when it comes to influencing the market. Due to the size of their asset bases, institutional investors routinely trading securities in large lots can affect market prices. Their high-volume purchases and sales can significantly affect the supply of or demand for a given security and move its price as a result. The demand created by a mutual fund executing a large purchase order may bid up a security's price in order to obtain the requisite number of shares to meet the fund's objectives. Conversely, an institutional fund needing to sell a large number of stock shares may have to accept a lower price for flooding the market with an overabundant supply of shares it made available for sale. In turn, this lower price becomes the market price for the security. Yet even the assets held by the largest institutional fund manager constitute less than 2 percent of financial assets in the world, which limits even their impact on the overall market.[7]

If the big players cannot significantly affect the market, the little guy does not stand much of a chance, either. The typical individual investor trading in small lots does not really carry enough clout to affect the market, or even a single security's market price, in any meaningful way. As an individual investor, you need to recognize that you are only a passenger along for a ride on the market roller coaster. As your therapist or trusted adviser may tell you, if you cannot control the situation at hand, at least you can control your reaction to the situation. Make sure your portfolio holdings are structured so as to put you in a position to participate in market advances while managing your exposure to risk.

Short of predicting future gyrations in the market, history does provide some general guidance in the form of rules of thumb useful in structuring a portfolio to generate the highest return for a given amount of risk. Once you buckle up for your ride on the market, you can make the most of your investments and trades by following these time-tested principles. Your investment success will depend on undertaking a disciplined approach involving asset diversification, patience, risk management, expense control, and tax efficiency. The day trading strategy also draws from these principles to generate additional returns in an uncertain market.

Diversify

People are unpredictable. As market participants, their unpredictable behavior affects security prices overall, as well as their own individual investment performance. Their different needs, desires, and dreams cause market volatility. So much is at stake when it comes to harnessing market volatility that vast armies of brilliant scholars and investment professionals devote countless hours analyzing market behavior to make some sense of it all. Their research has spawned fields of study devoted to behavioral finance and many sophisticated models that attempt to explain why the markets act as they do. From these efforts comes one universal finding that is useful for managing risk as it relates to the pooling of securities: **Asset diversification through pooling of securities in different asset classes and pooling of different securities within the same asset class can reduce a portfolio's risk.**

It really is not wise to put all your eggs in one basket, as the saying goes, since different asset classes have different risk characteristics. *Diversification* calls for a strategic allocation of your assets among asset classes. No, it is not like spreading peanut butter on every surface that sticks—you should not be equally allocating your retirement savings among all available plan funds. Since most fund options tend to be stock funds, you would probably end up with a greater degree of exposure to stocks than you realize or need. Rather, portfolio diversification among asset classes strives to strike a balance among stocks' capital appreciation and inflation protection, bonds' stability and income generation, and cash's liquidity and capital preservation qualities.

Most investment advisers wisely suggest that you invest your retirement savings for the long term in a diversified portfolio of stocks, bonds, and cash. This time-tested investment strategy tends to balance the underlying risk characteristics of each asset class. By its nature, a mutual fund embodies this diversification concept by holding a collection of securities that, in turn, tends to stabilize fund returns.

For someone seeking the benefit of portfolio diversification, the use of a hierarchical investment process may be suitable. In this situation, an investor allocates a portion of assets to each asset class. In a retirement savings account, this process takes the form of selecting from the plan's available fund options to fill the target asset allocation for each asset class. The question then becomes how much to dedicate to each asset class, which will be addressed later on in this chapter.

Although diversification provided through the pooling of securities generally reduces a portfolio's risk, a consistent approach involving some long-term exposure to stocks is key to a successful investment strategy.

Invest for the Long Term

Stocks are an essential, but risky, holding in every portfolio. Stocks' outperformance compared to other asset classes just does not occur overnight or every night. It takes time. You have seen that investors holding on to stocks over time earn superior returns over other asset classes. To experience the magic of stocks' superior returns requires an investor to take a long-term perspective toward managing an asset portfolio. Stock investments also provide the best hedge against inflation in addition to their potential for long-term capital appreciation. The patience required to obtain the extra returns offered by stocks makes them a perfect component of a retirement savings account, which, by design is not to be drawn upon for years.

Investing for the long term applies not only to stocks, but also to your entire portfolio. Chasing higher returns through frequent trading into and out of asset classes, as well as different funds within the same asset class, is not contemplated as part of a sound long-term investment strategy. Yet depending on market conditions, some type of periodic portfolio adjustments may be not only acceptable but advisable. Moderation is key in that trading costs and taxes would eat away at any gains generated by more frequent trading in a regular brokerage account.

By definition, long-term investing eliminates or reduces the need to buy and sell securities. In view of the brokerage commissions normally charged upon purchase and sale of securities, an investor or a fund with lower portfolio turnover resulting from long-term investing will incur lower trading costs. In a personal account, you pay your own way for trades and consequently incur lower trading costs for fewer purchase and sale transactions. Under a 401(k) plan, a fund with lower turnover passes along its lower trading costs to all shareholders proportionately. Participant accounts are generally not charged for normal fund exchanges that may or may not increase fund turnover.

Long-term investing also implies fewer security sales that could cause the realization of capital gains subject to immediate taxation in a regular brokerage account. Outside of a 401(k) account, less immediate tax is incurred under a long-term investment approach where securities are sold infrequently.

From a tax perspective, the holding period for an investment within a 401(k) account does not matter all that much. Short- and long-term capital gains and other income within a retirement savings account are taxed as ordinary income, but not until their receipt in cash as a plan distribution.

Fund switching frequency is where day trading differs profoundly from long-term investing—day trading relies on daily transfers between funds of different asset classes. Those switches set up or capture gains from a shaky stock market every day in a retirement savings account.

Investing for the long term also involves the sustained application of a well-thought-out process in managing your portfolio. Frequent changes in approach are not contemplated here. Day trading shares this long-term perspective. **Value is created through the sustained application of day trading a retirement savings portfolio over time.**

Patience is indeed a virtue. If good things come to those who wait, better things come to those who relentlessly pursue a worthwhile goal through a sustained effort using a well-thought-out approach. So it is with investing and trading a retirement savings portfolio. Once you set your sights on a goal, you need to implement a strategy and follow it through on a sustained basis until reaching that goal.

Remember that investing is for the long term, and trading is here and now. When not involved in day trading, investment holdings will continue to benefit from a long-term perspective applied to the management of a retirement portfolio.

Sometimes investors alter their desired asset mix to accommodate changes in personal circumstances or economic conditions. For instance, when a participant's investment horizon shortens as retirement approaches, a shift to a more conservative asset mix may be appropriate. To accommodate such a shift to more conservative holdings in a retirement savings portfolio, a 401(k) participant would execute fund exchanges from stock-heavy funds to funds with more bonds and cash.

Reduce Risk with Age

Life presents every individual with a series of transitions from one phase to another. A hippie (helper in promoting peaceful individual existence) guy grows into a yuppie (young urban professional), who settles down into a DINC (dual income, no children) couple, before becoming part of a MWC (married with children) family, and finally retiring to a life of golf and lunch with his ROMEO (retired old men eating out) crowd. With each passing phase, an aging investor needs to recognize that liquidity and security take on paramount importance in structuring a portfolio.

Young folks generally have a long time horizon when it comes to investing retirement savings. In theory, they should have no need to access their retirement savings during their accumulation. A need to draw retirement income from a 401(k) account is a distant, if not remote, event to a 35-year-old planning to retire at age 65. With such a long investment horizon, a young investor can afford to invest in an asset mix with more risk and potential for higher investment returns. There is plenty of time to recover from any short-term setbacks in more aggressive investments before needing to draw on accumulated savings for retirement income.

Young investors can take on a higher degree of risk by holding more stocks than other asset classes within their portfolios. History has shown that the additional risk of holding a heavier weighting of stocks is rewarded with higher portfolio returns over the long run. Patience and a long investment horizon become of paramount importance to attaining these better long-term returns afforded by stocks.

On the flip side, an older investor with a short investment horizon needs to take a conservative approach to investing. A recent retiree or one nearing retirement is more concerned with a portfolio's liquidity and ability to preserve capital than prospects of higher long-term investment performance. Green bananas are no longer on his shopping list. He is ready to get this party started and enjoy life now. Such a short-term investor may not be able to weather a temporary dip in the market when approaching or in retirement. Drawing down retirement savings at the wrong time in the market cycle (i.e., when the market is down) can be devastating to a retirement portfolio, in that account balances already eroded by poor investment performance are further depleted by drawdowns for support in retirement. Withdrawals in a down market put a permanent dent in a retirement portfolio by removing capital upon which future investment earnings otherwise may have accrued. These withdrawals and their forgone future investment earnings are lost forever, thereby hampering any chance that an eventual recovery in the market would fully restore this depleted retirement portfolio base to the level needed to sustain the retiree's previously projected retirement income.

In short, an individual's investment time horizon should serve as the basis for determining personal risk tolerance. The longer the time until retirement, the more an investor can afford to take on risk in the form of a higher concentration in stocks in a retirement savings portfolio. Younger investors in the accumulation phase have a long investment horizon during which they can tolerate higher risk. The shorter investment time horizon of an older investor calls for an investment mix with less risk. **With age, an investor's portfolio risk should be gradually decreased by reducing the portfolio's exposure to stocks in favor of bonds and cash.**

Once you settle on an appropriate level of risk in your portfolio, you need to monitor and manage the expenses extracted from each of the fund options in which your retirement savings accounts are invested.

Manage Expenses

Individual investors often do not get what they pay for. You can blame it on the high fees they pay, which in turn have to do with the way they shop for investment products. That old scream on the radio of "Books cost too much in San Francisco (or name your city here)" from the hawker advertising the now-defunct Crown Books retail chain applies also equally to investment expenses. Investments cost too much.

Whether investing through a retirement savings plan or an adviser, investors are presented with a limited selection of products with somewhat obscure disclosures. It is no wonder that investors sometimes forget to inquire about how much investment products actually cost. Then trading and management costs are collected discreetly before any investment earnings get to shareholders. So individual investors end up paying too much.

In order for investors to increase their chances of success in investing, they need to better manage their portfolio's investment expenses. This involves paying attention to the nature and amount of the different types of expenses charged in the course of buying, holding, and selling an investment. Only then can investors control their investment expenses.

Managing investment expenses essentially involves the selection of cost-effective investment options and control of transaction costs.

Select Cost-Effective Investment Options   A cost-effective investment offers the same or better investment performance than another higher-cost alternative. For investing in a retirement savings plan, it is important to consider the expenses associated with investing your account in the different investment options as well as their potential to meet your investment objectives. First, it is important to have available a wide selection of low-cost and high-performing investment options, which may involve accounts under both current and prior employers' plans. Then any decision to consolidate retirement savings accounts would consider the costs of the alternative existing and prospective investment choice platforms. Determining the cost-effectiveness of available investment options then includes an assessment of factors, such as whether the investment performance of an actively managed fund justifies its extra cost over that of a passively managed fund.

You Could Stand Pat   If you find yourself participating in a great 401(k) plan with a good fund selection and low costs, why not keep that account open when you change employers? Feelings aside, you can rest assured that, by law, your former employer may not touch your account, set aside in an irrevocable trust, for any other purpose than to pay plan benefits and expenses. There is nothing that requires you to transfer your account out of a former employer's plan unless you have reached age $70^1/_2$ (in which case you may need to begin receiving retirement distributions), or your account balance is less than \$5,000 (in which case your account may be automatically distributed to you without your consent).

Sure, a consolidated account statement summarizing your retirement savings account balances may sound enticing. Yet before you decide whether to consolidate accounts, you should weigh the relative advantages of the old and new plans. On the one hand, a rollover into your current employer's plan, but not an IRA, may offer access to more cash within your account through a loan, whereas a former employer's plan typically would not. On the other hand, retaining your account in a former employer's larger plan offering a variety of index and other good fund options subject to lower institutional-class fees may be a better alternative than transferring it to an IRA or your current employer's plan that may be subject to retail pricing. Also, an extra account in a former employer's plan will come in handy when employing the day trading strategy, as you will see later in Chapter 8.

When considering whether to roll over a distribution from a former employer's retirement savings plan, you should compare the former plan's features, fees, and potential fund performance offered under its menu of investment options with those of the prospective recipient plan. You need to decide whether account consolidation is worth giving up the fund option menu and fee structure applicable to investments under your former employer's plan.

Consider Passively Managed Funds   Whereas passively managed funds look to match a given market index, actively managed funds strive to beat the market through security selection and market timing. The opportunity to seek potentially market-beating returns in an actively managed fund generally comes at a greater cost to an investor than to settle for almost market-matching returns in a passively managed fund. Yet studies have found that 80 percent of mutual funds, most of which are actively managed, have underperformed the broad market over the past 15 years. Often it is the higher expenses themselves that prevent an actively managed fund's net returns from beating its passively managed brethren. When you also consider that most actively managed funds underperform the broad market over the long term, the average actively managed fund is not worth the extra cost. **Not only do actively managed funds cost more than passively managed funds, but studies show that most actively managed funds also underperform the broad market over the long term.**

As caretaker for your future way of life, you have the responsibility to invest in the best funds that will help you meet your savings goals. Although there are some exceptions, it is your call to decide whether the actively managed fund you are considering for investment of your retirement savings is just another subpar fund charging additional fees or a potential winner that can consistently beat the market. If you are willing to forgo the potential extra return and risk of an actively managed fund, you may conclude that the market returns offered by a passively managed fund with its lower fees are right for you.

If inconsistent investment performance is not enough to steer you away from actively managed funds into passively managed funds, consider the additional expense charged by actively managed funds. Although the difference in average expense ratios between actively and passively managed funds is nearly 0.5 percent, the actual expense difference between funds can vary dramatically. Fund expense ratios can range from a few basis points (hundredths of a percent) for institutional market index funds to over 2 percent per year for actively managed stock funds. These investment expenses are charged against fund balances each year regardless of whether the fund generates a profit. The drag on an account balance from the accumulation of these expense charges over time can be quite dramatic. An initial balance of $100,000 earning a net annual rate of 5 percent under a passively managed fund would grow to $703,999 in 40 years. That same $100,000 earning a net annual rate of only 4.5 percent under a similarly constituted but actively managed fund would grow to only $581,636 in 40 years. Assuming the 0.5 percent difference in annual return is attributable to the extra expense of investing in an actively managed fund rather than a passively managed fund, the resulting actively managed fund account falls short of the passively managed fund account by $122,363 (= $703,999 − $581,636). If the actively managed fund's return were instead 3 percent, or 2 percent less than the passively managed fund's return of 5 percent, its shortfall would be $377,795 after 40 years. That is quite a drag.

Passively managed market index funds provide the opportunity to mimic the market's performance at minimal expense. **The low cost of a passively managed stock index fund that tracks the market's performance makes it an attractive component of any retirement savings account.**

Steer Clear of Transaction Fees   Some investments carry the burden of some sort of charge for brokerage commissions and other trading costs. The astute investor will minimize these trading costs and avoid entering into certain other types of transactions that attract extra or unnecessary fees. If you are aware of the types of situations where transaction fees may be levied, you may avoid falling into their traps. In addition to paying a share of a fund's overall trading costs, you as a retirement savings plan participant may bear additional charges for any excessive trading or for a loan initiation on your part.

Trading Costs   The first area of investment expense management over which an investor has direct control relates to the volume of investment transactions on which trading fees are charged. Any trade in a normal brokerage account or within a plan's self-directed brokerage account is charged directly to the investor making the trade. Thus an investor limiting such trades incurs fewer trading costs.

In mutual funds and other funds within a retirement savings plan, overall trading costs are spread proportionately to fund holders based on their account balances. **The forced sharing of a fund's trading costs enables you to perform fund exchanges at no direct cost.** Instead, any trading costs attributable to your fund exchange are shared with your fellow fund holders. Likewise, next time another participant makes a fund exchange, you and fellow fund holders will bear any trading costs associated with that fund exchange.

Short-Term Trading Fees   As will be more fully discussed in Chapter 8, some stock funds assess a short-term trading fee upon redemption of shares held less than a specified period such as 90 days. These fees discourage trades into and out of such stock funds within a short period. You can avoid these short-term trading fees by not performing such exchanges within the same plan.

Loan Fees   If you must take a loan from your retirement savings account, note that loans typically involve initiation and ongoing maintenance fees charged to your account. Since such loan fees are assessed for each loan, your best cost-containment strategy would be to avoid entering into a loan in the first place, or alternatively, to minimize the number of loans outstanding at any one time.

Watch Out for Taxes

The tax treatment afforded any particular security should never drive your decision as to whether to own it. The issuing company's long-term prospects for earnings potential and how the underlying security fits within your objectives should be your primary considerations in deciding which securities are deserving of your investment. Nevertheless, a security's tax treatment often comes into play as part of the investment selection process. Taxes also influence whether an investment should be made either inside or outside of a tax-deferred retirement savings account.

In a taxable account where earnings are subject to immediate taxation, you need to consider the taxes associated with different types of investment earnings. Capital gains are not taxed until realized, and only then, if held for at least one year, they are taxed at lower rates than ordinary income. For tax purposes, you may prefer investments, such as growth stocks, offering potential for capital appreciation that are taxed when sold rather than those, such as bonds, paying taxable dividends each year. If you are in a high income tax bracket, you may also want to invest a portion of your taxable portfolio in tax-preferred investments, such as municipal bonds whose dividends are not subject to taxation.

In a retirement savings account where investment earnings are not taxed until distribution, you should invest in the funds that will generate the most earnings, regardless of whether the earnings come in the form of capital gains, dividends, or other income. Upon distribution, all earnings will generally be taxed as ordinary income. Therefore, the key investment objective in a retirement savings account should be to maximize earnings potential. The generally lower returns and tax-exempt status of municipal bond dividends would be wasted in a retirement savings plan where all earnings are taxed upon distribution.

Using these rules of thumb as underlying tenets, it then becomes necessary to formulate a specific strategy for managing your retirement savings accounts.

ALTERNATIVE INVESTMENT STRATEGIES

To some extent, an investment strategy relies on the systematic application of the foregoing rules of thumb based on conventional wisdom collected from years of experience with market economics. The best investment strategy guides an investor in optimally allocating assets among available investment options for the best returns within the constraints of the investor's objectives.

In managing your investments, you need to take a holistic approach encompassing all of your financial assets. Consider all financial assets held under your control, whether in taxable accounts or in tax-deferred retirement savings accounts. Then, to keep it simple, deal only with financial assets that are easy to value, such as stocks, bonds, and cash in bank, brokerage, and retirement savings accounts. Consistent with this streamlined approach, other less liquid and harder to value financial assets, such as options, derivatives, and limited partnerships, are left out of this exercise. Also, liquidity-challenged hard assets, such as real estate, cars, boats, and furnishings, are excluded from consideration.

Once you have identified all of your household's classifiable financial assets (and gained the necessary permission to manage them), you need to take an aggregate view in managing your portfolio. You measure how well diversified your portfolio is by the relative weighting of your aggregate holdings in taxable and tax-deferred accounts that are held in each asset class. The allocation of your holdings in any one particular account among asset classes does not matter as much as the allocation of your aggregate holdings. The quality of the holdings does indeed matter, though. You should make sure that your assets are invested in the best securities available that meet your objectives.

Investment strategies come in different varieties as to the levels of personal involvement and sophistication. At one extreme, you can manage your own investment portfolio, and at the other you can leave it to others. Do-it-yourself approaches run the gamut from outright neglect to overarching tinkering. Alternatively, you can put your investment strategy on autopilot by enlisting the support of an outside adviser.

Some strategies work better than others, depending on an investor's inclination, dedication, and background. Following are brief descriptions of five of the most commonly used investment strategies employed by individual investors. These strategies offer attributes valuable to day trading.

Three of the investment strategies (buy-and-hold, rebalancing, and market timing) deal with existing assets in a portfolio. Whereas a buy-and-hold investor pretty much relies on inertia, an investor who rebalances makes periodic portfolio adjustments in response to changing market and other conditions. Under a shorter-term strategy known as market timing, investors seek to capitalize on temporary swings in the market. The fourth strategy, dealing with regular purchases of the sort made from payroll contributions, is dollar-cost averaging. If these strategies do not fit your interest or inclination, you can always rely on a fifth strategy of seeking outside investment advice in the form of prepackaged funds of funds or personalized account management.

Buy-and-Hold

As with your spouse, your best investment is one that you intend to have and to hold for a long time, or so some say. Your best chance of picking a winner comes when you or your adviser do your homework to research the background of a prospective investment before making the plunge. As an astute investor, you are looking for solid company management, vision, strategy, track record, execution, and product lines indicating good long-term prospects before investing. If you are a buy-and-hold investor, you purchase a security with the intention of staying with it for the duration. Once you pull the trigger, you are going to sit and watch your investment grow, or not. You set and forget it.

In the real world, how an investor ends up using the buy-and-hold strategy is a little less straightforward. Whereas choice creates opportunities for sellers, more choices create anxiety for buyers. People have trouble making decisions about everyday life, let alone investing their retirement savings. Investing is hard enough for the pros. Not only do you have to know what securities to buy, but you also have to know when to buy and sell them. If you feel that way, you are in good company. As noted earlier, a 2008 survey found that 81 percent of employers cited where to invest 401(k) plan assets as a confusing aspect to their employees.[8] So many individual investors take buy-and-hold investing to an extreme by doing nothing—they are paralyzed by their own inertia. These people are like ostriches when it comes to retirement planning, preferring to bury their heads in the sand. If they do not check their account statements, it does not feel like they lost or made money. They are the ultimate buy-and-hold investors. Life goes on.

Inertia paralysis, an affliction prevalent in many buy-and-hold investors, strikes the type of person who balks when it comes time to deal with change, especially one dealing with personal investments. If their original investment election was good enough back when they joined the plan, it must still be good today. They may have decided, or had it decided for them if they joined the plan by default, to allocate their contributions to one or more funds and left their balances there to accumulate without any further direction. Never mind that time marches on, and investment options, market conditions, and personal circumstances change. Eventually the mix of their assets may very well become quite different from the original allocation designated in their contribution elections due to the differing investment performances of the various funds selected. Nevertheless they are sticking by that original investment election and committing to a course of sitting on the resulting portfolio, however that may turn out. They justify their neglect by saying they just do not have the time, interest, or expertise to make investment decisions.

Whether caused by inertia paralysis or not, the buy-and-hold approach appears to be the investment strategy of choice for most retirement savings plan participants. The overwhelming majority of participants exhibit very little, if any, interest in managing their retirement savings plan accounts, as shown by fewer than one in seven defined contribution plan participants making any fund exchange during 2009.

Not only does a buy-and-hold investment strategy minimize trading and its attendant commissions, but sometimes its aversion from trading also protects investors from their restless selves. It turns out that an investor's failure to decide is not necessarily a decision to fail. One study found that over the 20-year period ended December 31, 2009, individual investors in stock mutual funds earned an annual average return of just 3.2 percent compared with an 8.2 percent return that they could have earned by sitting on an investment in a fund (without expenses) tracking the S&P 500 index.[9] Instead of taking the trouble to make some ill-timed trades, the average investor could have enjoyed better investment performance by letting it ride in a market index fund. It turns out that the major source of the average mutual fund investor's shortfall resulted from putting money in and pulling it out of a fund at the wrong times, although picking subpar funds and paying too much in expenses also plays a part.

Successful investing in the long run still depends on how the portfolio stands up to continuously changing market conditions over the course of its initial investment, holding period, and eventual distribution. With your lifestyle in retirement hanging in the balance, you need to pay attention to the investment of your retirement savings portfolio. There are no investment Mulligans, or do-overs (at least for the little guy).

Even if you intend to stay the course with your investments, you should periodically monitor your holdings to see if they still meet your objectives. If not, a change in course may be necessary. Especially if you automatically joined the plan by default, you may want to review whether the initial contribution investment election made for you by default meets your current objectives. If your objectives change, you may want to reallocate your current account holdings as well as revise your investment election relating to future plan contributions.

Many investors go into an investment with the best of intentions to hold on to it for the long term. This requires discipline, detachment, or apathy. The buy-and-hold approach is but one investment strategy, and it may not be suitable for everybody. Among the reasons an investor may not want to stick with a buy-and-hold approach are: (1) it is boring, (2) economic conditions and personal circumstances change, and (3) investment advisers paid on a commission basis for trades may discourage it. So when conditions change, investors and their advisers wanting some action may decide to move on to something else.

Rebalancing

Balance is a subjective term when used to refer to lifestyle. An assessment of personal balance requires introspection of one's priorities. When it comes to work-life balance, one employee may consider her life to be balanced if she can work out for an hour before a 10-hour workday. Another employee may consider his life to be in balance if he can get home from work in time to eat dinner with his family. Balance can mean different things to different people.

Asset diversification provides balance to a portfolio by reducing its risk with stable fixed income investments while enabling growth through exposure to stocks. Optimal diversification potentially brings capital accumulation, all the while providing a buffer from losses on some investment holdings with gains from others. A diversified portfolio composed of stocks, bonds, and cash in the right proportions strikes a balance between risk and reward. Just what are the right proportions depends on an individual's risk tolerance, investment horizon, and objectives. A portfolio with a heavier weighting in stocks than bonds may be appropriate for a younger dude's long investment horizon, whereas one with less stocks and more bonds may be appropriate for older folks' peace of mind. There is no one right answer for everybody.

Over time, changing market conditions may cause an investor's actual asset mix to stray from its original blend. To *rebalance* an existing portfolio involves making an adjustment to right the portfolio to its desired mix of assets. Broken down into its component parts, rebalancing on a periodic basis involves the classification of portfolio assets, determination of a target asset allocation, and execution of periodic fund transfers.

Classification of Assets   Think back to the time you were tooling down the turnpike only to feel your car heaving up and down with each passing road marker. Once your cursing subsided, you vaguely recalled jumping that curb the previous day to avoid an oncoming car on your turn into the coffee shop's parking lot. Although your quick reaction may have avoided a collision yesterday, you were now thinking more about what was wrong here. So you pulled over to check your tires, only to find all four wheels still intact. Finally, the car doctor in you took over to diagnose a misalignment of the wheels, requiring a treatment of rebalancing at the shop.

Even if this road mishap never happened to you, you must realize that just as your ride's changes call for rebalancing, market changes necessitate portfolio rebalancing. Before you can determine whether your portfolio requires rebalancing at a particular point in time, you need to know what you have. A periodic comparison of your actual asset mix with your target asset allocation will determine when rebalancing is necessary.

To get a complete picture of your portfolio, you would need to aggregate all household assets. These household assets would include homes, cars, savings accounts, brokerage accounts, and retirement savings accounts held by you and your spouse or partner. Practically speaking, though, you are not going to sell a piece of your home or car if its value appreciates as rebalancing would require. So you will be left to parsing through account statements to determine your portfolio's current mix of financial assets among the asset classes. Rebalancing involves adjusting the mix of assets only within the financial accounts of your household when they run astray of your target asset allocation. It is this existing mix of assets in your household's financial accounts that will determine whether any trades or fund exchanges are necessary to rebalance your portfolio back to your target asset allocation.

The process of rebalancing a portfolio considers all of an investor's household assets in taxable and tax-deferred financial accounts. Of course, the tax preference of an account matters. However, the

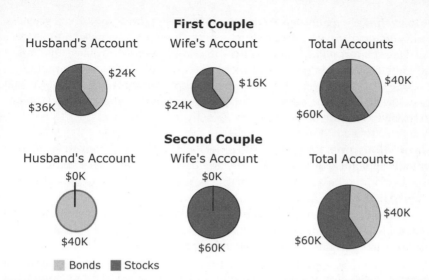

FIGURE 6.3 Aggregated Household Accounts with Same 60/40 Stocks-to-Bonds Split

asset mix in an individual account by itself does not matter, except to the extent of its effect on the asset mix of the entire household portfolio. As long as the aggregate portfolio, and not necessarily each of the individual accounts of which it is composed is balanced, the benefits of asset diversification reduce the risk of the portfolio.

Consider two couples, each with $100,000 saved in 401(k) plans (see Figure 6.3). With the first couple, the husband has $36,000 in stocks and $24,000 in bonds in his 401(k) account, and his wife has $24,000 in stocks and $16,000 in bonds in her 401(k) account. If they have no other savings, the first couple's household portfolio is equally balanced to that of a second couple, where the husband has a 401(k) account of $40,000 invested entirely in bonds, and his wife has her 401(k) account of $60,000 invested entirely in stocks. By aggregating their accounts, you will find that both couples maintain a split of 60 percent, or $60,000, in stocks and 40 percent, or $40,000, in bonds.

Target Asset Allocation As an investor, you need to determine, perhaps with some help from an adviser, how much of your household financial assets to allocate to each asset class. This target asset allocation sets the desired percentage of your portfolio's assets to be devoted to each asset class within the framework of your risk tolerance, investment time horizon, and savings goals. Rebalancing comes into play when adjustments are required to modify the holdings in your existing portfolio to meet your target asset allocation. These adjustments take the form of periodic trades or fund exchanges made at your discretion to bring the assets in your household's financial accounts into alignment with your target asset allocation.

The desired mix of a portfolio's assets among asset classes is generally defined in terms of a set of fixed percentages or floating percentages that vary by age. By rebalancing, you keep your portfolio properly balanced by staying aligned with a target asset allocation based on a static or age-based model.

Static Allocation Portfolio   An asset portfolio that retains a fixed percentage allocation of stocks, bonds, and cash over time has a static allocation. Periodic rebalancing ensures that its asset mix does not vary from the original fixed target allocation among asset classes.

Recently the aggregate value of stocks as a percentage of all financial assets in the world has been between 60 and 70 percent.[10] The remaining 30 to 40 percent is composed of fixed income securities (bonds and cash). Then it should come as no surprise that the most common target asset allocation for a static balanced portfolio does not diverge much from this range by being in the neighborhood of 60 percent stocks and 40 percent fixed income securities, such as bonds and cash. In keeping the asset mix consistent with the market, this 60/40 blend combines the potential for long-term appreciation of stocks with the lower risk of bonds and cash. In this blend, most of the fixed income securities are bonds, with the remainder going toward just enough cash to satisfy liquidity needs, such as for an impending loan or withdrawal.

Although the asset class allocations in a static allocation portfolio are intended to be unwavering, advisers and investors sometimes tend to modify their recommended portfolio allocations based on market momentum and conditions. A momentum shift to overweighting in stocks after the stock market has risen or to underweighting after stocks have fallen is usually a losing proposition and defeats the purpose of a static balanced portfolio. The discipline of adhering to the fixed percentage allocation is key to realizing the benefits of the static balanced portfolio approach.

The absence of change in the asset allocation percentages within a static balanced portfolio makes necessary portfolio adjustments simple and easy to track. Whereas rebalancing may be used to maintain an existing portfolio's static target asset mix under changing investment conditions, a portfolio overhaul involving a reallocation of existing assets may be necessary to accommodate a new target asset allocation. Another type of balanced portfolio shifts to a more conservative asset mix over time as an investor ages and approaches retirement.

Age-Based Balanced Portfolio   As noted earlier, conventional wisdom suggests that the amount of risk an investor should bear in a portfolio is directly related to his or her investment time horizon. Whereas a young investor has the benefit of time to wait out temporary setbacks that may result from an aggressive asset mix, an older investor cannot afford to take on risk that could irreparably harm an investment portfolio at the time it is needed for support in retirement. The almost retired or already retired investor's shortened investment horizon calls for a reduced amount of portfolio risk and consequently less exposure to stocks.

Unlike a static allocation portfolio, the target asset allocation in an age-based balanced portfolio drifts over time from an aggressive to a more conservative blend. The degree of the portfolio's conservative asset allocation at any particular time depends on the investor's time horizon until drawdowns for support begin at retirement. Although an investor's portfolio risk exposure should be based more on proximity to retirement, the most common floating target asset allocation is based on an investor's age.

Under the Rule of 100, an investor would allocate to fixed income holdings (bonds and cash) a percentage of the portfolio assets equal to the investor's age. Then the remainder of the portfolio would be invested in stocks. Therefore, the target asset allocation percentage of the investor's portfolio invested in bonds and cash would be the investor's current age, and for stocks it would be the difference between 100 and the investor's age. This Rule of 100 can be summarized as follows:

Portfolio's Percentage Invested in Bonds and Cash = Current Age

Portfolio's Percentage Invested in Stocks = 100 − Current Age

Under this simple rule, a 35-year-old investor would have 35 percent of his or her portfolio invested in bonds and cash, with the remaining 65 (= 100 − 35) percent invested in stocks. Table 6.2 depicts the investment allocations applicable under the Rule of 100 for investors of different ages.

Recognizing that people do not always retire at a fixed age such as 65, an age-based balanced portfolio should more appropriately reflect an investor's time until retirement. The Rule of 100 uses age as an acceptable substitute for investment horizon.

TABLE 6.2 Rule of 100 Target Asset Allocation

	Percentage of Portfolio Invested In	
Age	Bonds and Cash	Stocks
25	25%	75%
35	35	65
45	45	55
55	55	45
65	65	35
75	75	25

In a bullish stock market environment, it is not uncommon to find advisers who recommend a higher concentration of stocks (and consequently less in bonds and cash), such as what a Rule of 120 would accomplish. A Rule of 120 would allocate to stocks a percentage equal to the difference between 120 and the investor's age, with the rest going to bonds and cash. As with other investment strategies, an age-based target asset allocation approach requires disciplined portfolio monitoring and periodic rebalancing on the part of the investor to keep the asset mix in line with the specified portfolio allocation guidelines. For a more relaxed approach, an investor could consider prepackaged target-date funds or personalized investment advice.

Periodic Fund Transfers   Think of rebalancing as a lifestyle issue. Fat is good when it relates to investment portfolios, but is not so good for one's health or image. Look, but do not stare, at the chubby guy who sits at his desk all day constantly munching on junk food. Before he knows it, his snack consumption causes his body fat to grow faster than the rest of his body parts. Thus his body fat becomes a larger percentage of his body weight. Politely he may be considered overweight. Next check out his petite lady friend—again, no staring—who runs 10 miles a day while sustaining herself on a strict diet of figs and vegetables. Over time, her sacrifice will hopefully result in a leaner frame, reducing her body fat as a percentage of her body weight. When she reaches a size 0, she would love to be called underweight.

Asset classes, too, grow at different rates. When a portfolio's securities in one asset class grow faster than those in another, it is possible that a portfolio's asset mix gets out of kilter from its original or desired allocation. When one asset class grows to a larger percentage of the portfolio than the original target asset allocation over time, it is considered *overweight*. Similarly, an asset class becomes *underweight* when it constitutes less of the portfolio than it used to. An overweight or underweight state may result from an imbalance of earnings or cash flows among the asset classes within a portfolio.

Securities in different asset classes invariably grow at different rates, causing a balanced portfolio's asset mix held in each asset class to change from its original percentage allocation. As asset classes become overweight or underweight when compared with the original or target allocation, a balanced portfolio's assets need to be periodically shifted to restore the original or target asset class allocation percentages.

Portfolio rebalancing fixes the overweighting in one or more asset classes relative to the underweighting in others caused by the asset classes' different investment returns over time. The periodic trades or fund exchanges involved in rebalancing get the asset mix back to where you want it. Rebalancing captures some gains from the sale of asset class(es) whose securities have become expensive due to a run-up in prices to invest in other asset class(es) with relatively cheaper security prices because of lower returns. In a rebalancing fund exchange, you are selling some of your holdings in one asset class at a high price and reinvesting the proceeds in another lower-priced asset class.

The shift of assets from an overweight asset class to an underweight asset class through rebalancing captures gains from the sale of the faster-increasing asset class's securities for use in setting up future gains to come from an increased investment in a previously lower-performing asset class's securities.

Suppose an investor decides to hold 60 percent of a $100,000 portfolio in stocks and 40 percent in bonds. If stocks grow by 14 percent and bonds grow by 4 percent during a year, the stock portion of the investor's portfolio has grown to $68,400 (= 0.6 × $100,000 × 1.14), and the bond portion has grown to $41,600 (= 0.4 × $100,000 × 1.04). The value of the entire portfolio, $110,000 (= $68,400 + $41,600), at the end of the year is now invested about 62 percent in stocks and 38 percent in bonds. To rebalance to the original 60/40 stocks-to-bonds split, the investor would need to shift $2,400 (= $68,400 − 0.6 × $110,000) from stocks to bonds. Then the investor's portfolio would be rebalanced to the original 60/40 split with $66,000 (= $68,400 − $2,400) in stocks and $44,000 (= $41,600 + $2,400) in bonds.

Rebalancing is a fairly simple process when allocating assets among fund options that are each composed of holdings in only one asset class. In such a case, rebalancing involves making fund transfers out of overweight funds and into underweight funds so as to restore the original target asset allocation. This exercise becomes a bit more complicated when a participant has holdings in funds composed of more than one asset class. It then becomes necessary to sort out each fund's holdings by asset class and make any necessary fund transfers based on the funds' compositions to achieve the desired balance. To ease this process, some 401(k) administrators offer a feature that facilitates periodic fund rebalancing on an automatic basis when a participant's actual asset allocation gets out of kilter from its intended target allocation. Whatever you do, keep it simple.

Fund managers automatically perform this rebalancing process on a periodic basis for investors in their premixed balanced funds. Most investment advisers counsel their clients to rebalance their portfolios at least annually, if not more frequently. One such adviser advertises that he cozies up to his wife each year on their wedding anniversary to annually review and rebalance their combined retirement portfolios. Apparently they need more balance in their lives.

Market Timing

Conventional investment strategies favor a long-term approach toward accumulation of a balanced portfolio of stocks, bonds, and cash. The stability of a long-term, balanced approach provides an investor time, tax, and cost efficiencies as well as risk management through diversification. On the other side of the set-it-and-forget-it crowd of investors are market timing traders who often pay too much attention to their investment portfolios. They use market timing to buy and sell securities before anticipated changes in the direction of the market or particular securities. Market timing essentially amounts to placing bets on hunches as to the future direction of securities within the market in a quest to buy low and sell high. **By buying before a market advance, market timers obtain securities at low prices. By selling prior to a market downturn, they lock in gains at high prices.** Market timing may normally be considered more of a trading strategy for seeking short-term gains than an investment strategy setting the stage for long-term capital appreciation.

Security selection and market timing in a dynamic investment environment are no easy tasks. Those who can accurately predict the market, or even just a small segment of it, stand to make a boatload of money. There are three questions you need to get right to be a successful market timer: what to buy, when to buy, and when to sell. The accuracy of market timers' predictions and the size and term of their bets determine their success under this strategy. Just as a wrong guess on the direction of the market can prove disastrous, an accurate prediction could spell success.

Obstacles such as emotion, noise, and unforeseen events can complicate any market transaction based on a prediction. An investor's emotion, such as irrational exuberance or unrelenting panic, causing untimely purchases or sales, has a way of undermining the best-laid investment strategy. For example, individual investors often get sucked in by the expectation that actively managed funds touting past success can perform as well in the future, only to be disappointed with lower than market returns compounded by higher expenses. The noise of rumors or extraneous events may turn an investor's focus away from important aspects of an investment and cause an untimely trade. Potential buyers need to be wary of an unforeseen event, like a scandal, takeover, or war that could disrupt even what seems like a sure thing. Trades based on emotion, noise, and failure to consider unforeseen events can detract from investment performance.

Yet market timers think they are smarter than everyone else. In some cases, they are when they possess, and trade on, information not known to or understood by the other party. In an efficient market where rational parties to a trade have access to all available information, market timing for profit in a taxable account would be nearly impossible after taking into account trading expenses and taxes. On the practical side, information leaks do occur, thus creating opportunities to profit through trading. This breakdown in market efficiency relating to the flow of information enables savvy market timers to profit from trades with parties not as well informed.

Unlike professional investors with large sums of money to invest, individual investors are generally not privy to hot tips in time to profit. A hot tip may actually be stale and already built into a stock's share price by the time an individual investor gets it and thus useless for generating a quick profit. Without advance information, it becomes quite difficult to accurately predict the market with any consistency. Although market timing may not be considered an investment strategy of choice for individual investors, it has its place in day trading when it is combined with systematic purchases of stock at regular intervals.

Dollar-Cost Averaging

So far, the preceding rules of thumb have dealt primarily with the management of existing portfolio assets. Another time-tested approach to investing relates to the purchase of stock with new deposits made at regular intervals.

Conventional wisdom suggests that every investor should include stocks in his or her portfolio to get the best long-term return, because stocks have outperformed other asset classes and historically kept up with inflation and productivity advances. Therefore, at least some portion of ongoing retirement savings plan contributions should be invested in stocks.

When it comes to investing new money in stocks, it sure would help to be able to buy the stock at a low price. The thing is there are just no announcements beforehand as to when a low price point will be reached. Since stock prices are unpredictable, investors have resorted to a technique involving the gradual investment of recurring fixed deposits at regular intervals in the stock market. This somewhat scattershot approach results in investing regularly at all low points, as well as all high points and all other points in between. Under *dollar-cost averaging*, an investor buys the same dollar amount of stock on a recurring basis for whatever the current market price is at the time of the purchase. The price at each purchase will determine how many shares the investor buys with each recurring deposit. This technique eliminates the guesswork of trying to time the market with purchases when stock prices are perceived to be low.

Table 6.3 illustrates the use of dollar-cost averaging in the development of a portfolio resulting from the purchase of stock with three recurring deposits of $100 when the stock's share price dips from $5 to $4 from the first to the second day before recovering to $5 on the third day. The resulting portfolio value of $325 after three days exceeds the sum of its deposits of $300 due to the purchase of more shares when the share price temporarily dipped. This same scenario could very well have played out over different

TABLE 6.3 Dollar-Cost Averaging

(1)	(2)	(3)	(4) = (2)/(3)	(5) = Sum of (4)	(6) = (3) × (5)
Day	Deposit	Share Price	# Shares Purchased	Total # Shares Owned	Total Value
1	$100	$5	20	20	$100
2	100	4	25	45	180
3	100	5	20	65	325

pay cycles, such as months or weeks, as opposed to days, and generated the same result.

Dollar-cost averaging is particularly well suited to investing through a retirement savings plan, where participants' plan contributions are invested in a stock fund with each pay cycle. By making recurring stock purchases of the same dollar amount at regular intervals, you avoid trying to time your stock purchases. The recurring plan contributions made from each paycheck are used to buy stocks at the current prices in effect when the contributions are made. Thus your same contribution from each paycheck buys more shares of stock when the share price is low and fewer shares of stock when the price is higher. You profit when the share price increases above the average price you paid for the shares. Whether taxes are due upon the eventual sale or later of an appreciated security depends on the type of account in which it is held.

Outside Investment Advice

The best personal investment strategy provides a systematic way to allocate assets among available investment alternatives to generate the highest returns with the least amount of risk. The process forces do-it-yourself investors into the oftentimes uncomfortable position of making many difficult decisions on investment timing and selection. The process is further complicated by the variety of investment alternatives in the typical retirement savings plan, ranging from professionally managed collective funds to self-directed brokerage accounts. Then countless decisions on the timing of purchases and sales of these alternatives are critical to success.

With all of the choices involved in managing a retirement savings portfolio, many individual investors find the application of the foregoing investment strategies to be quite overwhelming. Therefore, many plans offer features that allow retirement savings plan participants to put the management of their accounts on autopilot mode. In such plans, participants not funneling their retirement savings into target-date funds may instead resort to obtaining outside help with investment advice or account management.

Investment Advice Employers sponsoring retirement savings plans put their employees in the position of having to save and invest well enough to provide themselves meaningful support in retirement. So plan sponsors began to enlist investment advisers to counsel their retirement savings plan participants in managing their investment portfolios. The advisers' assistance ranged from basic investment education to individualized investment advice of the type formerly provided only to institutional investors. Now the typical investment advice model has evolved into the delivery of specific recommendations as to the allocation of retirement savings plan and other portfolio assets among available investment alternatives. Increasingly, the advice is dispensed online by an independent investment adviser at the employee's request, although it may also be delivered in person, in writing, or by telephone. Depending on the sophistication of the advice model, the advice formulation may take into account an individual's age, projected retirement date, savings rate, risk tolerance, plan terms, and existing account and other asset balances provided by the plan administrator and participant. These factors will generally result in specific plan fund allocation recommendations that call for an asset mix with a gradual reduction in risk over time.

Most investment advice has historically been, and still is, provided by advisers compensated by commissions neatly tucked into the financial products they sell. Quite often, investors end up buying underperforming investment products offering generous commissions to brokers selling them. Risk-averse plan sponsors avoid situations in which they could be blamed for employees' investment mishaps in their retirement savings accounts by steering clear of giving even a hint of anything that could be construed as investment advice. Retirement savings plan sponsors remove some of the product-bias element of advice by carefully selecting and offering no-load funds as alternative investment options. They also may offer participants investment education that stops short of advice or, alternatively, enlist independent financial advisers willing to accept fiduciary liability for providing investment advice to plan participants.

In the past, retirement savings plan participants often received no help in managing their accounts due to plan sponsors' fear of reprisal from participants blaming investment losses on errant advice. With the law now granting employers some relief from fiduciary liability relating to investment advice dispensed by an independent adviser who is properly selected and monitored, more plan sponsors have stepped up to provide investment advice as an employee benefit.

To take advantage of investment advice offered by a plan sponsor, a participant must request the advice through whatever means are available. After providing the requested information, the participant receives individualized advice for use in rebalancing his or her retirement portfolio. It is then up to the participant to execute the necessary fund exchanges to complete the process.

Account Management   Individualized investment advice is part and parcel of the account management service. Whereas the process of obtaining investment advice stops just short of executing the necessary fund exchanges to implement the advice, account management includes the investment advice process as well as the periodic execution of the resulting advice. The difference lies in who (i.e., participant or plan) is responsible for executing the recommended fund exchanges in accordance with the advice. A plan offering investment advice relies on its plan participants to actually request and then execute the advice. The plan sponsor picking up the larger tab for providing the account management service still relies on its plan participants to access the advice but then can automatically deploy it with the participant's consent.

The extent of the service, if any, provided to plan participants depends on the arrangement between the plan sponsor and the investment adviser. Plan sponsors and participants using such advice or account management typically get charged based on service utilization or a percentage of assets under management.

WHAT STRATEGY?

The decision is yours. If you are someone who can be happy with somebody telling you how to invest your money, you may prefer the hands-off approach of investing in a target-date fund or using an investment advisory service. Otherwise, you need to define your portfolio's asset allocation target percentages based on your investment objectives, monitor your accounts, and periodically rebalance your assets to maintain this balance.

As a hands-on investor, you will want to use market economics and conventional wisdom to define your optimal asset allocation percentages, taking into account the benefits of asset class diversification, long-term stock holdings, portfolio risk reduction over time, investment expense management, and tax mitigation strategies. You will also want to take advantage of investing your contributions in stocks using dollar-cost averaging.

Whatever investment strategy you decide to use in managing your portfolio, keep it simple, maintain a disciplined approach, and avoid emotion. Once the foundation of an investment strategy is in place, you can turn your attention to adding a day trading strategy to enhance your returns under your retirement savings accounts.

CHAPTER 7

Getting an Edge

Buy Low and Sell High

In prosperity prepare for a change; in adversity hope for one.

—James Burgh

Kurt was an ambitious young freshman attending The University of Michigan on a needs-based Evans scholarship. Since his scholarship covered only room and tuition, he figured he would work to earn some spending money for books, food, and possibly some bar tabs. He needed to keep a car on campus, so he said, to commute to his weekend job some 40 miles away at the Birmingham (Michigan) Country Club pro shop. Anyone who has ever tried to keep a car on campus in Ann Arbor for any length of time knows what a hassle it can be and how expensive it can get to park it. Add the cost of gas to the parking fees and tickets (otherwise known as government tax revenue), and Kurt's fraternity brothers questioned whether Kurt was taking home any money from his job after paying car expenses. They viewed Kurt's break-even work venture as a consequence of being in an endless circle of needing a car to get to work and needing work to cover his fuel and other maintenance costs.

Instead, imagine, if you will, that Kurt lived in a car-loving land (like Michigan) that paid for his car maintenance and fuel costs regardless of how much he used his car. This land also allowed him to park his car anywhere at will, with payment for the parking deferred until his graduation. Kurt just might find himself tooling around town a little more with some extra money in his pocket. That Michigan does not exist, and Kurt was broke.

However, 401(k) and other tax-deferred retirement savings plans do exist. Just like the favorable treatment afforded Kurt driving a car in the pretend Michigan, retirement savings plans offer you similar advantages. In these plans, you get a free pass to gratuitous maintenance costs and deferred payment of taxes. That is, you generally do not have to pay for fund exchanges, and you need not pay taxes on realized gains from exchanges (as well as pretax contributions and other investment earnings) until retirement. Since you cannot get this kind of favorable cost and tax treatment on trades within regular brokerage accounts, retirement savings plans would seem like an ideal environment for trading funds frequently, and they are. Now if only there were a way to profit from frequent trading within a retirement savings plan, you could keep more of the gains you generate through the trades. This is where day trading comes into play.

DAY TRADING PURE AND SIMPLE

Nobody can predict the future. However, you can comfortably say that stock prices will go up, down, or sideways—you just do not know which or how much—on any given day. In trading stock, the trick is to know what, how much, which way, and when to trade in anticipation of the next move in the market. For a retirement savings plan, the questions pertain to fund selection, quantity, direction, and timing of fund exchanges while the market stumbles along. Although you may not have the prescience to anticipate the market's gyrations, your methodical use of the day trading strategy will guide you in correctly answering these questions enough times to profit from market fluctuations over time.

Some investors like to think of themselves as power hitters batting fourth in the lineup's cleanup spot. They swing for the fences every time at bat. The good ones will indeed hit some homers, but not every time. They get on base with hits, walks, or otherwise; or they end up miserably in the dugout when they strike, fly, or ground out. Overall, their success depends not only upon their home run counts but also on how many times they reach base on their own, especially in the clutch. Then there are leadoff hitters batting first in the lineup, who are just looking to put the ball in play on each trip to the plate. Their success relies on their consistency in reaching base and then advancing when opportunities arise. Like leadoff hitters, day traders look to set up or capture incremental gains each day through opportunistic trades resulting from market volatility each day.

The day trading strategy relies on the consistent execution of daily fund exchanges within a retirement savings portfolio to generate stock gains over time in an uncertain market. This simple strategy takes only minutes a day to execute one daily fund exchange from anywhere you have access to a phone or the Internet.

Buy at Every Low and Sell at Every High

The art of day trading involves the timely application (for these times in which we live) of the timeless principle of buying low and selling high in the right setting. The strategic execution of daily fund exchanges in retirement savings plans sets up and captures gains from stock purchases and sales without getting nicked by direct trading costs and immediate taxation. You get to keep your resulting stock gains, because individuals incur no direct trading costs related to fund exchanges and no immediate taxes on realized stock gains. Instead, trading costs are shared among fundholders, and income taxes are deferred on gains due to the existing cost and tax advantages applicable to 401(k) and other retirement savings plans.

The day trading strategy is truly a play on stock prices alone. As a pure price play, the whys and wherefores of stock market behavior are not as important as the market movement itself. Effective day trading relies on paying attention to market changes and making portfolio adjustments accordingly. A simple formula dictates the necessary retirement savings portfolio adjustments made in reaction to the direction and amount of each daily movement in the stock market.

Stock prices change continually. To take advantage of stock price changes, day trading incorporates a philosophy allegedly favored at times by Chicago voters—do it early and often. At every opportunity, you need to buy stocks on a dip and sell them on a rise in the stock market. In a retirement savings plan, this opportunity to buy low or sell high comes along once each day when funds are valued at the close of the market. Depending on the daily change in the stock market just prior to the market close, day trading calls for you to shift account assets by submitting one (and only one) daily fund exchange between a stock fund and a cash fund before the market close. The direction of the market determines whether the exchange is from stocks to cash or from cash to stocks. The amount of the change in the market dictates how much you will exchange according to a simple formula you establish, as you will see later in this chapter.

Since the specifications for each fund exchange depend on the market's daily movement, you will have to check the market just prior to its close each day to ascertain its direction and amount of change. When the market goes up, you transfer an amount based on the daily change in the market from a stock fund to a cash fund. In contrast, when the market goes down, you transfer an amount related to the daily change in the market from a cash fund to a stock fund. You make a fund exchange every day as long as you have an available balance in the fund from which you are about to make a transfer.

The reasoning behind these exchanges goes something like this. After a market rise, the corresponding stock in your portfolio is worth more than it was the day before. So it is time to take some of your stock off the table by selling it in order to preserve some of the gains earned that day. When you sell on a rise and park the sales proceeds in cash until the next buying opportunity comes around, you preserve a gain not previously realized that could very well erode in a future market decline.

When the market drops, your corresponding stock holdings suffer a decline over which you have no control. But you can take control when you recognize the drop as an opportunity to buy more stock at a price lower than yesterday's. So that is what you do. This current purchase added to your stock holdings puts you in a position to reap gains from a future sale if and when your stocks go up in value. Of course, your stock purchase buys you a chance for a gain only if your stocks subsequently rise.

In a sense, day trading involves hyperactive portfolio rebalancing, with portfolio adjustments made daily rather than less frequently as is commonly the case. You make daily fund exchanges in the cost- and tax-friendly environment of your retirement savings portfolio to buy into stock at relatively low prices and sell out of stock at relatively high prices. Its strategic use of daily rebalancing enables you to set up gains when you buy low and lock in gains when you sell high. On the buy side, the strategy uses a selective form of dollar-cost averaging to buy stocks at current price levels only on days the market drops. On the sell side, the strategy calls for selling stocks at current price levels—sort of like reverse dollar-cost averaging—only on days the market rises. Carrying out the day trading strategy on a disciplined basis over time, your accumulation of captured gains generates better returns than other portfolios, especially in an uncertain market.

Transfer between Stock and Cash Fund Options

To keep things simple, day trading involves fund transfers into or out of only two asset classes: stocks and cash. With each actual fund transfer, you as a retirement savings plan participant will exchange account assets between one fund option composed entirely of stocks and another fund option composed of cash-type securities.

Stock Fund   As the asset class with the most risk, stocks offer the most price volatility from day to day. It is this volatility in the form of daily stock price swings that renders day trading more than worthwhile. Stock share price increases result in account gains that are preserved (or realized, in accounting-speak) when stock is sold. Share price decreases create an opportunity to set up potential gains when stock is bought. Without volatility, there are no gains from day trading.

The type of stock fund most suitable for day trading is based on a broad stock market index for domestic companies that is easily tracked and serves as the basis for fund options commonly offered under retirement savings plans.

Market Index Modern portfolio theory suggests it is impossible for an investment fund to beat the market in the long run.[1] Consistent with this theory, studies have confirmed that most investment funds underperform the broad market over the long term.[2] Often it is the additional investment management expense charged by an actively managed fund that drags down its returns below the returns of less expensive passively managed stock market index funds. As exciting as chasing possibly higher returns under an actively managed fund may be, the odds are against you in finding an actively managed fund (with its higher fund costs) that outperforms a low-cost passively managed market index fund. It just does not make sense to earn inferior returns under most actively managed funds due to their higher expenses. Due to the likelihood of disappointing returns rather than possibly better returns from a typical actively managed fund, day trading involves the use of stock market index funds with their close-to-market-matching returns. Remember that index funds come close to, but cannot quite attain, the market's returns due to the expenses deducted from fund returns credited to shareholders.

Holding a fairly fixed market basket of stocks, a market index fund reflects the investment performance and volatility of the stocks of the companies included within the index. Therefore, an investment in a stock market index fund provides an opportunity to participate in the potentially higher long-term returns offered by stocks. More important for day trading, a stock market index fund investment can be expected to experience the kind of volatility associated with stocks—albeit somewhat muted by diversification—that fuels day trading.

Domestic Domestic funds invest primarily in publicly held companies domiciled in the United States. They offer the security of investments in some of the largest U.S.-based companies with worldwide operations. The funds themselves, as well as the companies in which they invest, operate under the jurisdiction of federal and state law. The comfort drawn from a domestic fund's investment holdings in large U.S. companies operating within the world's strongest economy with the protection afforded by consistent government regulation makes domestic funds desirable for day trading.

Easily Tracked Day trading relies on access to real-time investment performance information, especially near the end of each day, to determine that day's fund exchange. However, mutual fund options within retirement savings plans post their investment results but once per day at the close of the market. Therefore, a day trader needs to rely on surrogate real-time investment performance information, such as for a major market index, to determine a daily fund exchange involving a fund that mimics such an index. Following major market indexes has never been easier with today's ready availability of real-time market performance online, on television, by telephone, and at brokerage houses. This ease in tracking a major market index, such as the S&P 500 index, greatly facilitates day trading a retirement savings account offering such a market index fund.

Commonly Available   The theory behind using easily trackable domestic market index funds in day trading works only if such funds actually exist as fund options in 401(k) and other retirement savings plans. Fortunately, most 401(k) and other retirement savings plans offer a domestic market index fund as a fund option. In a 2009 survey, 98 percent of 401(k) plans offered a domestic stock market index fund.[3]

The most common stock market index fund found in retirement savings plans tracks the S&P 500 index. Although it goes under a variety of names, you will most likely find it labeled with terms such as "equity," "500," and/or "index" in its title. As a widely available domestic stock market index fund that may be easily tracked on a real-time basis, an S&P 500 index fund is an ideal representative of a stock fund suitable for day trading.

Cash-Type Fund   In contrast to stocks, cash represents the asset class with the least amount of risk or volatility. With its primary goal of preserving invested capital, a cash fund's most conservative bent offers stability in value and liquidity. Cash is the antidote to stock. What stock experiences in volatility, cash offers in stability. What stock lacks in stability, cash offers in abundance.

Although bonds may offer a higher long-term return than cash and somewhat of an inverse return to stocks to counterbalance stocks' volatility, they are not as liquid as cash. The purpose of parking money in cash is to preserve principal and facilitate liquidity for buying stock later. Cash generally does not react to changes in the overall stock market. When the market goes down, money held in a cash-type fund generally retains its value. When the market heads up, the value of account assets placed in cash (immediately following the sale of stock) remains pretty much the same except for some interest credited to the fund. Just as cash does not have much downside, it also has very little upside appreciation potential these days. This stability in value is precisely the reason that cash is used as the other asset class in the 401(k) day trading strategy.

The labels given to cash-type funds in retirement savings plans vary. A cash fund may come in the form of a money market fund, certificate of deposit, or other interest-bearing account. If these funds are not offered, a stable value fund or a short-term fund may also serve as a substitute for a cash fund.

Cash-type funds, too, are prevalent in retirement savings plans. In a 2009 survey, virtually all (99 percent) of 401(k) plans offered a money market or stable value/investment contract fund.[4] For plans that offer both a cash fund and a stable value fund, select only one and stick to it for day trading so as to avoid running afoul of any equity wash sale rules governing exchanges between cash and stable value funds.

Under the day trading strategy, each day's rise or fall in the stock market index determines whether you buy or sell stock that day. Each trade involves a fund transfer of a portion of your retirement savings portfolio from stocks to cash or cash to stocks. In this context, a cash fund, with its stability and liquidity, fills the role of being a temporary placeholder until the next stock-buying opportunity presents itself.

Determine Trade Amount Based on Market Index Daily Change

Perfect foresight would allow you to get completely out of a stock just before its share price drops and be entirely invested in the stock in time for its gains. Absent this foresight, you are stuck guessing about the next move of a particular stock or the entire stock market, as is the rest of the world. To prepare for that next move in the market, you need to make timely trades in the form of transfers between stocks and cash to gradually set up and preserve gains.

The day trading process adjusts your portfolio's exposure to stock through fund exchanges based on two factors: daily market changes and a preset *calibration formula* of your choice. There may be only one way to determine a particular market index's daily change, but there are countless ways to develop a calibration formula for weighting the amount of each trade in relation to the market index change. Under the simplest approach, you determine each daily fund exchange amount as the daily point change in an applicable stock market index multiplied by a preset calibration factor.

Daily Fund Exchange Amount = Market Index Daily Point Change

× Calibration Factor

This simple approach to determining the daily fund exchange amount offers the advantages of being both easy to remember and easy to apply. It merely involves the multiplication of two factors. The first factor, the market index daily point change, may vary from day to day, but the second, the calibration factor, is a fixed constant.

Market Index Daily Change   Think of a fund exchange in a retirement savings plan like a market order to sell shares in one fund and use the proceeds to purchase shares in another fund at the prevailing prices in effect, but at the close of the market. Therefore, you should determine the fund exchange amount based on your observation of the market index change as near as possible to the market close so as to minimize pricing uncertainty and to facilitate accuracy in the determination of the fund exchange amount. Not only will your exchange amount correspond more closely with the actual market index daily change that is not known until minutes after the closing bell, but you will also have less uncertainty about the closing price at which the order will be executed.

Each day just prior to the close of the market, you need to check the daily change in the stock market index that is tracked by the index fund involved in your day trading. Your access to a real-time quote for the market index change just prior to the market close will facilitate your determination of the type (stock purchase or redemption) and amount of that day's fund exchange to be executed at the market close. If the market index is about to close higher, you submit an order to exchange out of a stock fund into a cash fund. If the market index is about to close lower, you exchange out of cash into stock. Then you apply your calibration formula—in the simplest case, a constant factor—to the daily market index change to determine the fund exchange amount.

Calibration Factor   The amount of each incremental stock fund purchase or sale determines the extent of your success with day trading. Although you may not be able to control the direction or amount of the market's daily changes, you can still influence the size of your fund exchanges through your selection of a calibration factor.

In selecting a calibration factor, you need to take into account how your potential trades based on the stock market's volatility affect the fund balances within your retirement savings portfolio. Although day trading requires the consistent application of a fixed calibration factor over time, you may need or want to make adjustments as conditions warrant.

Under normal conditions, you could use a calibration factor of one thousandth of the initial amount of your retirement savings portfolio you decide to subject to day trading.

$$\text{Calibration Factor} = \frac{\text{Retirement Savings Portfolio}}{1{,}000}$$

In the case of an individual starting with a total retirement savings portfolio of $100,000, the calibration factor would be $100 (= $100,000 portfolio value/1,000). Do not underestimate the value of using a nice round number, like $100, for a calibration factor to be used in determining daily trade amounts on the fly day in and day out. Then each daily fund exchange amount can be expressed in equation form as follows:

Daily Fund Exchange Amount = Market Index Daily Point Change × $100

The fixed calibration factor used here represents but one easy way to determine the amount of each daily fund exchange or transfer between stock and cash. You can also select another calibration factor depending on expected market volatility and your risk tolerance. Whereas a higher calibration factor results in higher daily trade amounts, a lower calibration factor reduces risk and withstands more extreme market volatility by reducing each resulting trade amount. For the type of market volatility experienced from 2001 to 2010, it would have been necessary to use a divisor of over one thousand (more like 1,333) applied to the subject retirement savings portfolio to determine a calibration factor (of $75) that would have allowed you to continue day trading through all the market swings.

The simplicity of simply multiplying (a fixed calibration factor times the market index daily point change) simplifies an already simple calculation (of the daily fund exchange amount). Chapter 8 discusses other possible calibration formulas, such as ones involving the use of market index percentage (rather than point) changes or portfolio rebalancing to determine amounts to be exchanged between stock and cash funds.

Submit Exchange Order Just before Market Close

The day trading strategy derives its value from daily fund exchanges that take advantage of stock market volatility. Once you have determined the amount and type (purchase or sale) of the transfer, you are in a position to execute your daily fund exchange just before the close of the market.

Recall that retirement savings plan administrators generally execute all fund exchange orders submitted by retirement savings plan participants once per day at the close of the market based on the funds' closing prices. Instructions submitted early in the day receive the same pricing as those submitted later (but before the close of the market). Since any exchange order you submit before the market close for the day will be executed at the fund price in effect at the market close, you may as well submit your order just before the market close to get the best perspective for determining the fund exchange amount and pricing in effect for the exchange. Under the day trading strategy, you would then execute your one and only fund transfer for the day based on the daily change in the market index just before the close of the market (usually 4 P.M. EST), and not one second later.

Consider the case where you establish a policy to exchange $100 between the cash and S&P 500 index funds within your retirement savings portfolio for each one-point change in the Standard & Poor's 500 index. A negative change in the S&P 500 index calls for a purchase, and a positive change in the S&P 500 index calls for a sale of the equity index fund. If the S&P 500 index rises from opening at 1,000 to 1,005 at 3:55 P.M. eastern time (five minutes prior to the close), you would submit instructions before 4 P.M. to your plan record keeper to exchange $500 [–$500 = (1,000 – 1,005) × $100] from the S&P 500 index fund into the cash fund. If the S&P 500 index declines the next day from its opening at 1,005 to 990 just five minutes prior to the market close, you would exchange $1,500 [+$1,500 = (1,005 – 990) × $100] from the cash fund into the S&P 500 index fund.

THE SCIENCE BEHIND IT ALL

The day trading concept calls for you to buy into stock market weakness and sell off on strength. Daily fund exchanges are based on daily changes in the market index corresponding to the index fund options offered in your retirement savings accounts. At this point, you may want some proof of these wondrous claims about the generous returns offered by day trading. Before looking at how the day trading strategy has fared on a historical basis, first consider how day trading generates profits in a sideways market.

Arithmetic

John Bogle, the founder of Vanguard Investments, cites what Justice Louis Brandeis referred to as "the relentless rules of humble arithmetic" as responsible for how fees eat away at the returns delivered to investors. He notes that fund managers collect investment management, administrative, and trading expenses before crediting returns to shareholders.[5] That leaves the net return credited to shareholders as:

$$\text{Net Return} = \text{Gross Return} - \text{Fees}$$

Along the lines of the relentless rules of humble arithmetic, day trading uses not only subtraction but also addition, multiplication, and division to generate gains in a volatile market. The combination of these arithmetic operations enables you to profit from day trading in a shaky but sideways market. Strategic daily fund exchanges involving the purchase and sale of stock cause shifts in the allocation of your stock and cash holdings in your retirement savings portfolio. Gains result from an increase of your weighting in stock before an advance, and loss avoidance comes from a decrease of your weighting in stock before a decline.

Absent any fund exchanges to change your asset mix, your gain upon sale of stock would simply be its final sales price less the original purchase price. Instead, day trading in a wobbly but sideways market makes possible more gains through ongoing stock purchases at lower average prices and sales at higher average prices. These favorable weighted-average prices for the stock purchases and sales increase the overall profitability of your fund exchanges.

Day Trading under the Hood

How day trading generates gains in a sideways market is best illustrated in a hypothetical example involving only a single stock and cash as investment options. For the moment, this particular stock serves as a surrogate for a stock market index fund typically found in a retirement savings plan. Day trading would then involve the daily shifting of money between the stock and cash depending on the daily change in the stock's share price just before the market close.

Under the mantra of buying low and selling high, each day you would buy more stock when its price declines and sell a portion of your stock holdings when its share price rises. Specifically, you would buy stock shares just before the market close on a day when the share price is about to close lower than its opening price for the day. Conversely, you would sell shares just before the market close on a day when the share price is about to close higher than its opening price for the day.

Suppose you decided to commence day trading with respect to your current holdings of 100 shares of a particular stock with an initial share price of $4. Since you are not sure which direction the stock price will turn first, you will usually want to start off with a balanced portfolio including both stock and cash. However, to keep it simple, you will not need to start off with any cash in this case, where the stock price will turn out to rise at first.

Stock Price Goes Up, Then Down   Assume you have calibrated your day trades to call for the daily sale or purchase of stock in an amount of $100 for each $1 change in the stock's share price. If the daily share price increase is $1 just before the close of the market for the day, you will sell $100 worth of stock before the market close. Conversely, if the daily stock price decrease is $1, you will buy $100 worth of stock before the market close. Just as in a retirement savings plan, assume that all trades take place at the market closing price each day, but without any direct trading costs or immediate taxes applying in this example. Any proceeds from the sale of stock are assumed to be held in a non-interest-bearing cash account.

Over the first two days of your day trading, it happens that the daily share price just prior to the market close (and assumed to hold through the close) goes up $1 the first day and down $1 the next. On the first day, the stock opens at $4 and closes at $5. After opening at $5 on the second day, it closes at $4, where it had started on the first day. In declining the second day as much as it advanced the first day (in absolute, rather than percentage, terms), the share price ends up after two days exactly where it started.

At the start, your entire portfolio consists only of 100 shares of stock with a share price of $4, worth $400 (= 100 shares × $4 per share). When the share price increases to $5 by the market close on the first day, your stock is worth $500 (= 100 shares × $5 per share) by the end of the first day. Rather than holding the stock through the end of the day, the day trading strategy calls for your first day trade to be a sale (for cash) just prior to the market close of your entire one-day gain of $100 (= 1 point gain × $100 calibration factor) worth of stock, or 20 shares (= $100 gain/$5 share price at end of day 1). So after one day, you have a reconfigured total portfolio of $500, consisting of $100 cash (in realized gain) and 80 shares of stock (= 100 original shares – 20 sold shares) worth $400 (= 80 shares × $5 per share). When the share price goes back down to $4 per share by the end of the next day, your stock is now worth only $320 (= 80 shares × $4 per share), but you still have your cash of $100. Without any further trades, you have a total of $420 in your portfolio, consisting of $320 in stock and $100 in cash, after two days.

Although the stock price ended up two days later at the same $4 level that it started, your portfolio grew by $20 from $400 to $420 due to your shrewd trading. Had you kept your portfolio entirely invested in stock (or in non-interest-bearing cash, for that matter) for the entire two days, you would have the same $400 portfolio that you had started with. Instead you ended up with a larger portfolio of $420, resulting from cleverly preserving a portion of your first day's (temporary) stock gain by converting it to cash and thereby avoiding the erosion in value caused by the second day's decline in stock price. This simple example demonstrates how day trading can enhance your portfolio in a sideways market that goes up (the first day) and then goes down (the second day). Timing is everything in making something out of nothing.

The development of the interim portfolio values subjected to day trading in an *up and down*, but sideways, market over the course of the two days is summarized in Table 7.1.

TABLE 7.1 Day Trading Portfolio in Up, Down, and Sideways Market

(1)	(2)	(3)	(4) = (2) × (3)	(5)	(6) = (4) + (5)
Day	Share Price	Number of Shares	Stock Value	Cash	Total
1 (at opening)	$4	100	$400	$0	$400
1 (before close)	5	100	500	0	500
1 (sell stock)	5	−20	−100	+100	0
1 (at close) = 2 (at opening)	5	80	400	100	500
2 (before close)	4	80	320	100	420

You may not get too excited at this point, because you know the stock market may not always go up one day and down the next. You might ask, what if it went down before it went up?

Stock Price Goes Down, Then Up   This same day trading strategy works in reverse, too, when the share price goes down before going back up to where it started. If you extend the foregoing example another day, you start off just before the end of day 2 with a $420 portfolio, composed of 80 shares of stock (at $4 per share) worth $320 and $100 in cash. Just before the market close on day 2, the stock's share price had declined by $1 from its opening price of $5 to $4. Under the day trading strategy, this $1 daily stock price decline signals a buy of $100 (= 1 point decline × $100 calibration factor) worth of stock. So you use your entire $100 in cash to buy 25 (= $100 cash/$4 share price) shares of stock at the $4 share price before the market close on the second day. At the end of the second day and carrying through to the beginning of the third day, you have 105 (= 80 shares after first day + 25 new shares) shares of stock, valued at $420 (= 105 shares × $4 share price), and no cash.

When the share price goes from $4 at the beginning of the third day back up to $5 just before the market close on the third day, your 105 shares of stock with which you started the day are worth $525 (= 105 shares × $5 share price). Without any further trades, your portfolio is worth $525, composed of stock valued at $525 and no cash after three days. Only, as a day trader, you would have made a sale before the end of the third day to preserve some of your gain, and so on for the following days.

Again your shrewd trading resulted in a gain over the course of the prior two days when the market ended up just where it started. If you had just held on to your 80 shares of stock and $100 in cash at the beginning of

TABLE 7.2 Day Trading Portfolio in Down, Up, and Sideways Market

(1)	(2)	(3)	(4) = (2) × (3)	(5)	(6) = (4) + (5)
Day	Share Price	Number of Shares	Stock Value	Cash	Total
1 (at opening)	$4	100	$400	$0	$400
1 (before close)	5	100	500	0	500
1 (sell stock)	5	−20	−100	+100	0
1 (at close) = 2 (at opening)	5	80	400	100	500
2 (before close)	4	80	320	100	420
2 (buy stock)	4	+25	+100	−100	0
2 (at close) = 3 (at opening)	4	105	420	0	420
3 (before close)	5	105	525	0	525

the second day, your total portfolio value at the end of the third day would be worth the same $500 (= 80 shares × $5 per share + $100 cash) with which you started on the second day. Instead you ended up with a larger portfolio of $525 after the third day, by cleverly setting up a gain through a purchase of stock with your cash when the stock price temporarily declined on the second day, thereby generating a gain resulting from the third day's advance in the stock price. Although the stock price ended up on day 3 at the same $5 level at which it started day 2, your day trading generated a total gain of $25 in those two days. The story keeps getting better, as this $25 gain from two days earlier is $5 more than the previous cumulative gain of $20 after the first two days. This simple example demonstrates how day trading can also enhance your portfolio in a sideways market that goes down (the second day) before going up (the third day).

Table 7.2 extends Table 7.1 by one more day in the development of portfolio values subjected to day trading. During the last two days of the three-day period, the market goes down, then up, before ending sideways.

Granted, you probably will not come across too many situations where such dramatic stock price movements as two 25 percent gains and a 20 percent loss occur over the course of three days. However, the extreme share price volatility allowed for some easy mathematical computations. Suffice it to say that the numbers have been changed to protect the innocent, as stock price movements this volatile would rarely be found outside of the financial services industry in early 2009.

Why Day Trading Works

In the right environment, the day trading strategy works 100 percent of the time. Strategic daily trades in a shaky but sideways market take advantage of the relentless rules of arithmetic. When the market bounces around before ending up where it started, your consistent application of the strategy allows you to generate gains from trades that adjust your exposure to stock in anticipation of future market movements. You profit when you own more stock before the market advances and less stock before the market declines. How much you profit depends on the calibration formula used to tie market changes to trade amounts. You also get to keep more of your gains generated within the cost- and tax-friendly environment of a retirement savings plan.

Daily Fluctuation in Stock Prices   Daily changes in stock prices create buying and selling opportunities under day trading. Buying on the dip sets up future gains, and selling on the rise preserves those gains. The foregoing examples show how day trading took advantage of the equal but opposite stock price changes.

Timing of Trades   When the initial share price rose from $4 to $5, or by 25 percent [= ($5 – $4)/$4 × 100%], you sold $100 worth of stock at the higher $5 price and parked it in cash. When the share price subsequently declined from $5 to $4, or by 20 percent [= ($5 – $4)/$5 × 100%], the next day, you bought $100 worth of stock at the lower $4 price from your cash reserve. Your day trading gains resulted from locking in a portion of your 25 percent gain the first day by placing it in cash to avoid the second day's 20 percent decline in share price. Then you set up another gain for the third day's 25 percent rise in share price by buying with your cash more stock at the lower $4 price at the end of the second day. In essence, you are adjusting your portfolio daily to expose more of it to possible daily stock price increases and less to possible daily stock price declines.

Calibration Formula   For simplicity, the foregoing examples used a fixed calibration factor ($100) to determine the daily trade amounts for a portfolio consisting only of a single stock and cash. Using the flat $100 calibration factor in the prior example, you decrease your portfolio's exposure to stocks from $500 to $400 just before the first day's end, in time to partially avoid the second day's 20 percent stock price decline from $5 to $4. You then increase your portfolio's exposure to stocks from $320 to $420 just before the second day's end, in time to more fully experience the third day's 25 percent stock price increase from $4 to $5. In this example, the day trading strategy's gains come from a heavier stock exposure when the stock price rises and a lighter exposure when the stock price declines.

Although your day trading gains are derived from trading on the market's up and down movements, the magnitude of your gains is directly tied to the calibration formula or factor you select for determining trade amounts. If you did no day trading—or, in essence, had used a calibration factor of $0 instead of $100—you would have generated no gains from day trading. By contrast, you can enhance your gains in a net sideways market by increasing the calibration factor used in determining your trade amounts. A doubling of the calibration factor to $200 instead of $100 would have doubled your day trading gains. If a fixed calibration factor does not suit your fancy, a variety of other calibration formulas can be used in its place, as to be discussed in Chapter 8.

Expanding the Day Trading Notion to Retirement Savings Plans

The foregoing examples developed the gains from day trading a single stock over the course of three days. The same day trading principles that generate gains from the price volatility of a single stock also apply to a market basket of stocks or a market index fund. The typical retirement savings plan offers a stock market index fund of the variety from which day trading gains can be generated. Not only that, retirement savings plans usually offer a cash-type fund option into which captured gains can be parked until the next market index buying opportunity presents itself. When considered along with the tax and trading cost advantages, retirement savings plans provide an ideal environment for day trading. The terminology may be different, as a trade will otherwise be called a fund exchange or transfer among fund options within a retirement savings plan. The results are the same; your timely transfer or exchange of retirement savings account assets on a daily basis under the day trading strategy results in gains regardless of the movement along the way in a sideways market.

Day trading works because of market and environmental forces. This strategy allows for the harnessing of gains from a volatile market in uncertain times within the hospitable environment of a retirement savings plan.

Volatile Markets   A single stock's share price—or the broader stock market, for that matter—does not necessarily check in at the same level every other day as in the foregoing example; it tends to meander and cross back and forth over its initial level from days, weeks, months, or even years earlier. Market uncertainty characterized by these daily fluctuations presents daily opportunities to generate gains through day trading. If a market index eventually settles at or near the level at which you started a sustained day trading campaign, you have made money along the way.

Up and down is good, but big bounces are better when it comes to describing the type of ideal stock market price movements suitable for day trading. The more extreme the daily market changes, the larger the day trading gains are in your portfolio. The enhanced gains generated by these stock market fluctuations make volatility a day trader's friend.

Day trading works only when the stock market closes up some days and down other days. Both the up and down (or down and then up) daily closes are necessary. Selling on market rises preserves gains, and buying on market dips sets up future gains. Fortunately, history suggests that the markets do indeed both go up some days and go down others.

In the 5,050 trading days over the 20-year period from 1982 through 2001, the stock market experienced gains on 53 percent of the trading days, and consequently declines on the other 47 percent of the days.[6] Although this included both extended bull markets and crushing declines, it demonstrates the near evenhandedness with which the market rises and falls. This type of up-and-down movement is precisely what generates day trading gains. Otherwise, day trading would drag down the returns of a balanced portfolio in a market that unrelentingly goes down without interruption or forges ahead without pause.

Tax and Cost Advantages   The unfettered gains generated by day trading retirement savings accounts enjoy tax and cost advantages not otherwise available under taxable brokerage accounts. Whereas taxes on gains and direct trading expenses would eat away at gains generated in a brokerage account, the free trades and deferred tax treatment available under retirement savings accounts preserve the gains generated by day trading in such accounts.

SHOW ME THE MONEY

The stock market is defined by much more interesting daily movements than just advances followed by declines in the same amounts, or vice versa. It experiences long and short periods of up or down movement and in different amounts. Yet these are always interrupted with some directional turns along the way. The variations are endless. It is this type of market environment in which you will be day trading your retirement savings portfolio.

Brace yourself for some numbers. Just how good the day trading strategy really is can be measured by comparing its historical investment performance (as if it had existed) against that of other benchmark portfolios over various time periods. As an old concept in a new setting, day trading retirement savings accounts does not have an established track record. Its historical performance is constructed through simulations of day trades in the context of actual past market performance in a process called *back-testing*, before it is then compared against the performance of benchmark portfolios.

Since day trading involves a balanced portfolio comprised of the stock and cash asset classes, its performance is best judged against other balanced portfolios of the same initial composition. In order to show how day trading compares to stocks, its investment performance will also be compared against a stock market index portfolio.

For comparison purposes, all portfolios enjoy the tax and cost advantages afforded 401(k) plans and other retirement savings plans. Taxes are deferred on any realized gains and income. There are no direct trading costs associated with fund exchanges. This simplifying assumption of ignoring expenses makes for apples-to-apples comparisons and actually does not stray too far from reality for some of the larger institutional market index funds offered in retirement savings plans, which charge only a few basis points for investment management fees.

The comparison tracks the investment performance of the original assets within each of the portfolios. The difference in performance can be attributed entirely to the investment strategy used to manage the portfolio. No new contributions or deductions are taken into account in determining investment returns for any of the portfolios during the performance measurement periods. The investment performance for these portfolios is compared over different durations ending December 31, 2010.

At the beginning of a measurement period, each of the portfolios begins with $100,000 in assets. The balanced portfolios start off with $50,000 in stock and $50,000 in cash, while the stock portfolio starts with $100,000 that stays invested entirely in stock. All of the stock is invested in a market index fund that tracks the S&P 500 index, with no expenses. All cash is parked in a non-interest-bearing account, with no expenses. With the meager returns offered under cash funds these days, this simplifying assumption may not be too far from reality.

True to its name, the "Day Trading Portfolio" is subject to incremental daily trades executed at the end of each day based on daily changes in the S&P 500 index observed just prior to the close of the market (and assumed to carry through to the end of the day). To accommodate the market volatility experienced during the decade ended December 31, 2010, the amount of each daily trade is computed by multiplying a calibration factor of $75 by each one-point change in the S&P 500 index for the day. A rise from its opening price by the end of the day triggers a S&P 500 index fund sale before the market close, and a decline causes a purchase to the extent funds are available to complete the exchange.

Day Trading Compared with Balanced Portfolios

At this point you may be asking yourself just how worthwhile day trading is, as opposed to methods involving less of your attention. To answer this question, consider two types of balanced portfolios initially composed of stock and cash to be compared with the Day Trading Portfolio.

The "Set-It-and-Forget-It Balanced Portfolio" is set up to be identical to the Day Trading Portfolio in its initial composition. Its $100,000 value is originally made up of 50 percent in an S&P 500 index stock fund and 50 percent in a non-interest-bearing cash-type fund, both free of expenses. However, its composition remains static—that is, not adjusted or rebalanced—throughout the duration of the investment performance measurement period. This is indeed your typical set-it-and-forget-it portfolio.

The "Annually Rebalanced Portfolio" is also set up as identical to the Day Trading Portfolio in its initial composition, with $100,000 divided equally between an S&P 500 index fund and a non-interest-bearing cash-type fund, both free of expenses. Over time, the initial composition of 50 percent in an S&P 500 index stock fund and 50 percent in a non-interest-bearing cash-type fund will change due to the different returns of the funds. To get back to its original allocation, the composition of this Annually Rebalanced Portfolio is adjusted or rebalanced annually at the end of each year back to a 50/50 stock/cash split throughout the duration of the investment performance measurement period. If only the aforementioned investment adviser in Chapter 6 had invested in this type of automatically Annually Rebalanced Portfolio, he could have celebrated his wedding anniversaries with his wife (if she is still around) in ways other than rebalancing their portfolio.

Figure 7.1 compares the cumulative balances in the Day Trading Portfolio, Set-It-and-Forget-It (Static) Balanced Portfolio, and Annually Rebalanced Portfolio after one-, five-, and 10-year periods ended December 31, 2010.

When comparing the portfolios in Figure 7.1, remember that stuffing your money in a mattress would have let you keep your original $100,000 investment. Since the cash component does not grow in any of the portfolios, stock market changes alone generally cause the composition of the portfolios to diverge from their initial 50 percent in stock and 50 percent in cash allocation at the beginning of the investment performance measurement period. By definition, no subsequent adjustments are made to the Set-It-and-Forget-It Balanced Portfolio. The Annually Rebalanced Portfolio annually reverts back to 50 percent stock and 50 percent cash through portfolio rebalancing once each year. Daily trades in response to stock market changes continually modify the blend of stock and cash in the Day Trading Portfolio. These daily shifts in the Day Trading Portfolio's blend

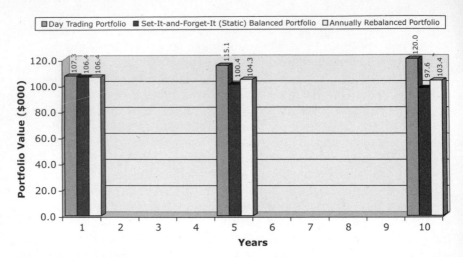

FIGURE 7.1 Comparison of Day Trading, Set-It-and-Forget-It (Static) Balanced, and Annually Rebalanced Portfolio Values after One-, Five-, and 10-Year Periods Ended December 31, 2010

between stock and cash are responsible for its outperformance over the Set-It-and-Forget-It Balanced Portfolio and the Annually Rebalanced Portfolio over the one-, five-, and 10-year measurement periods, each ended December 31, 2010.

For the one-year period ended December 31, 2010, the Day Trading Portfolio had a gain of 7.3 percent, compared to a gain of 6.4 percent for the Set-It-and-Forget-It Balanced Portfolio, which by definition is the same as an Annually Rebalanced Portfolio for a one-year period. The story gets better as the Day Trading Portfolio, with a gain of 15.1 percent, outperformed by far both the Set-It-and-Forget-It Balanced Portfolio with a gain of 0.4 percent and the Annually Rebalanced Portfolio with a gain of 4.3 percent over the five-year period ended December 31, 2010. Finally, the Day Trading Portfolio's cumulative gain of 20.0 percent bettered the Set-It-and-Forget-It Balanced Portfolio's loss of 2.4 percent and the Annually Rebalanced Portfolio's gain of 3.4 percent for 10 years. Under these market conditions, more frequent portfolio adjustments paid off in higher returns for a balanced portfolio.

Day Trading Compared with Stock Portfolio

Another useful comparison pits the Day Trading Portfolio's investment performance against that of a stock market index. For this purpose, the

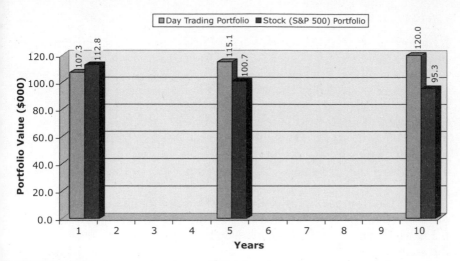

FIGURE 7.2 Comparison of Day Trading and Stock (S&P 500) Portfolio Values after One-, Five-, and 10-Year Periods Ended December 31, 2010

benchmark "Stock Portfolio" of $100,000 is a 100 percent stock portfolio that tracks the S&P 500 index, with no expenses. As with the Set-It-and-Forget-It Balanced Portfolio, this portfolio also retains its original holdings, but all in stock, with no adjustments to its composition throughout the investment performance measurement period. The Stock Portfolio is another set-it-and-forget-it type of fund.

Figure 7.2 compares the Day Trading Portfolio and Stock (S&P 500 index) Portfolio balances after one-, five-, and 10-year periods ended December 31, 2010.

Not only do day trading's returns beat balanced fund returns, but they also performed well against stock portfolios for the five- and 10-year periods. However, for the one-year period ended December 31, 2010, the Day Trading Portfolio's annual return of 7.3 percent fell short of the 12.8 percent return for the Stock Portfolio. That day trading performs better in a shaky but sideways market is borne out when the Day Trading Portfolio is compared with the Stock Portfolio over longer durations. For the five years ended December 31, 2010, the Day Trading Portfolio's cumulative 15.1 percent return betters the Stock Portfolio's 0.7 percent gain. Over 10 years, the Day Trading Portfolio's cumulative 20.0 percent return soundly beats the Stock Portfolio's 4.7 percent loss. Day trading performed better than the broad market by almost 25 percent over the first decade of the new millennium, suggesting it can significantly enhance the investment returns from retirement savings in choppy markets to come.

Caveat

As any experienced investor can tell you, a comparison of alternative asset management strategies relies heavily on the measurement period selected for use in computing the strategies' investment returns. Rapidly changing markets can dramatically affect the relative returns generated by alternative asset management strategies over different time periods. A 20-year comparison of alternative strategies becomes a bit more interesting, as it includes an unusual combination of time periods yielding wildly disparate stock returns. The market rose dramatically during the Internet and Y2K craze of the 1990s and settled somewhat during the first decade of the 2000s.

Day trading is a strategy of the times, but not for all times. It may perform well in a volatile stock market with little or no net change over time but does not fare as well by comparison in a rapidly increasing or decreasing stock market. The volatile but weak market performance of the first decade of the 2000s provided a hospitable environment for day trading that was borne out by its stellar returns in comparison with other strategies. However, day trading would not have fared well under conditions of unprecedented stock market growth like that experienced in the 1990s. When you combine the performance of these two decades, the Day Trading Portfolio's cumulative return was less than half of the Stock Portfolio's return and also less than the Set-It-and-Forget-It Balanced Portfolio's return for the 20-year period ended December 31, 2010.

If you think the U.S. stock markets are in for another ride like the bull market of the 1990s, you should ignore day trading and stick to stocks. If you believe in holding a balanced portfolio to weather oncoming market volatility in an otherwise flat market through 2020, you should consider day trading your retirement savings portfolio.

DAY TRADING TAKES DISCIPLINE

The stock market can be ruthless or giddy, or somewhere in between. Under the day trading strategy, you need to put away the fear that a market downturn will decimate your life savings and avoid the greed brought on by the euphoria of anticipated wealth that comes with market advances. Keep your emotions in check. Do not be the momentum investor who buys into a rally and sells into a decline. Yesterday's market movements are past history, as far as you are concerned. Instead you want to be the contrarian who buys at every daily market decline and sells at every market advance.

If you are not scratching your head at this point, you may be asking yourself what exactly distinguishes day trading from market timing or churning.

A Touch of Market Timing

Day trading is a distant cousin to market timing. Whereas market timing bets big on hunches as to the future, day trading bets smaller on what is happening right now before the close of the market. Market timers buy or sell a good portion of their portfolios based on anticipated stock price movements. They buy when they think a price is low and sell when they think it is high. Day traders resemble their market-timing brethren by buying when they think a stock price is low because it just dropped. They sell when they think a stock price is high because it just rose. In the process, they get the benefit of dollar-cost averaging in buying stock funds and a sort of reverse-dollar-cost averaging in selling stock funds.

The primary distinction between market timing and day trading lies in the process of determining the type (purchase or sale), timing, and amount of a trade. The day trader uses a methodical approach to determine the type and amount of an incremental exchange between stock and cash fund options in a retirement savings plan. The day trader then submits the fund exchange for execution at the same time each day before the close of the market. The market timer uses information, or perhaps a hunch, to determine the type, timing, and amount of a trade.

The disciplined approach to setting up and capturing gains is what makes day trading work when carried out on a consistent basis over the long term. By trading on each and every daily stock market movement, hindsight will show that the many stops and starts of the market may cause some selling before the market reaches the top and buying before it reaches the bottom. Yet these premature sale and purchase mistakes are overwhelmed by the lasting gains set up and captured through daily trades along the way in a choppy market. By taking advantage of every daily directional change in the market, even those that do not materially change the direction of the market on a long-term basis, you profit in a sideways market.

A Bit of Churning

Inertia continues to be an overwhelming force in the management of retirement savings plans, with only 13 percent of defined contribution plan participants making any fund exchanges during 2009. Some might take the view that the more frequent fund exchanges involved in day trading preclude it from being considered a long-term investment strategy. Granted day trading will never be considered a cornerstone of the buy-and-hold strategy, but sound daily trading activity sustained over a long period can be an important component of a long-term retirement savings investment strategy. It is best not to think of day trading as excessively trading, or *churning*, an account. Instead, it should be considered more as an exercise promoting fiscal fitness, which, carried out over the course of your life, will benefit you in retirement.

Day trading would probably not deliver acceptable net returns, after taxes and trading costs, if you tried it in a taxable brokerage account. Just like the ambitious young Kurt, who paid dearly to commute by car from school to work in the real world, you may end up broke using day trading in a brokerage account. Only this time you would owe your indigence to the trading costs and taxes eating away at your day trading returns. It is an entirely different story with a happy ending in a retirement savings plan, where its cost and tax advantages allow you to keep your day trading gains.

Almost There

Now that you have seen how the day trading strategy works and generates better returns than other portfolios in a sideways market, you may very well have decided to wash your hands of the buy-and-hold investment strategy and jump right into day trading your retirement savings. You may already know how to wash your hands, but drying them is another matter just as important to your health for warding off diseases lurking on door handles and such. Likewise, you will need to take an additional measure for maneuvering around potential obstacles that might otherwise inhibit your success in day trading. Only then can you ensure that your day trading will generate gains over the long term.

If you went out and tried day trading your retirement savings portfolio based on what has been covered so far, you might very well last only a few days before you could trade no more. It turns out that retirement savings plans impose restrictions that could get in the way of day trading. If you think you have been snookered, read on.

Like all good adventures, day trading presents some obstacles to overcome. Fortunately, an approach to be discussed in the next chapter will help you maneuver around these obstacles that attempt to thwart efforts to day trade retirement savings accounts. The road map in Chapter 8 guides you step-by-step on your way to day trading your retirement savings portfolio.

PART IV

Process

CHAPTER 8

Game Plan

The Art of Day Trading

Genius is 1 percent inspiration, 99 percent permission.
—Adaptation of Thomas Edison's quote "Genius is 1 percent inspiration, 99 percent perspiration" from *San Francisco Chronicle*, March 10, 2009

She called herself the Karma Queen—something having to do with one good act begetting another. Only this time it applied to parking her car. As a native New Yorker, but from the other part of the state, she could not exist without her car to get around at will. Parking it was a different matter entirely; such a hassle it seemed for everyone else but her.

She liked to believe she lived a simple but good life. For treating people well, she was rewarded with access to the finest parking spots in town. The parking problems the rest of the world faced were not hers, as the most convenient parking spot close to her destination seemed to await her every arrival. Once again a hectic day at work necessitated a perilous, but ever so courteous, car trip downtown. Only a quick parking job would allow her to make it on time to the day's most important engagement—her preschool daughter's ballet recital. She needed a parking spot, and she needed it now. How would she do it?

She had a strategy, confidence, and something magical like a little karma. Her strategy had something to do with slowing way down before arrival at her destination and looking at the big picture for any and every sign of people bidding a quick adieu to their parking spots. She would not wait very long, watching for signs of impending departure like tail lights, wheels turning, and adults entering cars (legally, of course). If you had parked in the right spot, your pulling out was an opportunity for her to pull in. She knew that once past the destination, the closest parking spots to it became more remote—it seems that everybody else needs to drive by to check out their destination before parking. She also had the confidence that only years of parking success (and good karma) can bring.

This time as always, she was on the prowl for that perfect parking spot. This day was no different, as she got the parking spot near the door, arriving just in time to catch her daughter's glance before the lights dimmed. But there just had to be something else, like divine intervention or access to an Internet site, to explain her parking success.

Life is not fair, you might say. Parking is tough in any city; how did she manage to navigate through busy downtown traffic to find the best spots? Whereas most drivers scramble aimlessly for a spot, she would swoop in with an advantage in her approach the world may never fully understand.

By this time, you probably have figured out that the Karma Queen's good fortune in parking her car in a crowded city somehow relates to managing retirement savings. Day trading deals with when and where to park your existing retirement savings account assets. You gain an advantage by consistently following a strategy and seizing the opportunities that come your way every day. You too will have to overcome obstacles along the way. However, that one piece that eludes the rest of the world in the realm of parking is right there for the taking in day trading a retirement savings portfolio. This chapter more specifically addresses how, when, and where to park your retirement savings account assets to overcome existing obstacles.

FREQUENT TRADING POLICIES

This is the part of the story where you as the hero are about to walk off into the sunset as a successful day trader. Only one obstacle remains in your way: Most plans will not allow you to perform the type of day trading described hereto in a single retirement savings account. You may not make frequent fund exchanges into and out of a stock fund in a retirement savings plan. That does seem like a pretty big obstacle. You may as well call it quits at this point. Thanks for reading, and have a good day.

Wait a minute! Did Columbus head back home after he hit a few waves in the great Atlantic? Did the Red Sox give in to the Yankees after losing the first three games in the 2004 American League Championship Series following an 86-year drought without hoisting a World Series trophy? Did the rest of the field fold up their tents before Tiger Woods cruised home with a 15-stroke victory in the 2000 U.S. Open championship at Pebble

Beach? Absolutely not (at least for the first two ... but it's not so clear in the last case).

You too shall succeed, as the day trading strategy has an answer to the trading restrictions imposed by fund companies. Before going there, consider first that retirement savings plans typically offer mutual funds and other collective funds as investment options. As noted earlier, these funds are professionally managed collections of securities that are offered for sale to retail and institutional investors. In a purchase, an investor pays cash for an ownership share in a fund. Upon sale, the investor receives cash upon surrender of fund shares. Under a retirement savings plan, purchases and sales are handled through fund exchanges. An exchange into a fund represents a purchase of fund shares, and an exchange out of a fund represents a sale or redemption of shares.

Each day the fund manager (or its transfer agent) aggregates all shareholders' exchange orders submitted throughout the day for execution at the market close. After settling shareholders' buy and sell orders for each fund, the fund manager executes a market trade in the net amount of all fund shareholders' exchanges in order to maintain the balance of securities within the fund portfolio necessary to maintain its consistency with the fund's investment policy, which is described in its prospectus. The fund manager's daily purchase or sale of securities in settlement of shareholders' exchange orders results in trading costs that are passed along to all shareholders as a reduction in net returns. The individuals submitting fund exchange orders are not directly charged for trading costs associated with fulfilling their exchange orders.

The day trading strategy calls for individuals to make daily fund exchanges. Although most retirement savings plan participants leave their account management on autopilot, the frequent trading of a few has caught the attention of mutual fund companies that manage the majority of assets held in 401(k) plans.[1] Fund companies do not like shareholders frequently trading into and out of stock funds. The settlement of these frequent fund exchanges necessitates additional exchange order processing, accounting, and oversight on the part of the fund manager. Recognizing the additional costs associated with these record-keeping functions and the potential threat that frequent fund exchanges pose to disrupt the management of a fund, mutual fund companies have stepped in to establish restrictions on frequent trading within a single retirement savings account.

These frequent trading policies applicable to stock funds are intended to prevent shareholders from making an excessive number of exchanges into and out of stock funds. Otherwise, the fund investment manager must pay more attention to fund liquidity for accommodating cash needs from shareholder liquidations and purchases, rather than the selection and timing of investments consistent with the fund's underlying investment policy. Not only does the frequent trading of shareholders potentially disrupt the management and administration of stock funds, but the cost sharing arrangement in most stock funds also results in any additional trading costs from frequent fund exchanges dragging down the fund's net return to all shareholders.

The prospectus of a mutual fund describes its frequent trading policies. The amount of detail regarding trading restrictions that is included in fund prospectuses varies from fund to fund. Some offer detailed descriptions of trading restrictions, while others make vague references, leaving the determination of a violation of such restrictions to the discretion of the fund manager.

Frequent trading restrictions typically do not apply to cash funds, which are intended to serve as a liquid source of funds available for withdrawal at any time. However, equity wash rules may restrict fund exchanges from capital preservation funds, such as stable value funds, directly to cash or other competing funds, without first going through a stock fund for a designated period, such as 90 days.

Nonetheless, stock funds discourage frequent trading by imposing limits on round-trip and short-term trades. Some plans limit a participant's overall number of trades involving any funds within a defined time period. An individual's violation of these trading restrictions may result in a suspension of some or all same-day fund exchange privileges or imposition of additional short-term trading fees.

Round-Trip Trading Restrictions

An individual making exchanges into and out of the same fund within a short time period, such as 30 days, is said to have made a *round-trip trade/exchange*.[2] By definition, a round-trip trade is an in-out transaction where a shareholder exchanges into a stock fund only to exchange out of it shortly thereafter. It differs in direction from an out-in transaction, or *reverse round-trip trade/exchange*, where a shareholder exchanges out of a stock fund and quickly back in again.

Because fund companies consider this frequent buying into and selling out of the same fund as disruptive to managing a stock fund, they impose round-trip trading rules to prevent investors from repeatedly exchanging out of a stock fund right after exchanging into it. Their restrictions effectively prevent day trading into a stock fund one day and out the next *within the same account*. Round-trip trading restrictions limit the number of times an investor may exchange into and out of a stock fund within the same account over a defined period of time. Other fund companies restrict reverse round-trip investments into a stock fund after just having pulled out of it.

Frequent trading policies applicable to stock market index funds typically impose rules to limit the number of round-trip trades a shareholder may make within a designated period of time, such as 90 days. These policies vary from one fund company to another. One major mutual fund company limits the number of round-trip trades (where an exchange into the fund is followed by an exchange out of the fund within 30 days) in its stock market index funds to two per 90-day period.[3] Another just flatly refuses an exchange into a stock fund within 60 days of exchanging out of it, as in a reverse round-trip trade.[4] To be safe, it is best to avoid exchanging into a stock fund within 60 days of exchanging out of it.

Once you complete the maximum number of round-trip (in-out) trades in a stock fund or attempt a reverse round-trip (out-in) trade within the defined period, the typical frequent trading policy's penalty is to preclude you from completing an exchange *into* that stock fund within a designated time period after having exchanged *out of* such fund. Both the round-trip and reverse round-trip trading restrictions act to preclude you for a designated time period from exchanging back into the stock fund you just left. In other words, the fund company does not want your stinking money in its stock fund if it thinks you are just going to pull it out shortly thereafter. However, you can still pull your money out of the stock fund even after you exceed the round-trip trading maximum limit. You may be suspended from exchanging into the fund, but the frequent trading policy usually does not prevent an exchange out of a stock fund into which you had just placed your money. In short, these restrictions on round-trip and reverse round-trip trades generally work in only one direction: they prohibit a fund exchange into a stock fund after having recently executed an excessive number of round-trip or reverse round-trip trades in a single account.

Round-trip and reverse round-trip trading restrictions resulting in a suspension of an individual's privilege to exchange into a stock fund typically apply to passively managed stock market index funds where competitive pressures have forced fund managers to offer these funds with minimal offsets from fund returns for management and trading fees. You may note that plans apply these trading restrictions to fund exchanges made within the same individual account. The day trading strategy provides a way to overcome round-trip and reverse round-trip trading restrictions that would otherwise keep you from making daily fund exchanges.

Short-Term Trading Fees

Closely related to round-trip trading is another potentially disruptive trading practice known as short-term trading, which involves a single round-trip trade where stock fund shares are purchased and redeemed within a preset period. To limit short-term trades, some actively managed funds have adopted a frequent trading policy that imposes a short-term trading fee based on the amount withdrawn from a fund within a designated period of its original placement. A typical short-term trading policy applicable to an actively managed stock fund would charge 1.5 percent of the amount an individual withdraws within 90 days of its initial placement in the fund. This short-term trading fee charged at redemption against the offending individual's account is then credited to the fund holdings of the rest of the fund shareholders.

Whereas round-trip trading restrictions apply to both passively managed and actively managed stock funds, short-term trading fees typically apply only to some actively managed stock funds. These short-term trading fees become significant when you are day trading in a retirement savings plan whose only stock fund is an actively managed fund that provides for such fees. It may be comforting to note that short-term trading fees are not assessed for exchanges involving passively managed stock market index funds of the type suggested for day trading.

Same-Day Trade Annual Limits

Although uncommon, some plans limit the number of fund exchanges a participant may initiate within a defined period of time. One such policy limits participants to 20 same-day exchanges initiated by telephone, Internet, or fax per calendar year. After reaching the limit, a participant may make no further same-day exchanges for the rest of the calendar year.

Violations of this type of frequent trading policy are usually handled through a suspension of the investor's privilege to execute same-day fund exchanges into stock funds by telephone, Internet, or fax. The suspension period lasts for the rest of the calendar year. Exchange instructions submitted by regular or overnight mail may still be honored in some cases. However, the uncertainty relating to the timing of the actual execution of the intended exchange submitted by snail mail would render the trading instructions ineffective in a day trading situation.

In more than one way, these frequent trading restrictions serve the fund manager. Not only does the fund manager avoid shareholders' frequent trading that may be disruptive to fund management, but the trading restrictions also discourage trading and lessen the administration of executing more frequent fund exchanges and associated fund portfolio trades. In addition, the round-trip trading rules' suspension of exchanges into market index funds steers investors away from low-cost stock market index funds into more profitable actively managed stock or other funds.

From an investor's perspective, the imposition of frequent trading policies may not seem all that intrusive. The typical buy-and-hold investor may never run up against a plan's trading limits. In addition, the penalty of restricting exchanges only into (but not out of) a stock fund may also allay the more active, but skittish, investors' fears by still letting them trade out of stock in a falling market.

Plan record keepers take responsibility for enforcing frequent trading policies established by fund managers to prevent constant exchanges into and out of stock funds. It may be interesting to note that enforcement of frequent trading policies seems to vary based on whether the affected fund manager also serves as the plan record keeper. For a full description of any of your mutual funds' frequent trading policies, you should check the fund prospectuses.

Since frequent trading policies limit exchanges involving stock funds within a single retirement savings account, it becomes necessary to use more than one account to effectively carry out the day trading strategy. If not for this tactic, frequent trading policies would take away the very essence of what day trading can accomplish in juicing the returns in your retirement savings portfolio.

DAY TRADING THE RIGHT WAY

Throughout this book, the key concepts of day trading have been highlighted in boldface letters along the way to lead you to the process involved in successfully day trading your retirement savings portfolio. It all comes together now.

The day trading concept sounds so simple: Just buy when the market goes down and sell when the market goes up. It really is, but there are a few wrinkles worthy of some attention to avoid getting caught in the web of frequent trading restrictions in carrying out this strategy.

Since day trading's fund exchanges into and out of stock funds within one account would normally violate these frequent trading policies, it becomes necessary to use two accounts: one account for buying stock and the other for selling stock. You can use not only 401(k), but also 403(b), 457, IRA, and other defined contribution plan accounts for day trading. In a way, trades through two parallel but reverse accounts mask day trading, as neither account record keeper tracks what trading activity is going on in an individual's other accounts. From a record keeper's perspective, fund exchanges within an individual account that flow in only one direction may appear as though an individual were trading pursuant to some type of 10b5–1 trading plan that insiders use to periodically dispose of or acquire company stock. Even for accounts handled by the same record keeper, it is as if a Chinese wall is in place to shield each account's transactions. Only through the use of two separate accounts does day trading generate aggregate gains not otherwise attainable with one account.

In short, the day trading strategy calls for a daily fund exchange in one of two separate retirement savings accounts. Each and every day you will use one account or the other to execute a daily trade in response to the market change for the day. You use one account for transfers just before the market close from a stock fund to a cash fund whenever the stock market is advancing for the day. In the other account, you transfer from a cash fund to a stock fund when the market is declining for the day. The stock-selling account captures and preserves gains, and the other (stock-buying) account sets up future gains. The proper use of two separate accounts ensures compliance with the frequent trading restrictions applicable to stock mutual funds within each account.

Each of these accounts will be used exclusively for stock sales or for purchases for as long as there is an applicable fund balance remaining in the account to support the necessary fund exchanges. When you reach the point where your cumulative transfers from a fund have exhausted that account's fund balance, you would introduce another retirement savings account to take over when day trading calls for another redemption from that fund type. For example, when your prior exchanges out of a particular account's stock fund leave no remaining balance, you would bring in a new account with an available stock fund balance to complete your next exchange out of a stock fund.

As day trading is explored here in more detail, keep in mind that the favorable tax and cost treatment afforded day trades applies only to funds within 401(k) and other retirement savings accounts. Within retirement savings accounts, you avoid the direct costs and immediate taxes normally associated with stock trades. The strategy does not address the investment of other savings, personal property, or ongoing contributions to retirement savings accounts.

This day trading process can be broken down into the two phases of setting it up and carrying it out on an ongoing basis. Once you set up your own personal routine, you will be in a position to carry it out within a few minutes each day. The following step-by-step approach will guide you through establishing a routine and carrying out the routine on a daily basis.

Setting Up Day Trading

Some people have a hard time getting going in the morning. Even the simplest of tasks seems to present a special challenge before that first cup of coffee. Others have it easier, but all go through some sort of routine to start the day. So it is with day trading—you need to establish a routine before using it on a daily basis.

Day trading involves navigating through plan, fund, and governmental rules designed to thwart your efforts to make daily fund exchanges within your retirement savings portfolio. Your ability to efficiently carry out the steps required to execute a daily trade depends on establishing a routine that not only complies with the rules but also fits comfortably within your lifestyle.

Step 1: Take Inventory of Your Defined Contribution Retirement Savings Accounts After working at a few companies and participating in their 401(k) or other retirement savings plans, you may be leaving a trail of plan accounts in your wake. That turns out to be a good thing when it comes to day trading defined contribution retirement plan accounts (i.e., those individual account plans).

Do you remember all those solicitations you've been continually receiving from fund companies to entice you into rolling over all of your retirement plan accounts held with prior employers into one individual retirement account (IRA)? The fund companies soliciting your business may tempt you with an offer to consolidate the accounting of all of your balances with former employers into one monthly report. They so want to make your life easier for a price. All they want in return for their asset management and custodial services is a small percentage of the assets you direct their way. Because they collect their fees as a percentage of assets under management, your consolidation of prior retirement plan accounts with their fund company would increase their revenue base.

Your former employer would also probably rather have you take a distribution of your retirement plan accounts once you terminate employment. Once you no longer have a plan account, your employer avoids the expense and hassle of keeping track of your whereabouts and your account for purposes of issuing required annual disclosures and statements for as long as you hold an account under the plan. Chances are your former employer does not mind the plan's fund manager soliciting you to roll over a distribution from your account into a rollover IRA.

Keep in mind that, if your retirement plan account balance is $5,000 or more, you are not required to take a distribution from a former employer's plan until April 1 of the calendar year following the year in which you attain age $70^1/_2$. Until then, you can leave your old accounts in place by taking no action whatsoever. You continue to be a participant enjoying the right to direct the management of your account through fund exchanges under the plan. However, as a terminated employee, you will no longer have some of the rights you had as an employee, such as contributing to the plan (since you no longer earn wages there) or taking out a loan. However, you retain most of the other rights you enjoyed while you were employed.

Another temptation to consolidate accounts may come from your *current* employer, who may accept rollovers of old 401(k) and other retirement savings accounts into your current 401(k) or other retirement savings plan. After all, you would be reducing your ties to your old companies and strengthening your bond financially with your current company. This may be to your advantage in that it would increase your balance available for a loan, if you are considering taking out a loan from the plan. This loan also binds you to your continued employment with the new company due to the cash outlay that would be required to repay the loan in full shortly after termination from your current employer.

You generally need to resist solicitations or temptations to consolidate your retirement savings accounts if you are to take advantage of the day trading strategy. Notwithstanding any overriding reasons to the contrary, you should leave those old 401(k) and other retirement savings accounts in place, as they may be needed to carry out the day trading strategy. Leave them be, and do not consolidate accounts by rolling them over to another plan or into an IRA.

However, there still may be a few cases where you may want to execute a rollover to get some flexibility in your investment options. If you formerly participated in a defined contribution retirement plan with only one fund option or a pension plan (like a cash balance pension plan) that allows for a lump sum distribution, you may want to roll over your lump sum benefit to an IRA—not to your current retirement plan. Such a rollover to an IRA will give you control within a separate account over the management of your assets in such a plan and access to the investment options available from the trustee holding the IRA.

Now dust off those old and current account records and list all of your 401(k), 403(b), 457, IRA, and other retirement savings accounts. From those records, list your account balances broken down by investment or fund option.

Consider the case of an individual with a retirement portfolio of $100,000 sitting in three different retirement savings accounts allowing daily fund exchanges. The aggregate assets within the three accounts are initially invested 50 percent in stock and 50 percent in cash. The sample inventory of retirement savings accounts in Table 8.1 breaks down each account by its funds, each of whose security holdings is dedicated to only one asset class (stocks or cash).

This retirement asset inventory process is something you should be doing anyway. It is always important to know what you have—especially when you are planning what to do with it.

Step 2: Earmark at Least Two Retirement Savings Accounts Suitable for Trading From your inventory of potential trading accounts, you will need to select at least two, preferably three, retirement savings accounts to implement this day trading strategy. You will use one account for all transfers from stock to cash and the other for all transfers from cash to stock. The first account should initially have a significant

TABLE 8.1   Sample Retirement Savings Account Portfolio

Retirement Savings Account	Fund	Current Balance
(AT) Advanced Tech 401(k) Plan		
	Cash/money market fund	$0
	S&P 500 index stock fund	40,000
(BG) Big Government 457 Plan		
	Cash/money market fund	40,000
	S&P 500 index stock fund	0
(CS) Charter School 403(b) Plan		
	Cash/money market fund	10,000
	S&P 500 index stock fund	10,000
Total		$100,000

weighting toward a stock index fund to support fund exchanges out of stock to cash, and the other should have a heavy concentration in a cash fund to support fund exchanges out of cash to stock. All daily transactions will initially occur within these two primary trading accounts, while a third trading account may be held in reserve until needed. More on that later.

If you have only one retirement savings account to your name, you may need to get creative. For example, if your family consolidates its finances, you may want to consider using a spouse's 401(k) plan account to carry out this day trading strategy. (What's mine is yours, and vice versa. Right, honey?) After all, it comes out of the same community pool, if both you and your spouse accumulated your retirement savings accounts while married in a community property state like California.

So your spouse or partner balks at the idea of offering up an account for day trading. For some reason, there are people who just do not like to try new things when it comes to money. You may need to explain the merits of day trading and how it requires at least two accounts to initiate. If your appeals for access to another trading account still fall on deaf ears, you can always approach your loved one with a touch of Father Mike Healy, who preceded a request to his congregation for donations to a church second collection for building a parish community center with: "We have the money; it's just that … it's in *your* pockets."[5] Somehow you need to come up with at least two retirement savings accounts.

It would get a bit more complicated to pull in another relative or friend for a part of the action, especially when you consider that day trading will cause one account to outperform the other at times and underperform the other at other times. The aggregated funds will perform better overall than the market in a sideways market, but the individual accounts from which the aggregated funds are comprised may very well experience different investment results.

In selecting these day trading accounts from your account inventory, you are seeking retirement savings accounts that each include a cash fund and a major market index fund that is trackable on a real-time basis with the following desirable features conducive for day trading:

- The account is valued daily, with unlimited daily exchanges between fund options available online or by telephone or fax. Such a facility to exchange between funds on a daily basis allows you to take advantage of stock market fluctuations through the execution of fund exchanges on a daily basis. The best type of accounts have no preset limit on the annual number of same-day fund exchanges transmitted by Internet, phone, or fax. You can always hold a limited trading account in reserve for emergency trading purposes when other accounts' capacity to trade has already been tapped out.

- The account has a low-cost stock market index fund and a cash fund as fund options. Within each retirement account that you have earmarked for trading, identify the stock market index and cash fund options with the lowest expense ratios. You can obtain a mutual fund's expense ratio by checking its prospectus, which must be made available to you on request. This expense information is probably also available online at the mutual fund's or plan's web site, where you can access your retirement savings account balances. Except for expenses, the investment performance of stock funds based on the same market index should be virtually the same. Therefore, make sure you use the market index fund option with the lowest expenses so that there is the least drag on returns.

- The existing account assets are already invested in a stock market index fund, cash fund, or both. The intent is to start day trading in earnest with aggregate assets in your retirement savings accounts about evenly distributed between a stock market index fund and a cash fund, although ideally one account's assets would be heavily concentrated in the stock market index fund and the other in a cash fund. Absent this initial balance between just these two fund options, you need to gradually direct portfolio assets from other types of funds into these two fund options by subjecting funds grouped by asset class to the operation of the day trading process until all retirement portfolio assets drift toward either a stock market index fund or a cash fund. Eventually the resultant fund exchanges will replace actively managed stock funds with passively managed stock market index funds and replace fixed income funds, such as stable value and bond funds, with cash and money market funds (although not necessarily directly, in order to comply with equity wash sale rules).

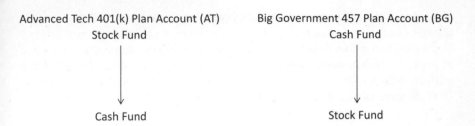

FIGURE 8.1 Purpose of Two Separate Day Trading Accounts

Using these criteria in the context of the sample account inventory in Table 8.1, you would select the Advanced Tech 401(k) Plan account (AT) and Big Government 457 Plan account (BG) as the two initial trading accounts. Each of these plans offers stock market index and cash funds, as well as a sizable balance in at least one of those funds. When market conditions warrant, you would use account AT to sell stock due to its sizable stock fund balance and availability of a cash fund. You would use account BG to buy stock due to its relatively large cash fund balance compared with its stock market index fund balance. (See Figure 8.1.) The Charter School 403(b) Plan account (CS), with its more balanced stock and cash holdings, initially remains idle while standing ready to step in to replace either account AT when AT's stock is depleted or to replace account BG when BG's cash runs out.

Step 3: Calibrate Your Daily Transfer Amount   Once you have identified your day trading retirement accounts with the desired fund options, you need to establish an approach for determining your daily trade amounts. Because each daily fund exchange will involve either one account initially loaded with stock from which exchanges will be made out of stock into cash when the market rises or another account initially heavy in cash from which exchanges will be made out of cash into stock when the market dips, you should make sure your necessary daily fund exchanges will not too quickly deplete your stock-heavy and cash-heavy accounts under different market conditions. The rate at which each account's cash or stock fund balance is depleted depends on the initial balance in the account, as well as on the actual market movements driving the cumulative amount of the daily fund exchanges.

Starting with an Already Balanced Portfolio   If the total of your two primary trading accounts' fund balances is initially split about evenly between stocks and cash, you are ready to start day trading. Normally you will determine each daily fund exchange under a preset calibration formula or factor of your choice applied to the daily change in the stock market. Although your choices are endless, you should use a calibration formula that is simple enough to remember, satisfies the frequent trading policies applicable to your accounts, and sustains fund balances that can withstand withdrawals in the form of fund exchanges between stock and cash for at least 60 days of day trading under normal market conditions.

As noted in Chapter 7, you could easily determine each daily fund exchange amount as the daily point change in the applicable market index multiplied by a constant calibration factor of your choice, expressed in equation form as follows:

$$\text{Daily Fund Exchange Amount} = \text{Market Index Daily Point Change} \times \text{Calibration Factor}$$

Successful day trading in a volatile market depends on the consistent application of a routine you can efficiently apply day in and day out. The use of a constant calibration factor to derive fund exchange amounts provides the type of straightforward approach that fits well into a day trading routine.

Chapter 7 described an easy way to derive a calibration factor by dividing your initial retirement savings portfolio to be subjected to day trading by 1,000. The calculation of exchange amounts seems to flow a little easier when you are multiplying, quite possibly on the fly, a market index daily change by a constant calibration factor. For an initial day trading portfolio of $100,000, the ease and efficiency of performing a simple multiplication of the market change by a nice round and constant calibration factor, like 100 (= $100,000 initial portfolio/1,000), to derive each day's fund exchange amount makes this approach effective for day trading.

Alternatively, you may want to use another way for determining your daily trade amounts to suit your accounts' frequent trading rules and your personal preference. You may also want to temporarily accelerate exchanges in one direction (toward stock or toward cash) in the event you are starting out with a portfolio that is not balanced enough to effectively day trade in both directions on an ongoing basis.

Gaining Initial Portfolio Balance   Day trading relies on the wherewithal of your stock and cash funds in each of your trading accounts to support daily fund exchanges from stock to cash or cash to stock, as appropriate. A shortage of one or the other is detrimental to the process. If your existing retirement savings portfolio is not about evenly split between stocks and cash when you are about to start day trading, you may want to temporarily tilt the amount of your daily fund exchanges in one direction until achieving a more balanced split of assets between stock and cash. The gradual shift in a portfolio's asset allocation carried out through incremental fund transfers over time avoids the detrimental impact a sudden large transfer would have at the wrong time of a market cycle. Any gradual shift to stock also recognizes the value of dollar-cost averaging, as day trading does, to make stock purchases at various price levels over time.

To gradually balance a portfolio initially skewed in one direction, you could adjust your calibration factor by a multiple of 2 until a more even balance between stocks and cash is attained. Then you could revert to your normal calibration of fund exchanges to maintain the consistency required to generate gains by day trading over the long term.

Under normal conditions, an initial portfolio asset allocation of 50 percent stock and 50 percent cash, as in the sample inventory in Table 8.1, would be an acceptable starting point to initiate day trading. In the event the initial portfolio were 70 percent stock and 30 percent cash, you may want to temporarily transfer twice as much as the normal amount from stock to cash in one account whenever the market rose, while transferring just the normal amount from cash to stock in the other account when the market declined. With a regular calibration factor of $100, a market rise of 10 points would have you exchanging $2,000 (= 2 multiple × $100 calibration factor × 10-point rise) out of stock and into cash. A market decline of 5 points would result in a transfer of the normal amount of $500 (= $100 calibration factor × 5-point decline) from cash into stock. This pattern of exchanges would continue until a more even distribution of assets between stock and cash is achieved. From that point on, you would consistently determine your fund exchange amounts in the normal way based on an unadjusted calibration factor.

Day Trading Process

The day trading strategy calls for daily responses to changes in the stock market in the form of buying and selling stock. In the context of a retirement savings account, buying and selling stock is done through fund exchanges. An account holder directs a fund exchange by submitting instructions to the account record keeper to transfer all or a portion of one fund to another fund within the same account.

Day trading works through the alternating use of two separate retirement savings accounts to set up and capture stock market gains. Within each of these two accounts, you must be able to make daily exchanges between two fund options: a stock fund and a cash fund. Each day you sell stock for cash to preserve past gains or use cash to buy stock for setting up future gains. In an ideal situation, the stock fund in each of your trading accounts will be a stock market index fund corresponding to a widely available index (such as the S&P 500 index) on which you will base your trades. When your account assets are not invested in stock, they will sit in the cash fund of each account.

If the stock market index goes up by day's end, one account's exchange out of a stock market index fund into the cash fund constitutes a stock sale that captures and protects a portion of the past gains from any future decline. If the market index goes down, the other account's exchange out of a cash fund into the stock market index fund constitutes a stock purchase that sets up, or takes advantage of, the next market rally with a portion of your account.

This is where you have to be careful. Each of the two mirror-image retirement savings accounts will be assigned the role of handling all exchanges going in only one direction (either cash to stock or stock to cash) in order to comply with frequent trading rules and avoid any short-term trading fees. In the beginning, you will use one primary trading account loaded with cash to execute all the exchanges from the cash fund to the stock fund, and the other stock-loaded primary trading account for transfers from stock to cash. When your holdings in an account's particular fund are eventually exhausted from the exchanges coming out of it, you will need to switch in a new account from your inventory to replace the exhausted account. The new account takes over where its predecessor left off.

Each daily exchange amount is determined under a preset calibration formula or factor of your choice applied to the daily change in the stock market index. The daily change in the stock market index just prior to the market close drives not only the amount of each daily fund exchange and the direction of the exchange, but also the account in which the exchange will be executed. For days when the stock market index declines, you transfer money at the market close from the initially cash-rich account's cash fund into its stock market index fund. When the market advances, you transfer money from the initially stock-laden account's stock fund into the cash fund. For day trading to work, you must submit your order for your one daily fund exchange just prior to the market close based on the daily stock market index change at that time. A graphic representation of three daily transactions for the two primary trading accounts picked from the previous sample account inventory is presented in Figure 8.2.

Recall that you are going through the trouble of using two accounts in day trading to satisfy stock funds' frequent trading restrictions. You cannot simply day trade with only one account. Fortunately, the fuss of day trading with two accounts, rather than one, is worthwhile, in that the improved aggregate investment performance generated by day trading with two accounts is identical to the impressive performance that would have been generated in one account, if so allowed.

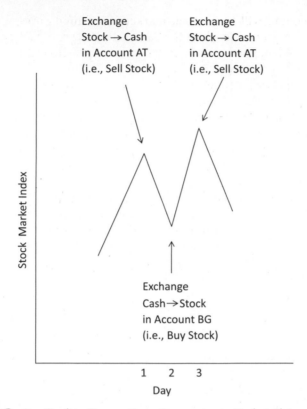

FIGURE 8.2 Day Trading Transactions Responsive to Market Changes

Refer back to the example in Table 7.1 in Chapter 7, in which day trading a single stock generated gains over the course of three days in a volatile market. Only now you need to relate it to exchanging into and out of a stock market index fund in response to changes in the market index. You also know that day trading requires the use of two separate accounts to satisfy frequent trading restrictions. So you use two accounts known as accounts A and B, each offering both cash and stock market index funds for day trading. Consider modifying that example to place the initial $400 of stock holdings entirely in account A and none in account B. Account A, with its initial composition of $400 in the market index fund and $0 in the cash fund, will be used for selling stock when the market rises. Then add $100 to account B's cash fund. Account B, composed initially of $0 in the stock market index fund and $100 in the cash fund, will then be used for buying stock when the market dips.

Using the same calibration factor calling for a trade of $100 for each one-point change in the market index, Table 8.2 develops the individual

TABLE 8.2 Day Trading in Two Accounts

(1)	(2)	(3)	(4)	(5)	(6)	(7)	(8) = (3) + (5)	(9) = (4) + (6)
	Stock Market Index	Account A		Account B			Total	
Day		Stock	Cash	Stock	Cash	# Stock Shares	Stock	Cash
1 (at opening)	$4	$400	$0	$0	$100	100	$400	$100
1 (before close)	5	500		0	100	100	500	100
1 (sell stock)	5	−100	+100	0	0	−20	−100	+100
1 (at close) = 2 (at opening)	5	400	100	0	100	80	400	200
2 (before close)	4	320	100	0	100	80	320	200
2 (buy stock)	4	0	0	+100	−100	+25	+100	−100
2 (at close) = 3 (at opening)	4	320	100	100	0	105	420	100
3 (before close)	5	400	100	125	0	105	525	100

and aggregate account balances that result from day trading with two parallel trading accounts over the same volatile three-day period from Table 7.1 without concern for future trades that may deplete one or the other account's fund source for exchanges.

Table 8.2 shows how day trading generates the same aggregate stock gains in two accounts as it did with one account in Table 7.1 over a volatile but sideways three-day period. Splitting the trades into two separate accounts had no effect on the aggregate results for the stock funds. As was the case for the single stock in Table 7.1, the total value of the aggregated stock funds within the two trading accounts in Table 8.2 grew from $400 to $525 over the course of three days. The $100 cash introduced to enable stock purchases ended unchanged in total, albeit ending up in account A rather than where it started in account B. It just goes to show that two accounts are as good as one in terms of performance, and even better when you consider that day trading would not otherwise be possible with only one account.

Figure 8.3 demonstrates the advantage day trading with two accounts has over holding stock by comparing, in a graphical format, the aggregate balances resulting from day trading with simply holding stock over only the first two days of these fluctuating market conditions where the stock market index ends up where it started.

Ongoing Day Trading

Day trading thrives on stock market volatility. Since a fairly priced market will have as even a chance of going up as it does going down, the best time

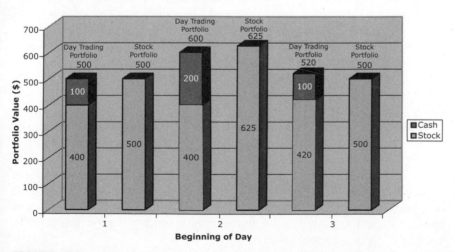

FIGURE 8.3 Comparison of Day Trading with Stock Holding in Volatile but Sideways Stock Market

to start day trading is when the stock market is fairly valued. Just when that happens is anybody's guess, as investors differ in their views as to any given security's true price at any point in time. The process of reaching a consensus among investors' different perspectives as to a security's worth is what makes a market. The changing perspectives of investors over time generate the market volatility upon which day trading relies to generate gains. Since no one really knows what the market will bring, now is as good a time as any to start day trading.

Step 4: Trade Daily in Mirror-Image Parallel Retirement Savings Accounts   Once you have selected your two primary day trading accounts and calibrated the amount of your trades to the market index, you are ready to start day trading. The ongoing process of day trading essentially involves taking a few minutes each day to observe the daily change in the stock market, determine a trade responsive to the market change, and execute the corresponding fund exchange.

Observe Closing Daily Market Index Change   These days people seem to have no lack of ways to access the latest news and respond to it. Modern technology has enabled Americans to get real-time news and conduct business in places ranging from the boardroom to the bathroom and even in more remote locations from the freeway to the fairway. It has gotten to the point where folks sometimes find themselves more connected to their smart phones and computers than to loved ones. This is not good if you have a life, but it can be useful for a few minutes each day around the close of the stock market if you day trade your retirement savings portfolio.

The major U.S. stock exchanges close precisely at 4 P.M. eastern time every weekday, except on holidays and other special occasions. Fund shares in most retirement savings accounts are traded at the market closing price in effect at day's end.

If you are like most people, you want to have a pretty good idea of what you are giving up or getting for something you buy or sell. You as a savvy day trader need to know at what price your stock fund shares will be traded. You also need the amount of the daily change in the market index to determine your trade amount for the day. Therefore, just before each daily market close, you need access to real-time market data relating to the daily change in the stock market index on which your trade will be based. Although continuous updates on major market indexes, such as the S&P 500 index, are generally available throughout the day online, by phone, and on television, day trading does not require tracking of such information until just prior to the market close.

The transmission of market index closing information is comparable to that of the Super Bowl halftime show on television, only the delay is more like a few minutes rather than a few seconds to view what just took place. Just as television editors need time to ensure a Super Bowl halftime show does not include any inappropriate content, market analysts take a few minutes to tally all the last-second trades, such as mutual fund exchanges, executed at the market close. Once this process is complete, the final market index closing price used for fund exchanges submitted before the market close is posted.

From the time you submit your exchange order before the market close until the time the market index fund's actual closing price is determined a few minutes after the close, you will not know the actual fund price at which your transaction was executed. Because you had to submit an exchange order just prior to the market close for it to take effect then, you will experience a brief period of uncertainty as to the actual price at which your exchange transaction will be settled. Your determination of the fund exchange amount may also differ from the amount you would have calculated had you known the actual market index closing price posted a few minutes after the market close.

To the extent that you minimize this period of uncertainty, you can get a better feel at the time you submit your exchange order for the actual market price at which your fund exchange transaction will be executed. Each day you submit a fund exchange order, you will want to base it on the most current market index information available just prior to the market close. In that way, you minimize the impact that the delay in the reporting of the actual closing price can have on your trade. (See Figure 8.4.)

Determine Trade Account, Direction, and Amount Armed with the direction and amount of the daily change in the market index, you are now in a position to determine the account source, type, and amount of the fund exchange you submit prior to the market close. Under the simplest approach, the amount of your daily fund exchange is simply your preset

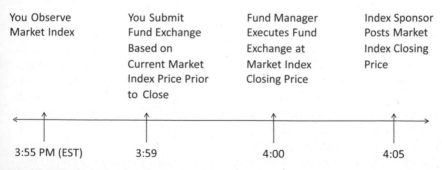

| You Observe Market Index | You Submit Fund Exchange Based on Current Market Index Price Prior to Close | Fund Manager Executes Fund Exchange at Market Index Closing Price | Index Sponsor Posts Market Index Closing Price |

3:55 PM (EST)   3:59   4:00   4:05

FIGURE 8.4 Time Line of Day Trade

calibration factor multiplied by the daily point change in the stock market index just prior to the market close.

You will use one primary trading account exclusively for selling stock by exchanging from the stock market index fund into the cash fund every day the market index advances. These daily exchanges after market index advances will continue in this same direction out of the market index fund and into the cash fund until you have exhausted all your assets in the account's market index fund. Another market advance at this point would necessitate switching to an idle, reserve account with a balance in a stock market index fund in order to continue making transfers out of stock into cash when the market rises. Because trading restrictions generally preclude immediate exchanges back into a market index fund from which you had just exchanged out, you will need to rest this stock-depleted account in trading limbo for the requisite waiting period (such as 60 days) before switching the direction of its exchanges from its new status as a fully loaded cash fund into its empty market index fund.

Under the other primary trading account, you will be buying stock by exchanging from the cash fund into the market index fund every day the market index retreats. You will keep making exchanges in this same direction out of cash into stock until you have exhausted your balance in the cash fund. Once the cash is gone from this account, you need to bring in a replacement account loaded with cash to facilitate exchanges from its cash fund into its stock market index fund. You may still be able to use this newly cashed-out, but fully loaded stock account now or rest it until it is needed later to carry on exchanges in the opposite direction from stock to cash in replacement of an account with a tapped-out market index fund. Although such an immediate turnaround from buying to selling a stock fund may trigger short-term trading fees in an actively managed stock fund, this type of exchange *out* of a market index fund by itself does not necessarily run afoul of the round-trip trading restrictions that preclude multiple in-out market index fund exchanges.

The foregoing discussion dealt with the transition of primary trading accounts when you have three accounts available for day trading. See Appendix A for an additional description of swapping in new accounts to replace exhausted accounts when you are working with three accounts. The actual process of swapping in a new account becomes a whole lot easier if you have more than three accounts to work with. In such an event, you replenish a tapped-out fund by replacing the account in which the fund was exhausted with a formerly idle account that has a corresponding fund balance.

Execute the Exchange   You can drive all the way to the basket, but you must still take the shot. As simple as it may seem, you have to execute in a timely fashion the trade you just determined. In a retirement savings plan, your trade takes place by submitting fund exchange instructions specifying the account in which a transfer is being made, the dollar amount of the transfer, the source fund option from which the transfer is being withdrawn, and the destination fund to which the transfer is being added. The account record keeper executes fund exchanges at the market close of the same day on which it receives properly submitted instructions before the market close.

Account record keepers typically facilitate your fund exchanges through their sophisticated online and telephone systems. Once you identify yourself with an account identification number (such as your Social Security number) and password to log into your account, you are in a position to submit fund transfer instructions. Be sure you get familiar with the account transaction process, whether it be online or by phone.

Although more cumbersome, some plans may also allow participants to submit fund exchange instructions in a specified written form. You would need to check with your account record keeper to see if a designated fund exchange order form submitted by fax would be an acceptable way to direct a same-day fund transfer.

You have a deadline to respect each and every trading day. Such discipline makes a difference in your retirement portfolio's investment performance. You must submit an exchange order *prior* to the close of the market for it to be executed that same trading day. That deadline is the close of the market at 4 P.M. eastern time sharp, unless it is a holiday or other special occasion—not one second later. This is tough love; it is a hard close with no ifs, ands, or buts. So take a few minutes to execute your daily fund exchange before wrapping up your coffee break when in Hawaii, lunchtime when on the West Coast, siesta in the Rocky Mountain states, after-school snack in the Midwest, and workday on the East Coast.

Any exchange submitted after the market close will not be executed until the end of the next trading day on which the market is open. If the market turns the other way the next day, a one-day delay in your trade causes you to forgo capturing some of the first day's market's gains or setting up future gains from the first day's market decline. However, if you get lucky and the market continues in the same direction for another day, your delayed trade has enabled you to capture or set up more market gains over the two days, rather than just the one day. The type of discipline required for day trading does not contemplate this type of good luck recurring on an ongoing basis.

Step 5: Keep Track   Your fund exchanges within each trading account will be independently tracked by your respective account record keepers or plan administrators. You can usually check and review your transaction history online in the web site dedicated to account record keeping.

For a consolidated view of your day trading account transactions, you should also keep a personal written record of your fund exchanges. This record will look like a checkbook or check register, but for tracking fund exchanges. In such a register, you should record the date, market index closing price, and market index daily change, as well as account used for the exchange, fund exchange source, destination, and amount.

You should keep this register for each day that the stock exchanges are open, regardless of whether you actually make a trade. This daily record is helpful in reviewing your exchange history for consistency or if you miss some day trades and want to make them up in a future trade. On the basis of the market index closing price you record for each day, the amount of the trade will be either a positive number indicating an exchange into a stock fund or a negative number indicating an exchange out of a stock fund. The listing of the account, fund source from which the exchange is transferred, and its destination for the exchange will be helpful in ensuring compliance with funds' frequent trading rules.

Table 8.3 presents an example of a weeklong register to record the day trading activity between the S&P 500 index and cash funds within accounts AT and BG from the sample day trading portfolio presented in Table 8.1. Each daily trade amount is determined by multiplying a calibration factor of 100 by the daily point change in the S&P 500 index and then rounded to the nearest $100. The different shadings of typeface for the register's lines distinguish between the S&P 500 index's daily positive and negative changes upon which the day trader's corresponding stock sales and purchases are based.

This daily register tracks the first two daily fund exchanges from cash to stock in account BG followed by no exchange, and then two successive daily fund exchanges from stock to cash in account AT. One flat week does not a market make. Once again you make something out of nothing with timely fund exchanges made in response to daily changes in a week of a

TABLE 8.3 Sample Day Trading Register

| Date | S&P 500 Index | | Account | Fund Source | Fund Destination | Trade Amount |
	Close	Change				
11/12/10	1,199.21	—	—	—	—	—
11/15/10	1,197.95	−1.46	BG	Cash	Stock	+$100
11/16/10	1,178.34	−19.41	BG	Cash	Stock	+1,900
11/17/10	1,178.59	+0.25	—	—	—	0
11/18/10	1,196.69	+18.10	AT	Stock	Cash	−1,800
11/19/10	1,199.73	+3.04	AT	Stock	Cash	−300

shaky S&P 500 index that ended just about where it started. With market volatility like that experienced during this otherwise unremarkable week, your additional return from day trading would amount to almost 2.75 percent on an annualized basis.

The process of determining and executing your daily trade in these Steps 4 and 5, respectively, is to be repeated each day the stock exchanges are open. Once you have developed your own personal routine, your daily trade should take no more than a few minutes per day.

Holding the Course within Reason

Here is where fear and greed come into play. Any reasonable adult can get really wrapped up in stock market momentum or gyrations to the point of panic selling out of fear or giddy buying due to greed. Remember that retirement portfolio day traders are a disciplined bunch going against the grain. They sell when others are bidding up the market and buying at ever higher levels. On the other side, they buy when others are dumping their stocks and driving the market lower. It may become really difficult to continue with this contrarian strategy in the face of adversity. However, day traders need to stay the course within reason in order for it to work.

Judgment comes into play with respect to how much of your portfolio to subject to day trading and whether to impose limits on an aggregate portfolio's exposure to stock. Although it is your call on when to rein in the day trading of your retirement savings portfolio, you must recognize that any such self-imposed limits you place on your day trading affect your investment performance.

How Much Portfolio to Day Trade   Since day trading works best within the tax- and cost-friendly environment of retirement savings accounts, it is likely that only a portion of your household assets is of the nature that would benefit from day trading. You may have financial and other assets in insurance, savings, and brokerage accounts; real and personal property; and an ability to earn a living that you cannot effectively subject to day trading. Even for your retirement savings accounts, you may be selective in which ones and how much you subject to day trading.

The portion of your portfolio you will want to day trade under normal circumstances depends on many things, including your current portfolio allocation, immediate and anticipated cash flow needs, investment philosophy, and personal preference. You should designate one account with the most stock holdings and another with significant cash holdings as your primary day trading accounts. Then you may separately manage (or leave out from day trading) other accounts invested in other holdings. It is your choice.

The extent to which you can continue to day trade your retirement savings accounts over time depends on your retirement horizon. When you approach retirement, you may need to scale back your day trading to accommodate your need to draw down your retirement savings in the near future. Your liquidity needs will take precedence over day trading. Think of your portfolio in two tiers: one used for living expenses and the other for day trading. Therefore, you would need to limit your day trading to retirement savings accounts that you need not access for at least the next five years. In retirement, you cannot afford to day trade retirement savings accounts you need to draw down by law or for supporting yourself in the next five years. That leaves the rest of your retirement savings portfolio for day trading to the extent it would not interfere with your liquidity needs.

Overall Exposure to Stocks   Regardless of your propensity for risk, it is never advisable to dedicate too much of your investment portfolio to stocks, especially as you approach retirement. You can limit your portfolio's stock exposure to a floating target allocation based on your proximity to retirement or to a reasonably fixed range dictated by prudence and experience. In either case, you would need to measure your investment portfolio's exposure to stocks by comparing your total stock holdings relative to all of your financial assets, such as stocks, bonds, and cash. No personal or real property, such as cars, houses, boats, or, for that matter, houseboats, is considered. This measure considers aggregate assets within both retirement accounts and personal savings and brokerage accounts.

Transition toward Retirement Ready

History has shown that stocks, while volatile, outperform all other asset classes over time. Because a swoon in stock prices late in your career could devastate your retirement dreams, time-tested advice suggests that investors reduce their investment portfolio's stock exposure as they approach retirement. Day trading's natural shift out of stocks in an increasing market should assist in accomplishing the goal of gradually reducing portfolio risk as you age. Yet it may very well happen that your exposure to stocks turns out to be different than what you would like as you approach retirement. The markets' tendency for volatility necessitates that you monitor your exposure to stocks so as to avoid the risk of undue stock exposure upon retirement at the wrong time of the stock market cycle.

Fixed Stock Exposure Boundaries

The renowned value investor Benjamin Graham recommended that investors maintain an exposure to common stocks within a range of 25 percent to 75 percent of their financial assets, with the rest to be invested in bonds (and other fixed income instruments such as cash).[6] To follow this guiding rule applicable to all household financial assets would seem to require continual monitoring to ensure that an individual's retirement savings portfolio's shifting exposure to stocks resulting from day trading did not cause his or her household portfolio's exposure to stocks to stray from the acceptable 25 to 75 percent range. Yet an easier solution would call for an earlier dedication to stocks and bonds (before the commencement of day trading) of a portion of assets that will not be subject to day trading. For example, an investor with $200,000 in household financial assets may initially decide to invest $50,000 in stocks and $50,000 in bonds outside of the remaining $100,000 in retirement savings accounts that will be day traded. Then the investor will initially have at least a 25 percent cushion of household assets each in stocks and bonds outside of day trading accounts. Any additional stock and fixed income holdings within retirement savings accounts only add to those held outside of retirement accounts. The initial cushion of stock and bond holdings outside of retirement accounts may justify only periodic portfolio monitoring at first until the aggregate portfolio's asset allocation between stocks and fixed income holdings gets significantly skewed by their different returns over time.

If you reach the point where your stock exposure would fall outside your (or Mr. Graham's) comfort level, day trading still presents opportunities for gains. Whether you continue to go forward at full bore or cut back is your choice. In either case, you are advised to proceed cautiously at your own risk.

Portfolio Adjustments   When a retirement savings portfolio adjustment becomes necessary, you have some alternatives. Although panic may cause some weaker souls to stop trading altogether, a better course would involve making necessary but gradual portfolio asset allocation adjustments through ongoing contributions or fund transfers.

Ongoing Contribution Redirection

If you are still contributing to a retirement savings account, you have an opportunity to alter your portfolio's asset allocation over time by redirecting the allocation of your ongoing contributions between stock and cash. If your portfolio becomes bloated with too much stock purchased in the course of day trading in a declining market, you can temporarily direct more or all of your new contributions into the cash fund. By contrast, if your portfolio is becoming too cash-heavy from day trading's stock sales in a rising market, you can direct new contributions into the stock fund. Although these temporary contribution elections may run contrary to the fundamental buy-low-and-sell-high philosophy behind day trading, preserving a reasonable portfolio balance may be more important to you.

For example, Lunchpail Lisa wants to adjust her retirement portfolio allocation between stock and fixed income investments to follow the Rule of 100. At her current age of 55, she seeks to have 55 percent in cash (for her fixed income portion) and 45 percent in stock. She has even gone to the extent of directing that her ongoing 401(k) contributions go 55 percent into cash and 45 percent into stock. However, upon reviewing her portfolio, she found that she currently has 60 percent in cash and 40 percent in stock. In order to adjust her portfolio toward a heavier stock weighting, Lunchpail Lisa may want to temporarily direct more of her ongoing contributions into stock and less into cash. So she could decide to temporarily change her ongoing contributions to be directed 100 percent toward stock and nothing to cash. In this case, she gets the benefit of dollar-cost averaging in buying stock.

Fund Transfers

In the event you no longer contribute to a retirement savings account or seek to rebalance your retirement savings portfolio quickly, you may resort to adjusting the mix of your assets by making gradual fund exchanges that get you to your target asset allocation. As noted earlier, you could accomplish such a portfolio adjustment by doubling up your normal trade amounts in the direction that will accelerate reaching your target asset allocation.

Temporary Trading Hiatus   If you stop day trading for some reason or are prevented from day trading because you have no account to replace an account with a completely exhausted stock or cash fund, you should note the level of the market index when you suspend day trading and wait until the market reaches that level again on its way back before resuming your day trading with an available balance. For example, if you had decided to stop day trading when the S&P 500 index dropped below a 750 closing price on February 27, 2009, you would not have resumed day trading again until it reached a closing price of at least 750 on its way back up on March 12, 2009. It was a pretty scary time, but you had better have a good reason for missing out on some opportunities for day trading gains during that period.

TWEAKING DAY TRADING TO FIT YOU

Volatile markets with wide market swings are ripe for day trading. Although you cannot control market volatility, you can harness it to your advantage through day trading. The possibilities of day trading are endless. You can fine-tune some of the components of day trading, such as the calibration formula, fund options, and trading frequency, to suit your risk tolerance and lifestyle. In making any adjustments to your day trading process, it is of paramount importance to keep it simple and consistent in its approach.

Calibration Formula

When you originally set out to day trade, you decide on a calibration formula to determine how much to trade based on each movement in the market index being tracked. This set formula serves as your guide in determining the amount of each daily trade.

A volatile market fuels day trading gains. In a less volatile market, a day trader may want to make larger bets on each market movement by adjusting the calibration formula. All other things being equal, a juiced calibration formula providing for increased trade amounts will enhance retirement savings portfolio returns in a sideways market. A calibration factor twice as large as another, such as 200 instead of 100, would set up and capture gains twice as fast. Because these larger daily trades would exhaust your stock and cash funds earlier, you may need to accelerate the replacement of these exhausted accounts with accounts replenishing these funds as necessary to continue day trading. More frequent replacement of trading accounts would necessitate mindful awareness of the frequent trading restrictions applicable to recycling a previously used account to take over trades in one direction shortly after completing trades in the other direction. These restrictions generally prohibit using an account for a stock purchase (exchange from cash to stock) right after having used it for a stock redemption (exchange from stock to cash).

However, a decrease in the daily trade amounts resulting from a calibration formula with less punch would reduce your returns from day trading. As a result, your funds would go longer without replenishment of new funds from other accounts. There are about as many variations in a calibration formula as your imagination can behold.

Market Index Daily Point Change   So far, a simple calibration factor, such as $100 for each one-point change in a stock market index, has been used to determine the daily fund exchange amount between stock and cash under day trading. Basing each daily trade on a constant calibration factor is an easy formula to remember and use on an ongoing basis. Of course, there are variations on this theme.

Market Index Daily Percentage Change   Instead of using a calibration factor of a flat-amount-per-point of daily change in the stock market index, one alternative calibration formula would provide for the use of a calibration percentage based on the daily percentage change in the market index for determining the daily trade amount. In this case, the trade amount would be derived as a percentage of the retirement savings portfolio equal to the percentage change, or factor thereof, in the market index. In the case of a calibration formula calling for each transfer to be a percentage of the portfolio that matches the daily percentage change in the market index, if the market index declined by 1 percent for a day, the amount of that day's fund exchange from the cash fund to the stock market index fund in a $100,000 retirement portfolio would be $1,000 (= $100,000 portfolio × 0.01 market index change). If the retirement portfolio initially comprises $50,000 in stock and $50,000 in cash at the beginning of the day, its balance after the fund exchange at the end of the day will be $99,500, composed of $50,500 (= $50,000 beginning stock fund balance × (1 − 0.01) + $1,000 fund exchange) in stock and $49,000 (= $50,000 beginning cash fund balance − $1,000 fund exchange) in cash.

Daily Rebalancing   Another alternative formula might call for daily portfolio rebalancing. In this case, the daily fund exchange amount between stock and cash is determined as the amount necessary to bring the retirement portfolio back to a target asset allocation between stock and cash after each daily change in the stock market. Again consider the case of a $100,000 retirement savings portfolio, allocated 50 percent to stock and 50 percent to cash. Starting with $50,000 in a stock market index fund and $50,000 in cash, a market index decline of 1 percent for a day would bring the portfolio value to $99,500, with $49,500 in stock [= (1 − 0.01) × $50,000 initial stock fund balance] and $50,000 in cash by the end of the day. To bring the retirement savings portfolio back to a 50/50 split between stock and cash before the market close, that day's fund exchange from cash to stock would then be $250 [= ($99,500 portfolio balance/2) − $49,500 end-of-day stock fund balance]. The total portfolio balance after the end-of-day fund exchange remains $99,500, but with $49,750 in stock and $49,750 in cash. This daily rebalancing process can get more complicated if you introduce other target asset allocations. Such complexity is not an attractive feature in a calibration formula intended to facilitate an easy calculation of fund exchange amounts responsive to stock market changes.

Periodic Rebalancing   If less involvement in portfolio rebalancing is your preference, some plan administrators and advice providers offer platforms with features to facilitate (through e-mail alerts) or actually perform less frequent rebalancing of retirement savings accounts. You should check with your plan administrator or plan web site to see if this offer for outside help in rebalancing your accounts is available.

Only a disciplined application of day trading over time will generate favorable investment performance in a volatile market. Any tinkering with the calibration formula should give due consideration to its potential impact on the viability of continuing to apply a balanced, methodical approach in the absence of emotion, where day trading derives its value. Also, do not underestimate the value of being able to quickly determine a trade amount just before the market close each day. Not only must a calibration formula be simple enough to remember and apply consistently, but it must also produce trades that you can reasonably expect will keep an entire portfolio's asset allocation within acceptable ranges, even after a string of market movements in the same direction over a short period of time.

Other Fund Options

The day trading strategy derives its value from daily exchanges between a stock fund and a cash fund. The volatility of stocks and the stability of cash drive the day trading strategy. The vast majority of retirement savings plans offer stock, bond, and cash investment options, as well as combinations thereof. The day trading strategy considers all but the straight stock and cash funds to be superfluous. As the architect of your own personal day trading system, you have some choices to make within these two categories of funds.

Stock Market Index Fund   The discussion so far has focused on the use of a broad-based stock market index fund, like one of the many based on the S&P 500 index, in day trading. Many fund companies managing 401(k) plans and other retirement savings accounts offer a fund that tracks the commonly referenced S&P 500 index. This index represents the composite weighted average stock price of 500 of the largest companies in the United States. Although you cannot invest directly in the S&P 500 index, you can invest in many passively managed funds that mimic the return of the S&P 500 index through investments in the stocks of a substantial number of companies constituting the index. Due to its broad holdings, the S&P 500 index can be considered to be reflective of the overall market.

Other passively managed funds based on other market indexes may also be worthy of consideration for day trading. Remember, you seek a stock market index fund for use in day trading that offers the key attributes of low cost, stability from primary holdings in domestic companies, broad-based diversification, wide availability as a retirement savings plan fund option, and correspondence with an easily tracked market index.

The three most widely publicized stock market indexes are the Dow Jones Industrial Average, the NASDAQ Composite index, and the S&P 500 index. The Dow Jones Industrial Average is an arithmetic average of the stock prices of 30 large U.S. industrial companies. The NASDAQ Composite index is heavily weighted with stocks of U.S. companies in the technology sector. Although easily tracked, the Dow Jones Industrial Average and the NASDAQ Composite index are not as suitable for use in guiding day trades, primarily because of their limited diversification and lack of availability as fund options in 401(k) plans and other retirement savings accounts. The wide availability of low-cost funds tracking the heavily publicized S&P 500 index makes these the favorites for day trading.

Other less publicized stock index funds with even broader exposure to the entire stock market, such as a total stock market index fund, are acceptable choices for day trading, although you may have problems getting real-time quotes for other than the three major indexes just before the end of a trading day. In this event, you may be trading somewhat blindly in one index fund based on a real-time quote for another index. You would have the same problem with trading actively managed stock funds which, by their very nature, do not track indexes and cannot be monitored until day's end when their closing prices are posted.

Despite the almost universal availability of actively managed stock funds, the diversification, low-cost structure, and near market-matching returns offered by a passively managed stock market index fund make it most suitable for day trading. So many of investors' hard-earned dollars are wasted on expenses charged by investment managers who produce little or no value. Granted, an investment fund that beats the market is worth the price. However, as noted earlier, few beat the market on a consistent basis. So the day trading strategy works best with passively managed index funds with low investment management fees.

If a retirement account does not offer a stock market index fund, you can use another well-managed stock fund with low expenses in its place. However, due care must be exercised to avoid some actively managed funds' short-term redemption fees for selling shares within a restricted trading period, such as 90 days.

Because the United States continues to stand out as the most powerful and stable economy in the world, the day trading strategy uses only domestic stock funds primarily invested in companies based in the United States. It also helps that these domestic stock funds available for investment in retirement savings accounts are highly regulated. Pure day trading does not contemplate the use of worldwide or foreign funds primarily invested in foreign companies that are not as tightly regulated as those in the United States. Furthermore, trading in foreign funds is even trickier due to the lapse in time between the close of foreign and U.S. markets.

Individual stocks are never a good choice for use in day trading due to their trading costs and, by definition, lack of diversification. Do not day trade any account assets held in individual stocks that would require a direct payment of commissions for trades, as these would be too costly to trade daily. Only if you decide to bite the bullet and sell these stocks to transfer the proceeds to mutual-fund-type stock or cash funds could these assets be useful for day trading. When a company goes bankrupt in an index fund, its impact is softened by the presence of other companies retaining their value and the bankrupt company's worthless stock eventually being replaced by that of another viable company. Such is not the case with an individual company's stock, which loses all its value if it goes bankrupt.

Cash   Cash is king in day trading. Cash is chosen as one of the fund options over other fixed income funds because of its stability, liquidity, and wide availability as a fund option. It serves as a temporary placeholder for idle money until called upon to purchase stock.

   If a retirement account does not offer a cash fund option, substitute a money market, stable value, liquid certificate of deposit with no term, or other similar type of fixed income fund instead. Because you would incur interest penalties upon liquidation of a term deposit, it is not an acceptable form of a cash fund for day trading. Although the inverse relationship of bonds' returns with those of stocks could distinguish a bond fund as a replacement for a cash fund, the stability and liquidity of cash complement the volatility of stock, making a cash fund the preferred parking spot for account assets not invested in stock funds.

Trading Frequency

The day trading strategy works most effectively when you track the market on a daily basis and make fund exchanges accordingly. But work, play, vacations, and other personal stuff happens; so you miss a day or more. Then there are those not willing or able to trade daily who prefer to undertake a strategy requiring less frequent trades. Keep in mind that you cannot place any retroactive makeup day trades that would enable you to recover any forgone gains from the intervening market volatility. Although you may miss out on capturing past gains and setting up future gains from the intervening market volatility during the period in which your trading was interrupted, you can perform a net trade upon your resumption of trading to get back in the game.

   Using the same day trading concept, you determine the amount of your next trade by applying your calibration formula to the net change in the market index since your last trade. Assume you use a calibration factor of $100 for each one-point change in the market index. If the S&P 500 index increased 25 points from 1,000 to 1,025 during your holiday from trading, you would exchange $2,500 (= $100 calibration factor × 25 points) from the S&P 500 index fund into the cash fund upon your return. This catch-up exchange gets your portfolio back to where it would have been except for any forgone gains that may have resulted from missing out on opportunities to capitalize on market fluctuations during your trading holiday.

If the stock market happened to go straight up or straight down during your trading hiatus, you lucked out. In a continually rising market, your single trade upon your return would enhance your investment performance by capturing more past gains in that single trade instead of presenting a drag on returns caused by daily trades that incrementally capture daily gains, which forgo future gains once they have already been placed in cash. Whereas volatile markets favor day traders, markets headed in one direction favor less frequent traders.

Consider the case of two traders who hold a stock fund initially valued at $1,000 that rises by 1 percent each day for two days. The first day trader sells his stock fund gain of $10 (= $1,000 × 0.01) the first day and has $1,000 in stock and $10 in cash at that point. On the second day, he again sells his stock fund gain of $10 (= $1,000 × 0.01). At the end of the second day, his total portfolio of $1,020 is composed of $1,000 in the stock fund and $20 in cash, resulting in a total gain for the two days of $20.

The second trader skips the first day trade and just sells her stock after the second day. Before the sale, her stock fund value grew to $1,010 (= $1,000 × 1.01) after the first day and $1,021 (= $1,010 × 1.01) after the second day. The sale after the second day brings her a gain of $21 (= $1,021 – $1,000) so that her total portfolio value is $1,021, composed of $1,000 in stock and $21 in cash. Such is the value of compounding. Whereas a rise and fall in the market during this two-day period would have favored the first trader (like the example in Table 7.1), the second trader's luck in skipping a trade in this instance earned her an extra $1 gain over that realized by the first trader.

Slippage

Each day the final closing price of market indexes is not known until a few minutes after the actual close of the market. In the course of day trading, you base the amount of your daily trade on a market index price posted just before the market close that, under normal circumstances, should be fairly close to the actual closing price at which the exchange is executed. However, in some cases, you may find yourself submitting an exchange order before the market close based on a published market index figure that turns out to be a little off from the final closing price. In this case, you need to adjust your next day's net trade amount to reflect the discrepancy between the preclose and actual closing prices due to the time lag between the trade amount calculation and execution. This adjustment in your next day's trade due to the time lag follows along the lines of the catch-up trade adjustment made on account of a trading hiatus or vacation, as discussed earlier.

Suppose you use a calibration factor of $100 for each one-point change in the market index. Then you submit, based on a reported market index decline of five points as of 3:58 P.M. one day, an order to exchange $500 (= $100 calibration factor × five-point decline) from the cash fund into the market index fund. When you later find out that the market index actually declined seven, rather than five, points for the day, you would reflect in your next day's trade an additional $200 exchange from the cash fund into the market index fund.

The same type of adjustment can be made for any errors made in submitting or calculating the amount or direction of your day trades. Just adjust the next day's net trade amount to reflect the adjustment due to the error.

As long as you have been tracking your last trade and the level of the market index at that point, you will be in a position to take your place back in the game. You may have missed out on capturing and preserving some gains, but at least you are ready for the upcoming market swings.

VARIATIONS ON THE DAY TRADING THEME

So you say you have a life, too. Day trading in its strictest form may not be your cup of tea. For those not able to trade daily, you may want to consider other less frequent forms of trading your retirement savings portfolio.

Day Trading Lite

What if you like the concept, but can't be near a telephone or at a computer when the market closes every day? Instead of day trading, you can carry out a comparable trading strategy on a periodic basis over regular intervals, such as a week, a month, or a year. Instead of checking the market and trading on a daily basis, you could do it on the last day of each week, month, or year by exchanging an amount based on the change since your last exchange.

Consider the case where you have decided to trade at the end of each week using a calibration factor of $100 for each one-point change in the S&P 500 index. If the index declined 15 points for a week, you would transfer $1,500 from the cash fund to the S&P 500 index fund in one of your primary trading accounts. Each week you would continue to execute a trade just prior to Friday's market close based on the weekly S&P 500 index change since the close of the market the previous week. Complying with frequent trading rules becomes a whole lot easier when you make less frequent fund exchanges.

Home-Made Dual Limit Orders

By using automated systems to monitor stock prices, brokers can provide stock traders with the facility to place a *limit order* to buy or sell stock at designated price points or better. When a stock reaches that price point designated by a trader's limit order, the broker automatically executes a trade to buy or sell a designated number of shares at the designated price or better. A trader can set up a buy limit order to provide for the purchase of stock at a price no greater than a designated limit price. If that buy limit price is currently below the stock's current share price, the trader is buying low. A limit order to buy stock at $35 per share when its current share price is $50 could be setting up future gains if its price rises after a decline that triggered a purchase at $35.

By contrast, a sell limit order could provide for the sale of stock at a price no less than a designated limit price. If that sell limit price is currently above the current price, the trader is selling high. A limit order to sell stock bought for $50 per share when its share price reaches $65 would capture and protect a gain of $15 per share upon a sale of the stock at $65.

The coincident use of these dual, but separate, limit orders could be set so as to surround a stock's current price for the purpose of buying low and selling high. Yet neither of these limit orders will be executed until the stock's price goes outside of the designated range of the dual limit orders.

If dual limit orders sound a little like the underlying philosophy behind day trading, then it must be adaptable to trading your retirement savings accounts. First you would need to establish a range around the current market index price that would trigger a purchase or sale. Normally this range would be set at limit price levels the same number of points below and above the current market index level.

When the market index goes outside of this range, you execute a fund exchange and set a new range about the new market index level on which the dual limit orders will operate. Similar to a buy limit order, a market index decline to a certain level triggers a stock purchase through a transfer from cash to the market index fund. Like a sell limit order, a market index advance to a specified level triggers a stock sale through a transfer from the market index fund to cash. The amount of each fund exchange would be determined in the normal manner by applying your calibration formula to the change in the market index.

Only under this home-made system, you, rather than a broker, would need to monitor the market index levels to ascertain whether a fund exchange is warranted. Depending on the range established for your dual limit orders, your trading frequency would probably be reduced, but not necessarily your daily stock-monitoring activities on which your trades are based.

Take the case in which Lunchpail Larry uses a calibration factor of $100 per one-point change in a specified market index to determine his trade amounts and sets dual limit orders of 10 points above and below the current market index level of 1,000. When the market index rises three points the first day and 12 points the following day to 1,015 (= 1,000 + 3 + 12), he makes one fund exchange in the amount of $1,500 [= $100 calibration factor × (1,015 − 1,000)-point change] from the market index fund to cash at the end of the second day. As a result of the transaction occurring when the market index reaches 1,015, a new 10-point *collar* is established around the new market index level of 1,015. Then a market index change outside of the 10-point collar to at least 1,025 or to no more than 1,005 would trigger the next market index fund sale or purchase, respectively. When the market index declines by 20 points the third day to 995 (= 1,015 − 20), he would make a fund exchange of $2,000 (= $100/point × 20-point change) from cash to the market index fund. The cycle starts once again, as Larry resets his dual limit orders this time around the market index price of 995, continues to monitor its daily changes, and executes trades when called for.

THERE YOU HAVE IT

Successful day trading involves trades at the right time (every day), in the right amount and direction (based on the daily market movement), in the right setting (retirement savings accounts), and under the right circumstances (market volatility). All you need is to develop a simple routine complying with applicable rules that will enable you to complete a daily fund exchange in minutes a day. Day trading must remain simple enough for you to carry it out effectively on an ongoing basis, but flexible enough to adapt to change.

In the right environment in which the stock market fluctuates on its way to a sideways direction, consistent day trading within retirement savings accounts generates gains every time through the relentless rules of arithmetic. So follow your routine with confidence to accumulate these gains over time, and get ready for good fortune. Like the Karma Queen, your success will come from opportunities that others have passed by. Take advantage of what you know, but stay ready to adapt your approach for any potential new obstacles that may come your way.

CHAPTER 9

Postgame Press Conference

Moving Forward

For every action, there is an equal and opposite reaction.
> —Sir Isaac Newton, Third Law of Motion

She was last in line to take her penalty kick with the score tied. The goalkeeper was the only obstacle between her and the game-winning goal. As everyone but her closed their eyes, she gritted her teeth and let loose the most blistering cannon shot a 12-year-old could muster. It headed toward the lower left-hand corner of the net. Her shot caromed off the sprawling goalkeeper's right forearm, causing the soccer ball to bounce up and down, but the ball was spinning—just before trickling across the goal line. That day she was the hero. She jumped for joy as she and her teammates celebrated their triumph. The goalkeeper slunk back to her fallen team on the other side of the field.

The winners' elation was matched by the losers' dejection. This type of equal but opposite reaction happens every day to some extent in stock market trades, but perhaps in more muted tones as consequences are not as immediately apparent. Although each party may feel pretty good at the time of a transaction, every financial transaction has an eventual winner and loser. If the market goes up, a buyer's hope to turn a profit becomes reality at the expense of the profit a seller forgoes. In a market headed down, a seller's hunch to avoid a loss turns into relief at the expense of the buyer getting stuck with the loss.

Day trading does not occur in a vacuum, but in a market full of investors with different aspirations, hopes, and dreams. Each trade has a consequence that affects more than just individual buyers and sellers, but also the overall market, record keepers, fund managers, plan sponsors, and ultimately regulators responsible for ensuring the smooth operation of the markets for the good of all. Individuals looking to score through day trading their retirement portfolios may face resistance from goalkeepers protecting their turf and potentially standing in their way. How each of these parties reacts to day trading retirement savings accounts affects its potential widespread use, and merits further discussion.

MARKET REACTION

The market reflects the collective vote of investors as to the value of each component security at any given moment in time. Buyers and sellers submit their votes as to security prices through their trades conducted throughout each day. The matching of trading partners determines the market price for a security at the time of the transaction.

The day trading strategy relies on the stock market's natural volatility that has a tendency to overshoot its mark. The science behind day trading works to enable the harvesting of gains on the market's way back to its target price. In any scenario that you can concoct in which the broad market fluctuates on its way back to where it originally started, a properly executed day trading strategy will generate retirement savings portfolio gains. In mildly increasing or decreasing markets, it also outperforms the broad stock market index on which it is based.

For purposes of determining the amount and pricing of each fund exchange, day trading concerns itself primarily with the closing market index level on which the fund exchange is based. A pure day trader considers all of the preceding market index levels to be just filler leading up to the rousing conclusion. On the basis of a stock market index preclosing price, the attentive day trader will sell stock when the market is up and buy when the market is down.

As day trading catches on, you may very well be wondering if the boat tips when everyone on board goes over to one side of a buy or sell trade. By the law of supply and demand, buyers and sellers execute a trade based on the equilibrium price point at which a stock's supply equals its demand. Ultimately they strike a deal at the price point the seller is willing to accept and the buyer is willing to pay. Too many buyers on the demand side or sellers on the supply side would seem to tip the deal in favor of the other direction.

Likewise, day traders executing the same type of stock buy or sell orders on a given day would collectively bump the closing share price in a direction adverse to their own trades. Day trading suggests a down day will bring out a slew of buyers, and an up day will bring a rash of sellers. A bunch of last-second buy orders by day traders for a relatively fixed supply of stock held by content investors should drive the stock price up, as these content investors turn greedy enough to be enticed to sell for a higher price. Similarly, day traders' last-second sell orders should drive stock prices down in order to attract previously content cash-rich opportunists to buy into the market.

Practicality suggests otherwise. Since fear and greed still rule the markets, independent investors trading in concert would be a sight to behold. Other market forces would also counteract the impact of day trades.

Forces behind Day Trading

Day trading involves contrarian trades that may reduce the market volatility on which it depends to generate gains. This unfortunate consequence may somewhat reduce the value of day trading to the extent that two forces behind day trading's effect on stock supply and demand lessen market swings. These forces that mute market volatility are (1) the contrarian nature of the trades and (2) the number of folks actually day trading.

Contrarian Nature of Day Trades   Day traders make proportionate contrarian daily trades that reduce price swings in response to large, as well as small, daily changes in the stock market index. These contrarian trades mute price swings by furthering a balance between stock sellers and buyers, regardless of the amount of the daily market index change.

A day trader provides stock market price support by increasing the demand for slumping stocks through purchases from sellers dumping stocks at lower prices on days when the market declines. The increased buying by day traders at relatively higher prices at the end of the day reduces what otherwise would have been a larger market index decline.

That same day trader weakens surging stock prices by increasing the supply of stock for sale to buyers bidding up stock prices on days when the market advances. The increased selling of day traders at lower-than-peak prices contributes toward reducing what otherwise would have been a larger advance in the market index.

Perspective on Impact of Day Trades   What if every 401(k) account holder started day trading? How would it impact stock prices and associated day traders' gains from stock price volatility? To answer these questions, you need to consider the market participants on the other side of the transaction in a stock market trade. Look at all the buyers when 401(k) day traders are selling, and look at all the sellers when 401(k) day traders are buying. At most, day trading could possibly represent but just a small proportion of the market's trading volume.

The extent to which day traders' contrary trades lessen market swings depends on the proportion of the stock market participants who day trade their retirement portfolios. In a hypothetical market where day traders' sales and purchases offset the rest of the market, the day trading act in itself would produce market neutrality or no changes in the market index levels. Fortunately for day trading's sake, those extreme conditions of no market volatility do not exist, as they would be devastating for day trading. Instead these trades running contrary to the market direction at the end of each day will have the effect of reducing, rather than eliminating, market volatility.

To get a feel for how much day trading could potentially affect the markets, it is important to bring some perspective to the amount of assets invested in U.S. retirement savings accounts. In the global economy of today, such perspective on the magnitude of U.S. retirement savings accounts is gained through a comparison with worldwide financial assets.

As of August 2009, Americans held $7.1 trillion in assets in retirement savings accounts like IRAs, 401(k) plans, and other defined contribution plans.[1] Compared to the world's financial assets, estimated to be $178 trillion around that time, retirement savings accounts comprise just under 4 percent of worldwide financial assets.[2] Day trading calls for the execution of daily fund exchanges in reaction to daily market changes that typically would amount to only a small proportion of day traders' retirement savings accounts. In the unlikely event that all defined contribution plan participants day traded on the day with the most extreme of market changes, their cumulative trades based on a standard calibration factor (based on dividing each retirement savings portfolio by 1,000) would amount to less than 0.5 percent of worldwide financial assets.

The most extreme trade amounts potentially generated by day traders in proportion to worldwide financial assets suggest that the act of day trading, in and of itself, by retirement savings account holders will have very little impact on the worldwide market. It would not significantly reduce market volatility, the lifeblood of day trading, but could possibly lessen it.

Other Crafty Market Participants' Reaction

Just as day trading may influence the investment behavior of 401(k) and other retirement savings account holders, it may catch the attention of other market participants and participants of other markets. Do not figure that these other traders on the other side of retirement savings account day trading will stand pat and not look for ways to cash in on transactions involving day traders.

There is probably some wise guy out there thinking he can profit from anticipating day traders' orchestrated trades at the end of each day. His opportunities derive from market changes that disrupt the normal flow of the day trading sequence of events. Buyers could disappear at the end of days when the market rises because they expect a big sell-off by day traders (all readers of this book). Likewise, sellers could vanish at the end of days when the market goes down in anticipation of the huge buy orders put in by day traders. These potential disruptions would cause end-of-day price swings that would lessen day traders' gains. Alternatively, in a market dominated by day traders, the wise guy could use options to take advantage of an anticipated price change at the end of the day. And this wise guy thinks he can herd cats, too.

Day trading will always be an undertaking by individuals with different dreams, priorities, and schedules. Some are trading on schedule, some are catching up on their trading, and some are skipping it altogether. In the aggregate, it would be hard for them to move in unison despite the best of intentions. This lack of an orchestrated trading pattern is what makes the markets ever so volatile and the world so wonderfully unpredictable.

Furthermore, the wise guy would need a boatload of capital and chutzpah to attempt to disrupt the market. Add the primal traders' instincts of fear and greed to this proposition, and you still have one fickle market that will be conducive to day trading.

Granted, day trading's tendency toward the narrowing of price swings would reduce stock market volatility. Due to the unpredictable nature of the balance between the collaborating and opposing forces behind day trading, the specific extent to which day trading would lessen daily market volatility is unknown.

FROM THE PERCH OF ACCOUNT SERVICE PROVIDERS

With the dramatic growth of 401(k) and other retirement savings plans over the years, a flourishing industry has developed around the performance of the two very important functions of administering retirement savings accounts and managing the assets within them. Account administrators, otherwise known as record keepers, facilitate account transactions and keep track of the funds in each individual's account. Fund managers invest the assets underlying the various funds in which accounts are invested. Some firms administer retirement savings plans and accounts, some manage the assets within the accounts, and some firms perform both functions as a bundled service for those parties seeking one-stop shopping.

Record Keepers

"Mathematicians are lazy," Mr. Rhoad would tell his freshman algebra class. That is why they cleverly invented shortcuts to save time and energy. Retirement savings plan record keepers tracking retirement savings accounts—and most smart businesspeople—come from this same school of thought. So they came up with sophisticated record-keeping systems to handle the dirty work involved in managing large amounts of financial data.

Not only do record keepers interface with account holders in processing their account transactions, they also organize, record, and report resultant daily changes in individual accounts due to deposits, withdrawals, and investment results within each fund held by account holders. This data-intensive work includes processing each fund exchange involving a withdrawal from one fund deposited into another.

In the interest of efficiency, record keepers use automated systems, supported by live telephone service, to assist in collecting and processing daily exchange orders for execution at the end of each trading day. Since relatively few—less than one in seven during 2009—defined contribution plan participants bother to execute any fund exchanges, record keepers build participant apathy into their cost structures. In pricing their record-keeping services, these fund companies are relying on the continued apathy of 401(k) plan investors to keep their fund exchanges at their current low level. Processing more daily fund exchanges called for by day trading would require more systems capability and support.

Day trading may cause an increase in account holders' use of administrative systems to submit and execute fund exchange orders. Widespread use of day trading would most likely require account service providers to add personnel and systems capacity to handle additional fund exchanges. As a result, account record keepers would incur some additional costs to provide these account service capacity enhancements. In some cases, passing along these additional record-keeping costs to account holders or plan sponsors has proven difficult.

Small plan sponsors and individuals with stand-alone accounts generally pay their own way for account record-keeping services. They may pay record keepers a fixed overall fee plus a flat amount per account regardless of trading activity. For large clients, mutual fund companies may give away account record-keeping services for the privilege of investing large asset bases. That leaves investment management, trading, and other administrative fees to cover record-keeping fees not explicitly charged. As a result, under the prevalent form of investment management and account administration fee structure, which does not vary by individual fund exchange activity, the record keepers within fund companies have very little interest in seeing an increased level of fund exchanges called for by the day trading strategy.

Fund Managers

When asked why he robbed banks, Willie Sutton allegedly replied, "Because that's where the money is." Fund managers have a similar mind-set when it comes to attracting and retaining assets for investment, since they get compensated pretty handsomely based on assets under management. Their compensation comes from the investment management and administrative fees they charge as a percentage of assets in the form of a reduction in net fund returns. Their fees are spelled out in mutual fund prospectuses and other plan- or fund-related materials.

Fund management involves the selection and timing of the investment of assets held in funds under a set policy. As such, it requires constant monitoring and investment of net cash flow from deposits and withdrawals. Outflows require liquidity, and inflows need to be invested. Any unforeseen variances in cash flow may require extra oversight to the investment and divestment of fund holdings in order to maintain fund holdings in accordance with the fund's set investment policy. With a predefined revenue stream based on assets under management and variable expenses depending on fund activity, fund managers find it a whole lot easier to manage the assets of complacent buy-and-hold investors with a penchant to consolidate their IRAs and other assets with one fund company.

Fund managers may fear that the increased number of trades generated by day trading could affect cash flow and require additional trades due to fund exchanges. Highly competitive index funds are already operating with razor-thin investment management fees. Any policy like day trading could be seen as possibly requiring additional trades that would require additional monitoring in the fund management process for which fund managers would want to be paid. Having set fixed investment management and administrative fees for a normal level of fund exchanges, fund managers have imposed frequent trading rules to discourage any strategy that would call for additional fund exchanges. Fund managers also pass along the trading costs associated with the security purchases and sales required to accommodate the net amount of the fund holders' fund exchanges indirectly to all shareholders within the respective fund.

By this way of thinking, the potential disruption of investment management, as well as the insufficient record-keeping systems capacity issues, brought about by day trading could be cause for retirement savings account service providers to resist day trading. Absent any resistance from interested parties such as account holders, plan sponsors, and competitors, fund companies may very well decide to tighten frequent trading restrictions by further restricting round-trip and reverse round-trip trades, imposing more short-term trading fees, setting tighter limits on the number of trades allowed, or establishing other more creative measures.

The increased number of fund exchanges caused by day trading is different. When fund managers take the time to review the impact of day trading's neutralizing fund exchanges on the amount of their net trades at the end of each day, they may actually find that day trading reduces a fund's cash flow and trading costs.

Each day, retirement savings account participants executing fund exchanges before the market close instruct fund companies to buy and sell fund shares at the respective funds' daily closing prices. These buy and sell orders are offset against each other during the day before a trade is made of the net amount of the fund exchanges at the closing prices in effect at day's end. In a way, a fund serves as a matchmaker of buyers and sellers for intraday trades. When the stock market declines, there is more selling than buying taking place in the overall market and quite possibly within individual stock funds. The day trader's buying at the end of a down day would likely reduce the net amount of stock needing to be sold by the fund at day's end. When the market advances, more buying than selling is happening. A day trader selling into a market advance would likely reduce the fund manager's buying at day's end.

The contrarian nature of fund exchanges submitted by day traders at the end of the day tends to offset some of the fund exchanges submitted by other shareholders earlier in the day. When the fund manager executes the net trade at day's end to maintain consistency with the fund investment policy, the manager will most likely find that the fund exchanges of contrarian day traders decrease the actual net trade required each day.

Day trading is an old concept in a new package. Any resultant attention it receives brings investment products anew into the public's awareness. This increased publicity brought to investment products and companies offering them is free advertising that is good for business. Fund companies must also weigh their reaction to day trading with respect to their attentiveness to the interests of their account holders and plan sponsors and their responsiveness to their competitors and regulators.

WHAT THE BOSS SAYS

If you have a workplace retirement savings plan like a 401(k), 403(b), or 457 plan, you have your employer to thank for the privilege of allowing you, and giving you the means, to save on a tax-deferred basis for retirement. You have yourself to thank for setting up an IRA. As long as you keep doing your job really well, the hand that feeds you is probably not going to bite.

Since a job represents a future income stream, your job represents your most valuable asset. Do not do anything to jeopardize it. That job provides you a means to save for retirement and hopefully more to enjoy all the rest that life has to offer.

Once you have established a routine, day trading takes only minutes a day. This is good when you consider that your employer would rather you work than trade on company time. If you are able to take a few minutes from your break or lunchtime without disrupting your work, your employer should not have a problem with your day trading, and in fact, may encourage such resourcefulness that improves your chances of retiring when you are ready.

When you leave a company, your former employer would rather you take your money with you. Employers usually have no interest in paying account administrators to send required annual disclosures to, or track the accounts of, former employees, no matter how valuable they were while employed there. Here is where your interest and that of your former employer may clash with respect to keeping your account under your former employer's plan open for day trading. Since your former employer cannot force a distribution upon you until age $70^1/_2$ as long as your balance is at least $5,000, you may want to retain it for day trading. Especially if you like the plan features and options, it is probably to your advantage to exercise your right to keep this account open and use it for day trading as long as you can.

THE GOVERNMENT'S TAKE ON IT ALL

As part of establishing policies with a public purpose, the U.S. government protects its citizens from themselves and each other. The Department of Labor, Internal Revenue Service, and Securities and Exchange Commission make and enforce rules designed to encourage retirement savings in an environment where you do not hurt yourself or get hurt by others. In this capacity, they promote fair and efficient markets and vehicles in which to save.

Markets facilitate liquidity for institutional as well as individual investors who supply investment capital on which American industry runs. Trading in the markets involves buyers purchasing stock of public companies from sellers cashing out stock holdings. As a variation on the trading theme, day trading takes a disciplined approach to create personal wealth in retirement savings from stock market volatility.

The United States' system of free enterprise generally allows markets to determine the viability of ideas with little government intervention. However, judging by the volume of legislation, the government has devoted a significant amount of attention to retirement savings. When it comes to setting the legal framework for dealing with retirement savings, legislators like to stand behind policies that help the little guy, encourage retirement savings, and cost next to nothing. Day trading is one such concept that meets these criteria and deserves to be left for the markets to decide.

On the other hand, government may discourage activities that do not promote a public purpose. To the extent day trading is not viewed as an activity promoting business investment, it could come under governmental scrutiny. Yet day trading with only one trade per day does not constitute high-frequency trading that might be disruptive to the markets. It should be viewed as promoting capital investment.

Less Market Volatility

The world has witnessed the devastating effect of sharp declines in the stock market on personal wealth. Regulators have responded by adopting policies, such as trading curbs and other mechanisms, to mitigate sudden changes in market conditions. To the extent that day trading can reduce stock market volatility, it should be accepted, if not encouraged, by government regulators.

Level Playing Field

Professional traders have access to information and strategies not generally available to individual investors to make money in both up and down markets. Professional traders use hedging strategies involving options and futures and make direct investments in a variety of securities not found in retirement savings plans. In contrast, you will generally find your investment options limited to long positions in stocks, bonds, and cash under a retirement savings plan.

Just as institutions have their own investment strategies, day trading represents a systematic strategy for individuals to buy and sell stock market index funds in their retirement accounts. In one respect, it levels the playing field so that small investors can take advantage of market swings as do institutional investors. It even offers the individual investor the dual advantages of tax and trading cost savings not generally available to the institutional investor. Now everyone, regardless of size, can play the ups and downs of the market.

Another Reason to Save for Retirement

The day trading strategy is designed to work in the cost-friendly and tax-favored environment offered by retirement savings accounts. The day trading strategy just does not work as well outside of retirement savings accounts, where trading costs and taxes associated with daily trading would eat up too much of the profits to render as much return. Since individuals determined to reap the gains available from day trading in an uncertain market can do this only through retirement savings accounts, they would need to save for retirement in the first place. Then once they have saved, they can grow their account balances faster through day trading.

Promoting future self-reliance through retirement savings is a public policy almost everyone can circle around. For those wanting to day trade, saving through a retirement savings plan is critical. When you add the savings buildup available from day trading in an uncertain market, you have another good reason for government regulators to let day traders do their thing.

Revenue-Raising Opportunities

In view of rising federal and state government deficits, it seems government regulators are always looking for new ways to support their programs through revenue enhancements—otherwise known as additional taxes. At the very least, new programs need to support themselves or be billed as revenue-neutral to gain the support or acceptance by government.

Under current law, day trading a retirement savings portfolio in itself would be revenue-neutral to the federal government in the zero-sum game of the stock market. Conceptually the tax due on the numerous short-term realized gains, net of losses, will continue to be deferred until receipt and still be taxed at ordinary income rates upon distribution. Yet to the extent tax is deferred on more current gains, it would affect the timing, but not necessarily the amount, of tax receipts. Of course, this cursory analysis could be refined further to reflect day trading's impact on other investors, taxpaying and otherwise.

The government made a promise long ago to encourage tax-favored savings under 401(k) and other retirement savings plans. Taxpayers took it up on its promise in a big way and invested trillions of dollars in tax-deferred retirement accounts. Despite the temptation to levy taxes on gains or even transactions under retirement savings accounts, it seems unlikely that the federal government would unwind what it so successfully accomplished in the first place by promoting retirement savings through tax incentives.

FACT OR FICTION

Would you act on a stock tip from the guy who shines your shoes? How about relationship advice from your plumber? How about buying underwear hawked by Michael Jordan? Of course not, unless in the third case, with MJ, you believe superstardom comes from avoiding a bunch in your undies. In the first two cases, you may recognize guys outside their areas of expertise blowing smoke where they have no business. In the third case with MJ, marketers count on people's tendency to generalize in accepting advice from superstars, even in fields that may be outside of their expertise.

You need to separate the wheat from the chaff and fact from fiction in determining whether day trading is for you. Your decision should consider your own interests rather than those of the companies that manage and administer your retirement savings accounts.

Old Retirement Savings Accounts

Other than independent advisers, financial service providers get compensated on the basis of assets under management. They generally get paid a percentage of assets they place in investment vehicles. The incentive to place your assets in vehicles providing your adviser—and not you—with the highest return can be pretty overwhelming. Make sure you find a trusted adviser who puts you first.

This compensation structure makes a compelling case for fund companies to continually solicit you to consolidate your IRAs and retirement accounts from former employers. If consolidated reporting is important to you, go ahead and roll over your accounts to one fund company. If you believe you can do better by day trading, leave your retirement savings accounts open so that you can use them to day trade.

Portfolio Rebalancing

Asset diversification is attained by maintaining a balanced portfolio. As a result, most financial advisers recommend periodic—typically annual—rebalancing of your investment portfolio to adjust to market conditions. Individuals rebalancing their portfolios usually pay no direct fees for fund exchanges made within retirement savings accounts but would incur brokerage costs for trades made in taxable brokerage accounts. Additionally, rebalancing within a retirement savings account results in no immediate taxation, whereas rebalancing a taxable account may subject realized gains to taxation. Therefore, the frequent rebalancing in day trading focuses on making fund exchanges under the favorable trading cost and tax conditions provided in retirement savings accounts. Rather than settling for annual portfolio rebalancing, day trading retirement savings accounts takes portfolio rebalancing to the extreme with its daily fund exchanges.

Fund managers and account administrators would rather you not make fund exchanges in your retirement savings accounts. Fund companies practically give away account administration services in order to attract fund management business from which they derive most of their fees. Under their current fee structure, they have no interest in seeing account holders making daily fund exchanges. Act in your own best interest in deciding whether day trading will work for you, and not that of fund managers and record keepers, persuasive though they may be.

GET OUT THE CRYSTAL BALL

Conventional wisdom suggests diversified portfolios of stocks, bonds, and cash minimize risk. Since day trading covers two of these three asset classes, day trading with stocks and cash is a great way to diversify the portion of your retirement portfolio you dedicate to day trading. Stocks, but not cash, carry the risk of market volatility showing up as price fluctuations. Cash provides liquidity and stability in value. Due to the stock market's continual fluctuations, day trading generates gains over and above what the stock market alone can generate in uncertain times when the stock market is headed nowhere.

All in Favor ...

Retirement savers should like it. Account service providers may not like it. Regulators may need to study it further to see whether they like it. The day trading gains of a retirement saver generated in a volatile market make more work for account service providers and no new tax revenue for the government. Any change that may threaten day trading's continued effectiveness in enhancing the returns earned on retirement savings depends on who carries the day.

Day trading works in the current regulatory, competitive, and administrative environment. Since we live in a world of constant changes, day trading's usefulness depends on the continuation of current conditions and rules that others may or may not want to change.

With the money now in their pockets, the fund companies hold the keys to whether day trading will allow retirement savers to improve their lot. They answer to their clients, competition, and the government as well as to their bottom lines. Their support or acquiescence, along with the government's, could further the spread of day trading retirement savings. Otherwise it is up to retirement savers to demand of their fund companies and government to support an environment where day trading remains a viable option for managing retirement savings.

Maybe someday fund companies will even come around to accommodate day trading exchange-traded funds (ETFs) in 401(k) and other retirement savings plans, where opportunities for gains would come more than once per day.

What Now?

Conventional advice offered for managing retirement savings accounts has heretofore focused primarily on three areas: personal savings levels, risk management, and expense control. Now, when you add day trading to the mix, there are four ways you can enhance your retirement savings portfolio:

1. *Maximize personal savings.* Contribute at least enough to your retirement savings account to receive the full available employer match offered under your plan.
2. *Manage risk.* Diversify your holdings among different types of stocks, bonds, and cash.
3. *Control expenses.* Minimize investment expenses by placing account assets in the best-performing low-cost fund options.
4. *Day trade.* Make strategic daily fund exchanges within your retirement savings accounts to take advantage of market fluctuations in an uncertain market.

So much has already been written here and elsewhere on the value of personal savings, risk management, and expense control. The introduction of day trading presents 401(k) investors with another option to consider for managing retirement savings assets in a volatile market. Pick a portion of your portfolio that you will dedicate to day trading, and stick with it.

Ideal Day Trading Conditions

It takes a combination of stock market conditions, retirement savings plan features, and personal qualities to perfect the art of day trading a retirement portfolio. The nature of day trading's ability to sow and harvest gains in a volatile but sideways stock market is indisputable. Its reliance on the relentless rules of humble arithmetic to generate gains from market volatility within the hospitable tax and trading cost environment afforded retirement savings accounts gives day trading its unique advantage.

Admittedly, whether the stock market will be volatile but end up around the same level in the near term is subject to debate. It is your call to determine whether future market conditions will show the type of volatility that is conducive to day trading. If the market is in the midst of a period of volatility with no apparent direction, your disciplined execution of day trading will be rewarded over time. Patience is key.

When all others are overcome by the forces of fear and greed, you as a day trader must maintain an even disposition. Do not get this wrong—you will still share in the delight of each stock market advance with the realization of gains upon your sale of stock. Yet your levelheadedness prevents you from getting overly disappointed by a market decline, because you recognize and seize upon it as a buying opportunity. Your methodical approach enables day trading to feed off of these natural (and unnatural) turns in the stock market.

The variations possible in designing a day trading strategy that works for you are endless. You could put much thought into it or leave it to others. Regardless of whether you day trade, you just cannot ignore the management of your retirement savings and expect it to all work out in the end. Just the process of attending to the development of a plan to manage your retirement savings, or perhaps selecting competent advisers for this role, is bound to get you closer to achieving your retirement dreams.

Whatever you do, keep it all in perspective. Money can be a way of keeping score for some people. In the end, life is about experiences, relationships, and peace of mind. If money is a means to get these, go for it.

Decision Tree Controlling Transition of Day Trading Accounts

A more detailed discussion of the transition of day trading accounts is presented here in the context of the sample retirement savings account inventory first presented in Table 8.1 of this book. This transition becomes necessary when the cash or stock in one of the two primary trading accounts is exhausted.

Initially, for each daily rise in the market, you would sell stock by transferring assets in stock-rich account AT from stock to cash. For each daily decline in the market, you would buy stock by transferring assets in flush-with-cash account BG from cash to stock. You hold account CS, with its more balanced holdings in stock and cash, in reserve until either account AT's stock or account BG's cash is depleted.

If account AT's stock is depleted before account BG's cash, account CS will replace account AT as the fund from which stock is transferred to cash every time the market rises. The newly cash-rich account AT is then left to rest in trading limbo until such time as any applicable trading restrictions have lapsed. Only then may it be used as necessary to relieve an account BG fully or partially depleted in cash. If account BG's cash subsequently runs out before account CS's stock does, a rested account AT with its replenished cash supply will be brought back to replace account BG to buy stock with cash every day the market declines. Alternatively, if account CS's stock is exhausted before account BG's cash runs out, you could switch over account BG, which had been buying stock, to sell stock and bring in a rested cash-rich account AT to buy stock. In this event, account BG's sudden transition from buying to selling stock would constitute

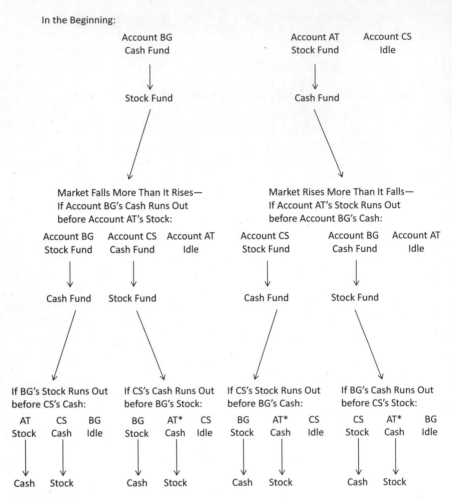

FIGURE A.1 Day Trading Account Replacement Decision Tree
*Before replacing fund, ensure compliance with stock market index fund frequent trading policies relating to round-trip and reverse round-trip fund exchange transactions within a designated time period.

one allowable round-trip transaction, of which typically two may be allowed within a requisite period such as 90 days under some plans.

  Alternatively, in the beginning, if account BG's cash is depleted before account AT's stock, account CS will take over to replace account BG as the account in which cash is used to buy stock every time the market dips. Although account AT could continue in its stock-selling role until exhausted, the typical frequent trading restrictions would allow account BG, all out of cash but chock-full of stock, to conceivably stay on to replace account AT when stock is sold for cash whenever the market rises. In this event, account AT would then be left to rest with a balance of stock and cash in trading limbo until needed as a replacement when either account BG's stock or account CS's cash runs out.

You can continue this cycle of switching in new accounts to replace exhausted accounts and swapping account roles as long as you do not run afoul of the frequent trading restrictions (applicable to a stock market index fund) relating to the number of allowable round-trip (in-out) transactions or preventing a reverse round-trip (out-in) transaction in the same individual account within a designated time period. Figure A.1 presents a decision tree diagram more fully describing the first few iterations of the day trading strategy's account replacement and role swapping for three accounts under alternative market conditions.

Although most stock market index funds are subject to a limit on the allowable number of round-trip trades in a designated period and restrictions on reverse round-trip trades, they typically do not also impose short-term trading fees. Therefore, an account's quick transition from stock accumulation to stock redemption should not pose a problem. However, the use of a stock fund subject to short-term trading fees would necessitate a rest for a stock fund in accumulation mode before switching over to redemption mode. In this case and most other cases, another account would come in handy.

Of course, you should review your particular plan's rules to determine whether your contemplated fund exchanges involved in day trading comply with applicable frequent trading restrictions.

Outside Assistance in 401(k) Day Trading through Systems, Services, or Funds

Although day trading retirement savings accounts is intended to be a process that can be easily performed on a do-it-yourself basis, at some point you may be able to enlist outside aids, services, or funds developed to facilitate or replicate the process.* Certain systems, whether they involve apps, spreadsheets, alerts, or other manual or electronic means, may become available to assist day traders in determining, submitting, and recording their daily trades or fund exchanges based on real-time market index data.

However, aspiring day traders without the patience, time, or attention required to successfully day trade on their own may choose to employ a service to day trade their retirement savings accounts or invest in a fund or fund of funds based on the 401(k) day trading process as described herein, to the extent available in the fund management marketplace.

Purveyors of an account management service would obtain permission from account owners to manage their retirement savings accounts. Such account management service may involve a manual or automated method or system to perform the necessary fund exchanges and account and market index tracking necessary to carry out day trading of 401(k) and other retirement savings accounts as described herein. Such method would involve electronic tracking of real-time data relating to a standard market index (such as the S&P 500 index); aggregation of individual accounts, including a fund based on such standard market index and a cash-type fund; formulaic computation of a daily fund exchange amount based on a

---

*Patent pending.

271

calibration formula or factor (chosen by investor or service provider) applied to the daily change in the market index as of a set time close to the market close; and execution of a daily fund exchange from the appropriate account prior to the daily market close. So as to avoid the stock fund's frequent trading restrictions, account exchanges involving stock fund redemptions would be directed through one account until its stock fund is exhausted and stock fund purchases through another account until its cash fund is exhausted. Either of these one-way accounts would be replaced as necessary, before or upon the exhaustion of the fund from which exchanges had been made, by another account with an available balance so as to maintain compliance with all funds' frequent trading restrictions.

A fund manager of a day trading fund or fund of funds would employ the 401(k) day trading methodology as described herein to buy and sell stock daily before the market close in amounts determined by applying a calibration formula to the daily change in a designated market index as of a set time before each day's market close.

Notes

CHAPTER 1 GAME ON: MAKING SOMETHING OUT OF NOTHING

1. 401(k) Benchmarking Survey, 2008 ed., Deloitte Consulting, LLP, 7.
2. Mary Williams Walsh and Tara Siegel Bernard, "In Need of Cash, More Companies Cut 401(k) Match," *New York Times*, December 21, 2008.
3. Everett T. Allen Jr., Joseph J. Melone, Jerry S. Rosenbloom, and Dennis F. Mahoney, *Retirement Plans*, 10th ed. (New York: McGraw-Hill/Irwin, 2008), 431.
4. *2011 Investment Company Fact Book*, 51st ed. (Washington, DC: Investment Company Institute, 2011), 128.
5. Charles Jaffe, "Motley Fool Rushes into Mutual Funds," *San Francisco Chronicle*, January 25, 2009.
6. Jeffrey A. Hirsch and Yale Hirsch, *Stock Trader's Almanac 2010* (Hoboken, NJ: John Wiley & Sons, 2010), 161, 162, 169, 170.
7. Ibid., 150.

CHAPTER 2 THE SHIFT: PENSIONS TO 401(k) PLANS

1. "Rethinking Retirement," Charles Schwab & Co. and Age Wave, March/April 2008.
2. Candice Choi, "Flexible Retirement Lets Firms Retain Wisdom," *San Francisco Chronicle*, July 30, 2008.
3. Everett T. Allen Jr., Joseph J. Melone, Jerry S. Rosenbloom, and Dennis F. Mahoney, *Retirement Plans*, 10th ed. (New York: McGraw-Hill/Irwin, 2008), 597.
4. Ibid., 608.
5. "Health, United States, 2009, with Special Feature on Medical Technology," U.S. Department of Health and Human Services, Centers for Disease Control and Prevention, National Center for Health Statistics, 44.

6. Social Security Online History, Agency History, Research Notes & Special Studies by the Historian's Office, Research Note #3: "Details of Ida May Fuller's Payroll Tax Contributions," Social Security Online History, www.ssa.gov.

7. "Health, United States, 2009, with Special Feature on Medical Technology," 44.

8. Social Security 2010 Trustees' 2010 Report, released Thursday, August 6, 2010.

9. Paul J. Lim, "Maybe This Time, It's Buy, Buy, Buy and Hold," *New York Times*, December 21, 2008.

10. "FAQs about Benefits—Retirement Issues, Retirement Question 14," Employee Benefits Research Institute, Figure 1, www.ebri.org/publications/benfaq/index.cfm?fa=retfaq14.

11. Edwin C. Hustead, "Trends in Retirement Income Plan Administrative Costs," in *Living with Defined Contribution Plans*, ed. Olivia S. Mitchell and Sylvester J. Schieber (Philadelphia: University of Pennsylvania Press, 1998).

12. Jeffrey A. Hirsch and Yale Hirsch, *Stock Trader's Almanac 2010* (Hoboken, NJ: John Wiley & Sons, 2010), 150.

13. "Defined Benefit vs. 401(k) Plans: Investment Returns for 2003–2006," *Watson Wyatt Insider*, June 2008.

14. Stephanie Ptak, "Investors Regain Footing," Dalbar, Inc., March 31, 2010.

CHAPTER 3   RULES OF THE GAME: 401(k) UNDER THE HOOD

1. "How America Saves 2010: A Report on Vanguard 2009 Defined Contribution Plan Data," Vanguard Group, 12.

2. Ibid., 18.

3. Everett T. Allen Jr., Joseph J. Melone, Jerry S. Rosenbloom, and Dennis F. Mahoney, *Retirement Plans*, 10th ed. (New York: McGraw-Hill/Irwin, 2008), 133.

4. "How America Saves 2010," 14.

5. Ibid.

6. 401(k) Benchmarking Survey, 2008 ed., Deloitte Consulting, LLP, 27.

7. "How America Saves 2010," 70.

8. Internal Revenue Code, Section 72(t).

9. "How America Saves 2010," 66.

CHAPTER 4   TOOLS OF THE TRADE: A LOOK AT YOUR ASSETS

1. *2011 Investment Company Fact Book*, 51st ed. (Washington, DC: Investment Company Institute, 2011), 128.

2. Marko Maslakovic, "IFSL Hedge Funds 2010—Recovery Begun in 2009 Looks Set to Continue," *Hedgefund Journal*, May 2010.

3. "How America Saves 2010: A Report on Vanguard 2009 Defined Contribution Plan Data," Vanguard Group, 49.

4. *The American College Dictionary* (New York: Random House, 1947), 1048.

5. Everett T. Allen Jr., Joseph J. Melone, Jerry S. Rosenbloom, and Dennis F. Mahoney, *Retirement Plans*, 10th ed. (New York: McGraw-Hill/Irwin, 2008), 431.

6. Amos Tversky and Daniel Kahneman, "Advances in Prospect Theory: Cumulative Representation of Uncertainty," *Journal of Risk and Uncertainty*, no. 5, 1992, 297–323.

7. Paul J. Lim, "When Nest Eggs Change Colors," *New York Times*, April 8, 2009.

8. Department of Labor Regulations Section 2550.404c-1 issued pursuant to ERISA Section 404(c).

9. "How America Saves 2010," 50.

10. *2011 Investment Company Fact Book*, 104, 119.

11. Ibid., 22, 32, 33.

12. M. P. Dunleavy, "That Rush to Beat the Market," *New York Times*, April 12, 2009.

13. "How America Saves 2010," 51.

14. Eleanor Laise, "Big Slide in 401(k)s Spurs Call for Change," *Wall Street Journal*, January 8, 2009.

15. Vivian Marino, "Big Dividends in Dangerous Terrain," *New York Times*, March 1, 2009.

16. Morningstar Target-Date Series Research Paper: 2010 Industry Survey, 31.

17. Christopher L. Jones, *The Intelligent Portfolio: Practical Wisdom on Personal Investing from Financial Engines* (Hoboken, NJ: John Wiley & Sons, 2008), 167.

18. "How America Saves 2010," 60.

CHAPTER 5 UNEVEN PLAYING FIELD: VOLATILITY IN A SIDEWAYS MARKET

1. "Prime Number," *New York Times*, September 12, 2010.

2. Christopher Hinton, "UAL Says Bankruptcy Rumor Is Completely Untrue," MarketWatch, September 8, 2008.

3. Conrad de Aenlle, "When Emotions Move the Markets," *New York Times*, October 11, 2009.

4. Whitney Tilson and John Heins, "Long and Strong," *Forbes*, January 18, 2010.

5. Kim Severson, "New York Gets Ready to Count Calories," *New York Times*, December 13, 2006.

6. Christopher L. Jones, *The Intelligent Portfolio: Practical Wisdom on Personal Investing from Financial Engines* (Hoboken, NJ: John Wiley & Sons, 2008), 126.

7. Jeffrey A. Hirsch and Yale Hirsch, *Stock Trader's Almanac 2010* (Hoboken, NJ: John Wiley & Sons, 2010), 161, 162, 169, 170.

8. "GDP (Official Exchange Rate)," in *The World Factbook*, Central Intelligence Agency (Washington, DC: Government Printing Office, 2010).

9. Paul J. Lim, "A U-Turn on Market Risk," *New York Times*, July 5, 2009.

10. Allen G. Rubin, "Oil and You," www.earthlink.net, p. 2.

11. www.bls.gov/news.release/history/empsit_09012000,
www.bls.gov/news.release/history/empsit_09032010.

12. "Employment Status of the Civilian Noninstitutional Population 16 Years and Over, 1970 to Date," Bureau of Labor Statistics, Household Data Historical, September 2009.

13. Robert N. Butler, M.D., *The Longevity Revolution: The Benefits and Challenges of Living a Longer Life* (New York: PublicAffairs, 2008).

14. Christopher Rugaber, "Movie industry's short-sighted fight," *San Francisco Chronicle*, March 10, 2009.

15. Harry Hurt III, "A Generation with More than Hand-Eye Coordination," *New York Times*, December 21, 2008.

16. Ibid.

17. Ben Stein, "The Smoot-Hawley Act Is More Than a Laugh Line," *New York Times*, May 10, 2009.

18. Gretchen Morgenson, "Debt's Deadly Grip," *New York Times*, August 22, 2010.

19. "Prime Number," *New York Times*, September 19, 2010.

20. Doug Anderson, "Below the Topline: The Recession & Declining Immigration," Nielsenwire, September 1, 2009.

21. Doug Anderson, "Below the Topline: Women's Growing Economic Power," Nielsenwire, October 6, 2009.

22. T. J. Matthew and Brady E. Hamilton, "Trend Analysis of the Sex Ratio at Birth in the United States," National Vital Statistics Reports, Center for Disease Control and Prevention, National Center for Health Statistics, Vol. 53, No. 20, June 14, 2005, Table 1, p. 10.

23. Hsiang-Ching Kung, Donna L. Hoyert, Jiaquan Xu, and Sherry L. Murphy, "Deaths: Final Data for 2005," U.S. Department of Health and Human Services, Centers for Disease Control and Prevention, National Center for Health Statistics, National Vital Statistics Reports, Vol. 56, No. 10, April 24, 2008.

24. "Facts for Features: Women's History Month, March 2010," U.S. Census Bureau Newsroom, January 5, 2010.

25. Frank Hobbs and Nicole Stoops, "Demographic Trends in the 20th Century," Census 2000 Special Reports, U.S. Department of Commerce, Economics and Statistics Administration, U.S. Census Bureau, November 2002, 62.

26. Hurt, "Generation."

27. "Monthly Budget Review," Congressional Budget Office, October 2010.

28. Jackie Calmas, "Budget Gap Is Revised to Surpass $1.8 Trillion," *New York Times*, May 12, 2009.

CHAPTER 6   PLAYBOOK: RETIREMENT SAVINGS INVESTMENT STRATEGIES

1. Stephen C. Goss, Chief Actuary, Social Security Administration, April 14, 2010, presentation at Enrolled Actuaries meeting.

2. "Defined Benefit vs. 401(k) Plans: Investment Returns for 2003–2006," *Watson Wyatt Insider*, June 2008, 5.

3. Aswath Damodaran, "Annual Returns on Stock, T.Bonds and T.Bills: 1928–Current," http://pages.stern.nyu.edu/~adamodar/New_Home_Page/datafile/histretSP.html.

4. Jeremy J. Siegel, "What's Ahead for the Markets and the Economy," Pension Group Investment Forum, March 23, 2010.

5. "Global Capital Markets: Entering a New Era," www.mckinsey.com/mgi/publications/gcm_sixth_annual_report/executive_summary.asp.

6. Matthew Miller and Duncan Greenberg, eds. "The Forbes 400," *Forbes*, September 30, 2009.

7. Douglas Appell, "Worldwide Assets Rebound 18% in 2009," June 28, 2010, www.pionline.com/article/20100628/PRINTSUB/306289977.

8. 401(k) Benchmarking Survey, 2008 ed., Deloitte Consulting, LLP, 7.

9. Stephanie Ptak, "Investors Regain Footing," Dalbar, Inc., March 31, 2010.

10. Christopher L. Jones, *The Intelligent Portfolio: Practical Wisdom on Personal Investing from Financial Engines* (Hoboken, NJ: John Wiley & Sons, 2008), 80.

CHAPTER 7 GETTING AN EDGE: BUY LOW AND SELL HIGH

1. Stephen Kotkin, "A Bear Saw around the Corner," *New York Times*, January 3, 2009.

2. Charles Jaffe, "Motley Fool Rushes into Mutual Funds," *San Francisco Chronicle*, January 25, 2009.

3. "How America Saves 2010: A Report on Vanguard 2009 Defined Contribution Plan Data," Vanguard Group, 51.

4. Ibid.

5. John C. Bogle, "The Relentless Rules of Humble Arithmetic," *Financial Analysts Journal* (November/December 2005), 1.

6. Kim Johnson and Tom Krueger, "Market Timing versus Dollar-Cost Averaging: Evidence Based on Two Decades of Standard & Poor's 500 Index Values," 2003, 3. www.valueaveraging.ca/docs/Analysis_Dollar_Cost_Averaging.pdf.

CHAPTER 8 GAME PLAN: THE ART OF DAY TRADING

1. Diya Gullapalli, "ETFs Seek Room in Your 401(k)," *Wall Street Journal*, September 10, 2007.

2. "Spartan 500 Index Fund," Fidelity Investments, April 29, 2010, 9.

3. Ibid.

4. Vanguard Institutional Index Fund prospectus, April 29, 2010, 27.

5. Father Mike Healy's sermon at Saint Bartholomew Parish Community, San Mateo, CA, June 14, 2009.

6. Benjamin Graham, *The Intelligent Investor: The Definitive Book on Value Investing*, rev. ed. (New York: HarperCollins, 2006), 89.

CHAPTER 9   POSTGAME PRESS CONFERENCE: MOVING FORWARD

1. Janet Morrissey, "New Ways to Shelter Your Retirement," *Fortune*, August 19, 2009.

2. "Global Capital Markets: Entering a New Era," www.mckinsey.com/mgi/publications/gcm_sixth_annual_report/executive_summary.asp.

Glossary

401(k) plan Tax-deferred savings plan offering eligible employees the opportunity to save and invest a portion of their wages in available plan funds on a before-tax basis, with earnings posted periodically.

403(b) plan Tax-deferred savings plan, similar to a 401(k) plan, offering eligible employees of educational institutions and certain nonprofit organizations the opportunity to save and invest a portion of their wages in available plan funds on a before-tax basis, with earnings posted periodically.

457 plan Tax-deferred savings plan, similar to a 401(k) plan, offering eligible governmental employees the opportunity to save and invest a portion of their wages in available plan funds on a before-tax basis, with earnings posted periodically.

absolute priority order The preset order established for satisfying a company's obligations and interests in the event of its bankruptcy.

actively managed fund Fund in which an investment manager carries out an investment strategy based on security selection and market timing that is intended to beat the market.

anchoring Inertia or reluctance investors have to change their original convictions, causing stock share prices to respond only gradually to new information.

annuity Series of periodic payments payable as income over a specified period, such as a lifetime or period certain.

back-testing Simulation of investment performance of a fund or strategy in the context of past market performance.

balanced fund Fund holding a mix of more than one asset class.

bond Form of debt issued by a company or government entity with a repayment term of five years or longer.

buy-and-hold investment strategy Purchase of a security with an intention to hold it for a long time.

calibration formula The weighting assigned to a market index change in determining the amount of each daily trade in 401(k) day trading.

callable   Form of debt where the issuer has the right to prepay the loan prior to maturity.

capital appreciation   Increase in the value of a security or portfolio over its original purchase price.

capital gain   Gain resulting from a security rising in value to a level higher than its original purchase price.

capital loss   Loss resulting from a security declining in value to a level lower than its original purchase price.

cash   Most liquid form of debt; currency.

cash or deferred arrangement   401(k) plan or other tax-deferred savings plan offering eligible employees the opportunity to save and invest a portion of their wages in available plan funds on a before-tax basis, with earnings posted periodically.

churning   Excessive trading of securities within an investment portfolio.

collar   Establishment of an upper and lower limit around a price at which a trade is to be executed.

common stock   Security evidencing equity ownership in a publicly traded company.

contrarian   Investor who buys or sells securities against the direction of the current overall market trend.

day trading   In the context of a 401(k) plan, exchanging funds between cash and stock investment options each day that the market is open.

default election   Automatic enrollment in retirement savings plan of newly eligible employees, calling for employee contributions to begin when first eligible at a designated employee contribution rate into a designated fund.

defined benefit pension plan   Type of tax-deferred employer-sponsored retirement plan paying a retirement income annuity stream based on service and/or pay that is taxable upon receipt by the participant.

defined contribution retirement plan   Type of tax-deferred retirement plan providing each participant with an individual account into which contributions and investment earnings are accumulated until distribution.

disposable personal income   Earnings and investment income after payment of income taxes.

diversification   Reduction of portfolio risk accomplished by holding different securities potentially in different asset classes whose values do not tend to move in concert.

dividend   Periodic (or special) distribution of a company's earnings to stockholders or a promised periodic interest payment to bondholders.

dollar-cost averaging   Purchase of securities on a regular periodic basis over an extended period so as to take advantage of securities' price fluctuations over time.

Dow Jones Industrial Average (DJIA)   Composite average price of the 30 largest industrial companies in the United States weighted by market capitalization, as determined by Dow Jones, Inc.

efficient market   Market in which prices for securities are set by negotiation between buyers and sellers who have access to all available information.

equilibrium   Point toward which true value or price gravitates over time.

exchange-traded fund (ETF)   Market basket of securities priced on a real-time basis.

excise tax   Penalty levied by federal and/or state government, such as on a premature or late distribution from a qualified plan like a 401(k) plan.

expense ratio   Percentage of assets under management deducted from a fund's gross returns to cover direct expenses for a fund's administration and management.

fiduciary   Party responsible for the administration or investment of plan assets in retirement savings plans.

fixed income security   Debt of a company or government.

fund exchange   Transfer of individual retirement savings account funds from one alternative fund option to another as directed by participant account holder.

gross domestic product (GDP)   Economic value of goods and services produced by a country's workers within a given period.

herding   Momentum investing, or gradually buying into a rally or selling into a decline, that reinforces advances or declines in stock prices until the valuations it creates can no longer be sustained, causing prices to revert back in the other direction.

individual retirement account (IRA)   Tax-deferred savings account allowing an individual to contribute a portion of wages before tax, which accumulate with investment earnings in an account that is generally not taxed until distributed to the individual.

institutional fund   Collection of securities managed by a professional investment manager for large clients like retirement plans.

investing   Buying a security with an intention of long-term ownership.

investment   Ownership stake in a security.

law of supply and demand   Structure relating to the balance of availability and purchase intentions in determining the price of a good or service.

life cycle fund   Fund of funds comprised of an underlying asset mix that becomes more conservative over time.

limit order   Direction given to a broker to execute a trade when a security reaches a set price designated by the holder of the security.

liquidity   Ability to sell a security at a moment's notice with little or no loss of principal.

margin   Type of loan taken out by an investor from a broker to purchase a security that typically requires the borrowing investor to maintain assets in a brokerage account equal to a designated percentage of the outstanding loan.

margin call   Demand by a lending broker for a cash deposit to bring a borrowing investor's brokerage account balance to a designated percentage of the outstanding loan balance.

market capitalization   Aggregate value of common stock shares of a publicly traded company computed as the product of outstanding shares and the current share price.

market index   Composite weighted-average price of corporate or government securities of a collection of entities included within a defined group, such as the Dow Jones Industrial Average, NASDAQ Composite index, and Standard & Poor's 500 index.

market index fund   Passively managed fund composed of a collection of securities intended to match the performance of an underlying market index.

market order   Instruction to buy or sell a block of common stock shares at the current market price.

market timers   Traders who time their security purchases and sales to correspond with anticipated changes in the direction of the market.

momentum investor   Investor buying or selling securities in the direction of the current overall market trend.

mutual fund   Collective fund composed of market basket of securities priced on a daily basis that is managed by a registered investment company.

NASDAQ Composite index   Weighted average price of all stocks listed on the NASDAQ stock exchange.

negative election   Automatic enrollment in retirement savings plan of newly eligible employees, calling for employee contributions to begin when first eligible at a designated employee contribution rate into a designated fund.

net asset value (NAV)   Average price of securities included in a particular mutual fund, weighted by market capitalization, at which shares are bought and sold.

noncallable   Form of debt where the issuer has no right to prepay the loan prior to maturity.

note   Form of debt issued by a company or government entity with a shorter repayment term between one and five years.

overweight   Condition where one asset class becomes a larger percentage of the portfolio than its original target asset allocation over time as a result of securities in different asset classes growing or declining at different rates.

passively managed fund   Fund composed of a collection of securities intended to match the performance of an underlying market index.

pension   Income stream payable in periodic installments for a specified period, such as a lifetime.

personal savings   Amount of personal income set aside after paying taxes, housing, food, clothing, transportation, utilities, entertainment, health care, and interest payments.

personal savings rate   Personal savings as a percentage of disposable personal (after-tax) income.

pooling   Aggregating securities to reduce risk, such as in a mutual fund.

portability   Ability for a former employee to receive immediate distribution of retirement benefits upon leaving an employer.

portfolio turnover   Level of trading, as measured by the volume of securities bought or sold in relation to the value of the fund, undertaken by a fund manager in managing an investment fund.

preferred stock   Class of security interest in a publicly traded company that usually pays the owner a fixed income stream in dividends and payout of principal at the end of the term.

productivity   Measure of workers' output, usually in relation to their wages, for performance of their jobs.

rebalance   Trade or exchange of securities, usually on a periodic basis, intended to maintain a target allocation of assets in each asset class over time.

replacement rate   Comparison of income after retirement with final earnings just before retirement, expressed as postretirement income as a percentage of preretirement income.

reverse round-trip trade/exchange   Selling a stock index fund one day only to purchase shares in it shortly thereafter.

risk   Volatility of a particular investment's return in relation to that of the market.

rollover   Transfer of a tax-deferred account, such as an individual retirement account (IRA) or qualified plan distribution, from one plan or account to another without immediate tax consequences.

round-trip trade/exchange   Buying into a stock index fund one day only to sell out of it shortly thereafter.

security   Financial instrument of value that is composed of a single issue or combination of issues, such as stock, bond, cash, or mutual fund, that entitles an investor to set payments in the future from the issuer.

self-directed brokerage account   Individual trading account established within a retirement savings plan that allows the participant to direct, often on a real-time basis, the allocation of account assets among investment vehicles other than standard plan fund options.

sideways   Direction of the market that may fluctuate on its way to ending up at the same level at which it started.

Standard & Poor's 500 (S&P 500) index   Average common stock share price of the 500 largest companies in the United States weighted by market capitalization, as determined by Standard & Poor's.

stock   Equity ownership in a company conferring rights to its residual earnings.

Summary Plan Description (SPD)   Abbreviated description of plan terms in enough detail so as to be understood by the average participant.

target-date fund   Fund of funds with an underlying mix of assets that becomes more conservative over time as the investor approaches retirement.

term   Duration or time to maturity, or period of time over which the entire loan evidenced by a bond or note is to be repaid.

trade   Purchase or sale of a security, such as stock of a publicly held company.

trading   Generally a series of trades over a short time period.

Triple Witching Hour   Third Friday of the final month of each calendar quarter when stock options, index options, and futures contracts all expire at the same time.

underweight   Condition where one asset class becomes a smaller percentage of the portfolio than its original target asset allocation over time as a result of securities in different asset classes growing or declining at different rates.

vesting   Entitlement upon termination of employment to different types of plan benefits that may depend on a participant's service with an employer.

About the Author

RICHARD SCHMITT is an adjunct professor teaching retirement planning at the Edward S. Ageno School of Business at Golden Gate University in San Francisco. Having worked in the retirement plan industry since the origin of 401(k) plans, he has assisted companies in the design, implementation, and administration of 401(k), 403(b), 457, and other retirement savings plans for over 25 years. Before joining academia, he worked as a corporate manager overseeing compensation and benefits plans for a couple of the largest U.S. companies based in Silicon Valley. He also worked as a consultant at major international consulting firms serving other Fortune 500 companies. Mr. Schmitt is a Fellow of the Society of Actuaries, a member of the American Academy of Actuaries, and an Enrolled Actuary licensed to practice before the Internal Revenue Service. He graduated with distinction from the University of Michigan with a bachelor of business administration degree and subsequently earned teaching credentials at San Francisco State University.

Index